Speaking the Language of Power: Communication, Collaboration and Advocacy (Translating Ethnography into Action)

Social Research and Educational Studies Series

Series Editor
Robert G. Burgess,
Professor of Sociology,
University of Warwick

Social Research and Educational Studies Series: 11

Speaking the Language of Power:
Communication, Collaboration and Advocacy
(Translating Ethnography into Action)

Edited by

David M. Fetterman

 The Falmer Press

(A member of the Taylor & Francis Group)
Washington, D.C. • London

USA   The Falmer Press, Taylor & Francis Inc., 1900 Frost Road, Suite 101, Bristol, PA 19007

UK   The Falmer Press, 4 John Street, London WC1N 2ET

First published in 1993

A catalogue record for this book is available from the British Library

Library of Congress Cataloging-in-Publication Data are available on request

ISBN 0 750 70 202 8 cased
ISBN 0 750 70 203 6 paperback

Jacket design by Caroline Archer

Typeset in 11/13pt Bembo by
Graphicraft Typesetters Ltd., Hong Kong.

Printed in Great Britain by Burgess Science Press, Basingstoke on paper which has a specified pH value on final paper manufacture of not less than 7.5 and is therefore 'acid free'.

Contents

Contents

Series Editor's Preface

The purpose of the *Social Research and Educational Studies* series is to provide authoritative guides to key issues in educational research. The series includes overviews of fields, guidance on good practice and discussions of the practical implications of social and educational research. In particular, the series deals with a variety of approaches to conducting social and educational research. Contributors to this series review recent work, raise critical concerns that are particular to the field of education and reflect on the implications of research for educational policy and practice.

Each volume in the series draws on material that will be relevant for an international audience. The contributors to this series all have wide experience of teaching, conducting and using educational research. The volumes are written so that they will appeal to a wide audience of students, teachers and researchers. Altogether the volumes in the *Social Research and Educational Studies* series provide a comprehensive guide for anyone concerned with contemporary educational research.

The series will include individually authored books and edited volumes on a range of themes in education including qualitative research, survey research, the interpretation of data, self-evaluation, research and social policy, analyzing data, action research and the politics and ethics of research.

In recent years there has been much discussion about research, evaluation and policy making. In this volume David Fetterman has brought together a range of contributors who are able to discuss the way in which ethnography can be used in the policy-making process and to conduct qualitative evaluations. The papers that are presented in this volume will therefore be of use not only to those engaged in the study of ethnography but also to non-ethnographers, evaluators and policy-makers.

Robert G. Burgess
University of Warwick

This collection is dedicated
to our daughter
Sarah Rachel
who is just discovering
the power of language
and
whose joy
at every step
teaches us to see the world anew.

1   Words as the Commodity of Discourse: Influencing Power

David M. Fetterman

Ethnographers recognize multiple realities in their fieldwork. They observe the various ways individuals perceive the world and attempt to record these differing perceptions in their ethnographies and ethnographic reports. However, in delivering their findings to their various audiences — sponsors, program clients, courts, legislators, Indian tribes, colleagues, school districts, informants, media representatives, community members — ethnographers must again observe and distinguish differing realities. Further, they must speak in the several languages appropriate to those realities. To convey their findings in a manner that each of many audiences will understand is a task requiring the ability to assume many voices. Policy-making, programmatic, legislative, funding, and even academic audiences require different foci, styles, and levels of abstraction.

Any speaker must adopt his or her discourse and manner to suit the expectations and biases of the audience. Ethnographers face the additional challenge of communicating findings based on ethnographic techniques and concepts to a non-ethnographic audience. This collection addresses the importance and difficulty of communicating qualitative research findings to policy-makers and other power brokers. It is unique in defining power brokers more broadly than most traditional discussions. In an educational setting, not only the legislator but the teacher, administrator, parent, and the child are power brokers. They possess the power to accept or reject a finding or recommendation. A recommendation or the implementation of a recommendation will not have a significant impact if it does not make sense to the child who it is designed to benefit. Lack of support on the part of the teacher, administrator, or parent, boredom, inattention, and indifference on the part of the child, are real forms of power. In dealing with the many power brokers in the educational research setting, the researcher finds that collaboration, negotiation, and advocacy are instrumental tools. These tools engage the audience and facilitate change — they enable the researcher to have a powerful impact. However, in using these tools, researchers depend ultimately on the foundation of language.

This introductory chapter explores the topic of researcher as rhetorician. Ethnographic educational evaluators represent a useful example of how ethnographers must respond to the multiple realities they live with to communicate their findings and to survive and prosper. Subsequent chapters provide specific strategies for translating knowledge into action and examine ethical, methodological, and other conceptual concerns. (See Angrosino, 1976; Elliott, 1985; Nixon, 1981; Rynkiewich and Spradley, 1976; Spradley, 1970; and Weaver, 1973 for exemplary discussions and examples of translating knowledge into action.)

Ethnographic Educational Evaluation

Ethnographic educational evaluation is part of the intellectual landscape of educational research and educational anthropology. The roots of this hybrid subdiscipline are firmly planted in the rich soils of anthropology, education, and evaluation. Ethnographic educational evaluation is the process and product of applying ethnographic techniques and concepts to educational evaluation. Key elements of this approach involve conducting fieldwork and maintaining a cultural perspective. Concepts that guide this effort involve maintaining a holistic and contextual perspective, eliciting the emic or insider's perspective about their reality, and adopting a nonjudgmental attitude. Additional ethnographic tools include key informant interviewing; informal, semistructured interviewing; and triangulation. These methods and concepts, traditionally used to understand sociocultural systems, are applied to educational evaluation in an attempt to assess more accurately the relative merits of a given educational approach, setting, or system. This field is described in some detail in *Ethnography in Educational Evaluation* (Fetterman, 1984), *Educational Evaluation: Ethnography in Theory, Practice, and Politics* (Fetterman and Pitman, 1986), *Ethnographic Educational Evaluation* (Fetterman, 1987) and *Ethnography: Step by Step* (Fetterman, 1989). In addition, also see *Qualitative Approaches to Evaluation in Education: The Silent Scientific Revolution* (Fetterman, 1988b) and *Excellence and Equality: A Qualitatively Different Perspective on Gifted and Talented Education* (Fetterman, 1988a).

In ethnographic evaluations, the ethnographer must learn to work effectively with federal and/or state policy decision makers, internalizing their needs and understanding their values and perceptions as a significant constituent. At the same time, the program-level audience may include such various groups as students, teachers, parents, and administrators. This intracultural diversity — added to intercultural diversity of different audiences — further complicates the communication requirements of the ethnographer. Sensitivity to their multiple realities and to the different languages they speak and understand is requisite if the ethnographer is to successfully navigate the rapids of fieldwork and reporting. Beyond ensuring mere survival, this approach will improve the ethnographer's effectiveness. Before presenting a few examples to illustrate this point, the central theme of this discussion — the ethnographer as rhetorician — warrants examination.

Ethnographer as Rhetorician

We all wear many masks in the course of our daily existence. We try to match our self-presentation with our perception of the needs of the situation or the people we face (Goffman, 1959). Obviously, we establish boundaries of acceptable forms of self-presentation within which we can roam. Ethical, political, and pragmatic forces — social norms, as individually interpreted — shape and constantly define these boundaries. These forces keep us from trespassing on both the defined and the undefined territory of others. Socially effective individuals, who are able to accomplish their objectives, believe that they are in control of these social and cultural forces (Rotter, 1964). Whether or not their belief is an illusion, their perception shapes their behavior. These forces and the individual's perceived control over them may in fact be nothing more than a self-made prison — unnecessarily restricting that individual's abilities, talents, and creativity.

The ethnographer as rhetorician provides a model of effective communication. Language is a powerful force that can shape thoughts and influence minds. (See Burke's [1966] *Language as Symbolic Action.*) The rhetorician wants an audience to understand a particular message in a certain way. Therefore, the rhetorician shapes each presentation to the specific listeners who constitute the audience. The rhetorician designs each speech, each written expression, with this guiding image and audience in mind. The rhetorician is aware that the most intricate, carefully crafted speech will fall on deaf ears if it is not spoken in language the listener understands and appreciates.

Thus, an effective ethnographer is an effective communicator. The presentation of research findings, within scientific and moral boundaries, can assume infinitely varied forms depending on the particular audience and the ethnographer's specific purpose for communicating information. The ethnographer must not only write well, but must know and address the listeners in their own tongues.

The traditional audience for ethnographers is other ethnographers. However, to be effective outside our own camp we must learn to speak many other languages and accept many other views of reality. The people we work with in the field have specific needs and a language and level of abstraction that differ significantly from those of policy decision makers. Ethnographers clearly have an equal obligation to speak to both. The obligation to the informant or participant is moral and professional, whereas the obligation to the policymaker or sponsor is legal and contractual as well. The ethnographer may be able to speak to the informants or participants more easily than to policy-makers because of the time spent with them in the field, learning their customs and their language.

Access to policy-makers may be minimal, and opportunities to learn their language and their ways may be limited to brief encounters and exchanges. Lack of access does not lessen the ethnographer's responsibility to learn the ways of a more distant tribe. Failure to communicate effectively with policy-makers can have devastating results for people whose lives are affected by their decisions. The language may be bureaucratese, the focus administrative, and the reality or world view widely disparate from that of the people we work with on a daily basis, but policy-makers have as great a need for and right to knowledge as the participants we observe every day in the field.

In ethnographic evaluation studies, the number of stakeholders compounds this problem. In these cases, ethnographers must distinguish between program concerns and policy matters. Program personnel live in a different world from that of policy-makers. Ethnographers need to learn how the program personnel's world works. Parents of program participants represent yet another interest group — with their own need to know about the program their children participate in. The ethnographer must address their particular focus, dialect, style, and level of abstraction. Inadequate or inappropriate communication with this group of stakeholders can undermine the support structure of the program under review and result in resentment, disenfranchisement, and rebellion against the program, school, or sociocultural entity.

Few people would argue with the role of ethnographer as information source. The difficulty comes when the ethnographer is perceived as a politician, manipulating these various vested interests. The model of the ethnographer as rhetorician poses two potential dangers: First, that ethnographers manipulate truth as well as language, and second, that ethnographers adapt to so many audiences and so many realities that they become chameleonlike, with no center, personality, consistent message, or findings. This state reduces the ethnographer's language to what Malinowski called 'phatic communion' or sheer chatter. (See Spindler, 1987, for a more detailed discussion of self and others.) This danger is real, but should not constrain the ethnographer's versatility or contradict discipline and experience. Ethnographers need not lose their message or their center of gravity just because they function in a complicated and conflicting world. In fact, their training makes them uniquely qualified to sort through and identify conflicting realities. Ethnographers can apply the same analytical tools they use in fieldwork to maintain communication with various parties and to make sense of it all through the presentation of their descriptions, findings, and re-commendations. A nonjudgmental orientation, a holistic view, and the emic or insider's perspective are as important to the communication of research conclusions as they are to data collection and analysis. These basic guiding principles will help make formal communication less threatening and more meaningful to the varied audiences in question. They will also enable ethnographers to keep their message intact despite multiple translations and to maintain their identity despite their many different masks.

Case Examples

Final reports represent the most common medium through which ethnographic evaluators express their research findings, conclusions, and recommendations. The final report is shared with the participants of the study, the sponsor of the study, and the public. Often, much is riding on what is said and how it is said in these reports. These written expressions may signal the life or death of a program, affecting future funding, political endorsements, and public credibility. Three case examples are presented to illustrate the significance of maintaining a sensitivity to power brokers' concerns particularly as expressed through the written word.

Conflict Resolution

I was asked to conduct an ethnographic evaluation of a conflict resolution program in San Francisco schools. The program was designed to teach young children in school how to resolve arguments and settle fights on school grounds without resorting to violence. The sponsor of the program required an evaluation to determine future support and to improve the program. The program officials wanted an evaluation because the sponsor required it, they wanted to use the evaluation findings to secure political endorsements and entry into other school districts, and they wanted to improve their own program — in that order.

The founder of the program explained that it was going through a significant transition. He said he wanted new ideas and bold recommendations about the program, before it was too late to make significant changes in any features of the program — including the name of the program. In my draft final report, I made a bold recommendation. I suggested that they consider renaming the program 'the peacekeeper', 'the peacemaker', or 'the peacekeeping program'. He agreed that the suggested name more accurately reflected what they were doing, it was more positive, and it was more acceptable than the word conflict to many parents in the community. However, his staff rejected it. They were concerned that the potential clients (school districts) might confuse it with another program with a similar name but a poor reputation with neighboring districts. After some probing into the issue, I agreed with them and removed the recommendation. In this instance, the wording of the title itself required sensitivity and responsiveness to those who knew best — the program staff who worked in the school districts.

Another problem that emerged during the review of the draft report involved the length of the report. Program management wanted a longer document. They did not object to the content. They simply believed that a physically weightier document would be more useful to them to help sell the program in the future. The sponsor was perplexed by the program managers' request, preferring a brief report that described the program and highlighted strengths and weaknesses of the program. The evaluator and the sponsor explained to the program manager that it often takes more time to write a concise report than an extremely lengthy one. This was ironic because most ethnographic reports are faulted for their extreme length, as most policy makers desire a brief, readable report. The sponsor was particularly concerned about the program managers' request because one of the sponsor's chief criticisms was that the program managers' correspondence and training materials were unwieldy in size and displayed an unedited stream-of-consciousness style. A solution to the dilemma was found. I doubled the length of the report by describing some of the less critical features of the program in more detail and added a useful and lengthy appendix for the interested reader. The issue here was one of bulk (from the native's perspective) and it was no less important to them than style, subtle connotations, or delicate and refined descriptions.

While a compromise was made in the presentation of the findings, no compromise was made on the content. Conflicting roles in the organization were described in detail to help program managers prevent maladaptive behavior in the future. Similarly, significant achievements, including receiving high-level political support, were discussed.

Alternative High School for Dropouts

The significance of wording in a final report reached the height of absurdity in the production of a national evaluation report about a program for dropouts. I spent a week going over every single line of a 340-page single-spaced document. In many cases, the words served as pawns in a power play as each party established its turf and displayed its muscle. Each side used selected words to test each other to establish the boundaries of acceptable behavior.

During this wordsmithing marathon, the program managers brought numerous legitimate concerns to my attention. In my zeal to reflect their terminology accurately, I had reported the number of staff who were fired as a result of what they labeled incompetence. They indicated that in the reporting stage this term might not reflect well on the program. Although they had used the term in their own documents and language at the sites, they feared that using the term in the final report without any caveat or qualification might be problematic in front of a larger audience. The advisory panel was also concerned that this term might not reflect well on social welfare programs in general. The finding about staff turnover was important to me; the term used to communicate it was not as important to me. I rephrased the finding, using terms such as voluntary and involuntary terminations and lack of appropriate qualifications (specifying weaknesses in management skills) to serve as a supplement to the insider's own term. (This resulted in a more sensitive and accurate phrasing.)

The absence of any words about a topic or problem can be as significant or powerful as the most artfully crafted phrasing. In one delicate situation, the director of the program and I observed a student and counselor engaged in an extremely compromising sexual position. After much thought and discussion, I decided that the act and observation were atypical of program behavior and did not merit discussion in a formal report to the government. It was clear that a description of this anomaly would have closed the program without any consideration given to the positive, successful efforts that more accurately characterized the program. However, I discussed this incident with the program director, and immediate remedial action ensued. (Fetterman, 1986).

Just as the absence of language requires thought and judgment, the use of literary conventions to communicate insights requires careful thought and judgment. The author may assume the voice of different speakers, may appear omniscient or transparent. The author can expand or contract through narrative pace. Use of concrete metaphors, rich similes, parallelism, irony, and many other devices on a larger plane convey the true feel, taste, and smell of a moment.

I used Shakespeare's resonant phrase 'a comedy of errors' in my 'Blaming the Victim' article about this dropout program. The phrase aptly characterized in a concise and instantly comprehensible fashion the misuse of the treatment-control design and the federal bureaucratic intervention in the study. The phrase — as a description of the behavior of educational agencies and researchers in a national research effort — conveys the absurdity of the experience, as well as its comedy of errors (misevaluation). (Fetterman, 1981).

Henrik Ibsen's play, *An Enemy of the People*, provided a powerful image that accurately reflected my experience in attempting to publish my research findings about the misapplication of the treatment-control design in the dropout study. In this play, Dr. Stockmann, the play's protagonist and a medical official of the town's baths, attempted to publish his discovery of contaminants in the town's famous baths. He encountered significant resistance from the townspeople, who derived their income from tourists frequenting the baths. I used this poignant story to convey my frustration and capture the emotional tension and outrage I experienced in the face of harsh resistance to a public discussion of the misuse of a paradigm fundamental to educational research. (Fetterman, 1982.)

Stanford University's Health and Safety Program

The use of language in a report is always dependent on the purpose of the effort. While it is necessary to use bold language to raise people's awareness of important but largely overlooked events, it is equally important to avoid inflammatory language in already controversial and sensitive (as well as litigious) atmospheres. A level-headed and neutral-sounding report will typically facilitate rational discussion of the problems and more easily enable stakeholders to confront the problem in a constructive and responsible manner. In preparing a report about a controversial evaluation of Stanford's health and safety program, I struggled with the title for some time. I had evaluated the program a few years ago and found a variety of serious management problems. Little had been done to rectify the identified problems, and the 'lid blew off' when a health and safety officer resigned a few years later, making a number of allegations and charging — in some cases accurately — that nothing had been done to remedy a multitude of health and safety problems. My first impulse was to use a striking title for the second report to attract the attention the problem deserved — 'Fact and Hyperbole: A Report on the Allegations'. However, the health and safety official's resignation and allegations were already widely publicized in the news media, and the event resembled a three-ring circus. Therefore, I decided to use a more neutral-sounding title — 'A Report on Allegations' — to encourage everyone to deal with the problems in a less hysterical and sensational fashion. In fact, publicity and the findings of the evaluation did result in a massive reorganization of the health and safety function at Stanford and ultimately created a much safer environment. (It has also had an impact on research universities throughout the United States.)

One of the findings in this health and safety report concerned the question of whether or not a coverup had occurred. The health and safety employee had accurately claimed that the hospital and medical school incinerators were not burning infectious wastes long enough or hot enough to complete the job. This meant that infectious materials were entering the atmosphere and being blown back into the offices (re-entrainment). The dark soot had been seen by and complained about by employees for years, and there were memoranda about the problem and documentation of repairs over the years. I determined that no coverup had taken place, focusing on the fact that a coverup requires secrecy and that if people throughout the university knew about it then the test of a coverup failed on that criterion alone. However, the administration had been selective in its formal communications about this problem. They discussed the dangers only with those employees who complained about it in writing. They did not discuss the implications of incomplete combustion and re-entrainment with all concerned (potentially affected) employees in the Medical Center. The fact that they continued to burn infectious waste with this knowledge was unethical (although not a coverup). A gentle but forceful turn of phrase was used to characterize the unethical aspect of the institution's behavior. 'While Stanford did not make a concerted effort to conceal, it did not make a concerted effort to reveal.' This phrase had high saliency as it was quoted often in the press and in administrative discussions. It appeared to ring true for all concerned. The phrasing — although certainly not positive — allowed senior administrators to accept the blame for what had happened in a manner that motivated them to correct the problem and contributed to a more zealous regard for the community's welfare in the future.

Chapter Conclusion

Ethnographic work can only be appreciated when it is read, and ethnographic research will only be read if it is presented in the right fashion to the right people. No one way to present ethnographic research exists, but basic parameters can guide effective communication. The first is to know your work and yourself; the second is to know your audience. Sharing knowledge requires great ability and is a weighty responsibility. The dangers of miscommunication should be recognized, but they should not paralyze an ethnographer and prevent the dissemination of research findings. To dismiss an audience is to dismiss that audience's reality and thus jeopardize the foundations of our phenomenological bias as ethnographers. Fear of miscommunication and an arrogant refusal to adapt one's language to suit an audience are powerful obstacles to communication. A non-statement, like a non-decision, is both a statement and an act with grave implications — for ourselves and for the people we work with day to day. Rhetoricians learn to master many languages to communicate their thoughts more effectively. Such precision and mastery are susceptible to abuse, but can remain tools of integrity and truth so long as they are guided by honesty, compassion, and good science.

Abuses will occur, but no one is above the law or above others, as Dostoevsky's Raskolnikov notes in *Crime and Punishment*. We have moral and scientific obligations. It is impossible to legislate morality. External, explicit social forces, ranging from ethical codes to government laws, strengthen and reinforce — but do not replace — a healthy moral fiber.

We are complex beings operating in a complex world. We deliver good news and bad. The worst news can be made to sound like the best, and the best news like no news at all. Ethnographers have the power and the obligation to shape their information in ways meaningful to their many audiences, both inside and outside the ethnographic tribe. They must pursue this difficult task under the guidance of their individual consciences, their professional ethics, and their social obligations.

Overview of the Collection

These socially concerned scholars are making their ethnographic insights and findings useful to decision makers. They address a host of significant issues, including conflict resolution, the dropout problem, environmental health and safety, homelessness, educational reform, AIDS, the situation of American Indians, and the education of gifted children. Myriad strategies are being used by practicing anthropologists to ensure that they have an impact on sponsors and policy decision makers. This chapter has focused on the use of language and rhetorical style to enhance communication and effectiveness. Within that framework, the approaches presented in this collection range from translating qualitative information into quantitative forms, to testifying about specific legislation on Capitol Hill. The chapters artfully blend the three themes of this book — communication, collaboration, and advocacy. Some chapters focus on one theme more than another, but all display more than one of these overlapping strategies. Building on the enormous contributions made by qualitative researchers throughout the world, the aim of this discourse is to explore successful strategies, share lessons learned, and enhance our ability to communicate with an educated citizenry and powerful policy-making bodies. (For references from Canada, Israel, Switzerland, Sweden, the United Kingdom, and the United States see Burgess, 1982, 1983, 1984a, 1984b, 1985, 1988, and 1992; Denzin, 1989; Erickson, 1976; Fetterman, 1984, 1988a, 1988b, 1989; Fetterman and Pitman, 1986; Glaser and Strauss, 1967; Goetz and LeCompte, 1984; Goldberg, 1984; Hammersley, 1983; Hammersley and Atkinson, 1983; Marton, 1988; Miles and Huberman, 1984; Ogbu, 1978; Pelto and Pelto, 1978; Patton, 1980; Shaffir and Stebbins, 1991; Spindler, 1982; Spradley, 1979, 1980; Spradley and McCurdy, 1975; Stake, 1978; Stenhouse, 1977; and Van Maanen, 1983; Whyte, 1984; Wolcott, 1990; and Yin, 1984.) The spirit driving the dedication displayed in each chapter is simple — to improve the world we live in, to make it a better place for our children and our children's children.

Kim Hopper's chapter, 'On Keeping an Edge: Translating Ethnographic Findings and Putting Them to Use — NYC's Homeless Policy', speaks directly to the topic of 'attending to context' with the homeless. He speaks with the voice of an advocate and a scholar, drawing on over a decade of advocacy and research on homelessness in New York City. Hopper has drafted enabling legislation, co-founded a local advocacy organization, worked in program design and evaluation, and served as an expert witness in public interest litigation. Hopper's chapter provides an additional framework for this collection by bringing ethnography's potential for advocacy to bear within real-world constraints and by discussing the ethnographer's own position in relation to real issues. He reminds us of the power of anthropology to respond critically to cultural givens. Hopper highlights the ethnographer's role as a corrective in public debates concerning the homeless poor, properly framing issues at hand and correcting distortions and the misuse of research findings. He also discusses candidly how it can be difficult to see the forest when you must focus on the trees. He discusses a case in which ethnographic endorsement of the native's point of view resulted in the implementation of surface remedies, instead of engaging some of the long-lasting structural problems underlying homelessness. Hopper focuses on present-day problems with the understanding that only history will tell whether we made a difference.

Fred Hess's chapter, 'Testifying on the Hill: Using Ethnographic Data to Shape Public Policy', provides a powerful picture of how anthropologists are participating in the political process of social and educational reform. Hess was an author of one of the most significant educational reform efforts in the United States, the Chicago School Reform Act. The Act is designed to establish a demonstration project that relaxes federal regulations on schools in exchange for higher achievement for students. It shifts the role of decision making from administrative bureaucracies to parents. It also establishes local school councils with the authority to hire principals, develop and approve school improvement priorities, and establish budgets. In addition, it abolishes life-time principal tenure. Hess was invited as an educational anthropologist to testify on a variety of bills, including one before the US House Committee on Education and Labor. This chapter presents Hess' activities on Capitol Hill, where he used ethnographic research to document the failures of the Chicago Public Schools to adequately educate its disadvantaged students and to explain to Congress people the local effects of changing state and federal policy requirements. Hess presents a credible picture of the fundamentally political nature of this activity and the role research plays in the game.

Margaret Weeks and Jean Schensul's chapter, 'Ethnographic Research on AIDS Risk Behavior and the Making of Policy', speaks to a compelling contemporary social concern. They present a case study about a project designed to evaluate the effectiveness of three prevention oriented programs: culturally appropriate programs for African Americans and Latinos and a non-culturally specific intervention program. Weeks and Schensul highlight the value of ethnographic research and specifically ethnographic evaluation in AIDS behavior research. In their research, ethnographic evaluation is used in combination with quantitative outcome measures within a quasi-experimental design. Program staff on various levels participate in the qualitative data collection effort. The chapter also discusses some of the ways the project has used qualitative and quantitative data to influence local and national policy on AIDS prevention among injection drug users and their sex partners, including the role of needle exchange.

Linda Parker and Bertney Langley (a member of the Coushatta Tribe of Louisiana) focus on strategies for turning ethnographic data into action plans in their chapter, 'Protocol and Policy-making Systems in American Indian Tribes'. They provide an insight into what is required if anthropological research is to be useful to Indian tribes, as well as to other groups. Some of the lessons were learned the hard way, others were simply a function of living with the people you work with and being told how to behave. The basic guidelines include: explaining who you are and what you are doing, determining who makes the rules, following the appropriate protocol, trying to be impartial and consistent, communicating clearly and simply, providing a road map or action plan for implementing recommendations, and trying not to take over. These basic guidelines were effective in helping the authors make their ethnographic data applicable to the real-world concerns of the Coushatta Tribe of Louisiana.

Jolley Christman and Elaine Simon's chapter, 'The Case for Delayed Gratification: Communicating Evaluation Findings as a Process', highlights the role of collaboration in evaluation. Their study of a district-wide curriculum project demonstrates many ways to collaborate in an evaluation, ranging from negotiating the evaluation purposes to conducting pilot studies and involving stakeholders in decisions about evaluation design. Their chapter brings to the fore the issue of who defines the focus of the evaluation, grounding their evaluative stance in an emic perspective. (See Abascal-Hildebrand, 1993; Adelman, 1985, and Elliott, 1985 for another set of excellent discussions on this topic.) They provide a model of how to communicate effectively with clients by breaking the communication process down into analytical steps. They illustrate the importance of communicating the purposes and values of ethnographic evaluation and provide sensitive, instructive, and effective techniques for ensuring that clients understand, welcome, and become engaged in the research approach.

Mary Jo McGee Brown's chapter, 'Massaging Soft Data, or Making the Skeptical More Supple', represents a shift in the tone of this collection. It focuses on working with a difficult, if not adversarial audience. Brown has been working to change policy-makers' world views, concerning the value of qualitative evaluation findings about educational innovation projects. She provides useful approaches that have been successful in demystifying the ethnographic approach and expanding the belief system of policy makers and evaluation colleagues. One approach involves exposing colleagues to the nature of ethnographic work through coursework. Another effective approach involves inviting policy makers and adversarial colleagues to join in the field experience and observe how ethnographic research is conducted first hand. Brief informational exchanges, emphasizing the value of 'hearing the voices' of participants of a project and understanding why they are saying what they are saying about the project, have been an albeit less successful, but nonetheless good start and a useful alternative when combined with other approaches.

Joe Maxwell's chapter, 'Gaining Acceptance from Participants, Clients, and Policy-makers for Qualitative Research', reinforces Mary Jo McGee Brown's message in resonant tones. Maxwell recognizes that ethnographers still encounter misunderstanding and hostility, despite the increasing adoption and acceptance of ethnographic approaches and methods. Paralleling Brown's discussion, Maxwell is aware that the absence of shared values and assumptions can be a part of the problem. However, Maxwell focuses on compatibility and complementarity, rather than similarity. He provides conceptual frameworks and techniques that help ethnographers justify their approach and findings to those who possess conflicting world views. These tools are borrowed from the diffusion of innovations and negotiation literature, as well as from ethnography itself.

Ron Mertz changes the pace of the collection by providing an Orwellian tale. His chapter, 'An Evaluation Fable: The Animals of United Farms', crystallizes Brown and Maxwell's message about conflicting world views. Mertz highlights the role of communication in making a policy impact by contrasting the world views of evaluators and program managers in an educational evaluation. This fable describes how two stakeholders with the same objectives (a successful evaluation) can be at odds with each other, erecting road blocks and other obstacles throughout the effort, simply because they come to the party with clashing or conflicting cultural baggage. The contrast in world view shapes how each behavior is interpreted and acted upon. Ideally, this caricature of roles and relationships enables us to see ourselves more clearly, providing a useful mirror in which to see unproductive patterns.

Mary Lopez de Abascal-Hildebrand's chapter, 'A School Board's Response to an Ethnographic Evaluation: Or, Whose Evaluation Is This Anyway?', is a confessional tale. She discusses the politics of rejection, drawing on her own ethnographic evaluation, which was rejected by a school district. Abascal-Hildebrand evaluated a program designed to provide inservice training for teacher aides who work with primarily Asian language-speaking students. Like most ethnographic researchers, the author was interested in promoting the participants' voices 'in telling their tales of the field'. The school board refused to accept the evaluation, and she was told there were 'no data in it'. They were interested in attendance and other numerical presentations. She came to the same conclusion as her colleagues in this collection — the heart of the problem was the conflicting world views about what constitutes data and how data should be presented. Abascal-Hildebrand had to wrestle with some of the ethical questions involved in this case, but she did come to a constructive solution and resolution that respected multiple audiences and their realities.

Barbara Rylko-Bauer and John van Willigen's chapter, 'A Framework for Conducting Utilization-focused Policy Research in Anthropology', helps us to step back and reflect on the vast array of useful strategies used to convert knowledge into action. They present a framework of strategies that enhance the use of anthropology in the policy process, based on an examination of knowledge utilization studies from a variety of disciplines. They apply this framework to the analysis of fourteen case studies in anthropology to develop a model for increasing the use of anthropological knowledge. Their discussion about basic strategies includes: collaboration with potential users; agency, community, political, research process, communication, and time factors; as well as advocacy and ethical issues.

This collection concludes with a brief examination of where we have been and how far we have to go to improve our effectiveness as we speak the language of power. This concluding discussion is presented within the context of 'playing the game' or participating in the process of decision making. It is titled 'Ethnography and Policy: Translating Knowledge into Action'. Two national studies are used to highlight the importance of the role of collaboration and advocacy, as well as timeliness and language. Underlying methodological and ethical tensions are also explored. Ethnography and policy share a long history and a rich tradition. This collection is designed to contribute to the historical dialogue and to enrich our understanding and practice as we translate knowledge into action.

References

ABASCAL-HILDEBRAND, M. (1993) 'A School Board's Response to an Ethnographic Evaluation: Or, Whose Evaluation is this Anyway?', in FETTERMAN, D.M. (Ed.) *Speaking the Language of Power: Communication, Collaboration, and Advocacy (Translating Ethnography into Action)*. London, England, Falmer Press.

ADELMAN, C. (1985) 'Who Are You? Some Problems of Ethnographer Culture Shock', in BURGESS, R.G. (Ed.) *Field Methods in the Study of Education*. London, England, Falmer Press.

ANGROSINO, M. (1976) (Ed.) *Do Applied Anthropologists Apply Anthropology?* Athens, GA, University of Georgia Press.

BURGESS, R.G. (Ed.) (1992) *Learning About Fieldwork*, London, England, JAI Press.

BURGESS, R.G. (Ed.) (1990) *Reflections on Fieldwork*, London, England, JAI Press.

BURGESS, R.G. (1988) (Ed.) *Qualitative Methodology*, London, England, JAI Press.

BURGESS, R.G. (1985) (Ed.) *Field Methods in the Study of Education*, London, England, Falmer Press.

BURGESS, R.G. (Ed.) (1984a) *The Research Process in Educational Settings: Ten Case Studies*, Lewes, England, Falmer Press.

BURGESS, R.G. (1984b) *In the Field: An Introduction to Field Research*, London, England, George Allen and Unwin.

BURGESS, R.G. (1983) *Experiencing Comprehensive Education: A Study of Bishop McGregor School*, London, England, Methuen.

BURGESS, R.G. (1982) (Ed.) *Field Research: A Sourcebook and Field Manual*, London, England, George Allen and Unwin.

BURKE, K. (1966) *Language as Symbolic Action: Essays on Life, Literature, and Method*, Berkeley, CA, University of California Press.

DENZIN, N. (1989) *Interpretive Biography*, Newbury Park, CA, Sage.

DOSTOEVSKY, F. (1927) *Crime and Punishment*, New York, Grosset and Dunlap.

ELLIOTT, J. (1985) 'Facilitating Action Research in Schools: Some Dilemmas', in BURGESS, R.G. (Ed.) *Field Methods in the Study of Education*, London, England, Falmer Press.

ERICKSON, F. (1976) 'Gatekeeping Encounters: A Social Selection Process', in SANDAY, P.R. (Ed.), *Anthropology and the Public Interest: Fieldwork and Theory*, New York, NY, Academic Press.

FETTERMAN, D.M. (1981) 'Blaming the Victim: The Problem of Evaluation Design and Federal Involvement, and Reinforcing World Views in Education', *Human Organization*, **40**, 1, pp. 67–77.

FETTERMAN, D.M. (1982) 'Ibsen's Baths: Reactivity and Insensitivity (A Misapplication of the Treatment-Control Design in a National Evaluation)', *Educational Evaluation and Policy Analysis*, **4**, 3, pp. 261–279.

FETTERMAN, D.M. (1984) *Ethnography in Educational Evaluation*, Newbury Park, CA, Sage Publications.

FETTERMAN, D.M. (1986) 'Conceptual Crossroads: Methods and Ethics in Ethnographic Evaluation', in WILLIAMS, D.D. (Ed.), *Naturalistic Evaluation, New Directions for Program Evaluation*, No. 30. San Francisco, CA, Jossey-Bass.

FETTERMAN, D.M. (1987) 'Ethnographic Educational Evaluation', in SPINDLER, G.D. (Ed.) *Interpretive Ethnography of Education: At Home and Abroad*, Hillsdale, N.J., Lawrence Erlbaum Associates.

FETTERMAN, D.M. (1988a) *Excellence and Equality: A Qualitatively Different Perspective on Gifted and Talented Education*, Albany, NY, State University of New York Press.

FETTERMAN, D.M. (1988b) *Qualitative Approaches to Evaluation in Education: The Silent Scientific Revolution*, New York, NY, Praeger Publications.

FETTERMAN, D.M. (1989) *Ethnography: Step by Step*, Newbury Park, CA, Sage Publications.

FETTERMAN, D.M. and PITMAN, M.A. (Eds) (1986) *Educational Evaluation: Ethnography in Theory, Practice, and Politics*, Newbury Park, CA, Sage Publications.

GLASER, B. and STRAUSS, A.L. (1976) *The Discovery of Grounded Theory: Strategies for Qualitative Research*, Chicago, Ill, Aldine.

GOETZ, J.P. and LeCOMPTE, M.D. (1984) *Ethnography and Qualitative Design in Educational Research*, New York, NY, Academic Press.

GOFFMAN, E. (1959) *The Presentation of Self in Everyday Life*, New York, Doubleday and Company.

GOLDBERG, H.E. (1984) 'Evaluation, Ethnography, and the Concept of Culture: Disadvantaged Youth in an Israeli Town', in FETTERMAN, D.M. (Ed.) *Ethnography in Educational Evaluation*, Beverly Hills, CA, Sage.

HAMMERSLEY, M. (Ed.) (1983) *The Ethnography of Schooling*, Driffield, England, Nafferton.

HAMMERSLEY, M. and ATKINSON, P. (1983) *Ethnography: Principles in Practice*, London, England, Tavistock.

MARTON, F. (1988) 'Phenomenography: Exploring Different Conceptions of Reality', in FETTERMAN, D.M. (Ed.) *Qualitative Approaches to Evaluation in Education: The Silent Scientific Revolution*, New York, NY, Praeger.

MILES, M.B. and HUBERMAN, A.M. (1984) *Qualitative Data Analysis: A Sourcebook of New Methods*, Beverly Hills, CA, Sage.

NIXON, J. (Ed.) (1981) *A Teachers' Guide to Action Research*, London, England, Grant McIntyre.

OGBU, J. (1978) *Minority Education and Caste: The American System in Cross-cultural Perspective*, New York, NY, Academic Press.

PATTON, M.Q. (1980) *Qualitative Evaluation Methods*, Beverly Hills, CA, Sage.

PELTO, P.J. and PELTO, G.H. (1978) *Anthropological Research: The Structure of Inquiry*, (2nd ed.) Cambridge, England, Cambridge University Press.

ROTTER, J.B. (1964) *Clinical Psychology*, New Jersey, Prentice-Hall, Inc.

RYNKIEWICH, M.A. and SPRADLEY, J.P. (1976) *Ethics and Anthropology: Dilemmas in Fieldwork*, New York, NY, Wiley and Sons.

SHAFFIR, W.B. and STEBBINS, R.A. (1991) *Experiencing Fieldwork: An Inside View of Qualitative Research*, Newbury Park, CA, Sage.

SPINDLER, G.D. (1982) *Doing the Ethnography of Schooling: Educational Anthropology in Action*, New York, NY, Holt, Rinehart and Winston.

SPINDLER, G.D. (1987) 'The Self and the Instrumental Model in the Study of Culture Change and Modernization', presented at the 86th annual meeting of the American Anthropological Association, November 18–22, Chicago, Ill.

SPRADLEY, J.P. (1979) *The Ethnographic Interview*, New York, NY, Holt, Rinehart, and Winston.

SPRADLEY, J.P. (1980) *Participant Observation*, New York, NY, Holt, Rinehart, and Winston.

SPRADLEY, J.P. and MCCURDY, D.W. (1975) *Anthropology: The Cultural Perspective*, New York, NY, John Wiley.

STAKE, R.E. (1978) 'The Case Study Method as Social Inquiry', *Educational Researcher*, **7**, pp. 5–8.

STENHOUSE, L. (1977) 'Case Study as a Basis for Research in a Theoretical Contemporary History of Education', East Anglia, England, Centre for Applied Research in Education, University of East Anglia.

VAN MAANEN, H. (Ed.) (1983) *Qualitative Methodology*, Beverly Hills, CA, Sage.

WEAVER, T. (1973) *To See Ourselves: Anthropology and Modern Social Issues*, Glenview, Ill, Scott, Foresman, and Company.

WHYTE, W.F. (1994) *Learning from the Field: A Guide From Experience.* Newbury Park, CA, Sage.

WOLCOTT, H. (1990) *Writing Up Qualitative Research*, Newbury Park, CA, Sage.

YIN, R. *Case Study Research: Design and Methods*, Beverly Hills, CA, Sage.

2 On Keeping an Edge: Translating Ethnographic Findings and Putting Them to Use—NYC's Homeless Policy

Kim Hopper

Introduction

In order properly to situate these remarks on ethnography's potential as a tool in the local struggle for reform — as *advocacy*, in Singer's sense of 'putting knowledge to use for the purpose of social change' (1990)[1] — a brief overview of the problem area within which I work will be useful.

As I read it, the American way of relief is grudging at best and punitive as a rule. It is built upon a fundamental ambivalence toward dependency, especially on the part of those who convention tells us *ought* to be working: able-bodied and sound-minded men of laboring age, in particular. Accordingly, the provision of assistance to such men has historically been, as Matthew Josephson put it some time ago, 'premised on the theory of the bum' (1933). Official relief, especially the design of 'indoor' relief (almshouses, workhouses and, later, shelters), has been made so forbidding, so onerous, as to constitute an active disincentive to its use. The rationale is to encourage men to make do any other way they can; usually this means relying upon the hospitality of friends and family. Put simply, institutional relief lowers its costs and keeps sharp the spur of necessity by transferring much of the burden of support to the informal sector of kinship.[2] The ledger costs are buried; the social ones often remain untold.

Any attempt to challenge the terms and conditions of relief extended toward these men must begin by confronting what is commonly an unstated and long-settled stock of assumptions about their worth and the legitimacy of their need. I have in mind the sort of deep-rooted assumptions that, for example, are illustrated by the query from a standard I.Q. test for children meant to draw on a simple question of 'smarts', not a complicated one of morality: 'Why is it better to give to organized charity than to the beggar on the street?' (WISC). More pertinent here is the characterization, unremarked at the time it was made, of a New York State Supreme Court judge in the initial ruling of what was to be a landmark right-to-shelter case, *Callahan v. Carey*. Deciding in favor of the three homeless men who brought the case, Andrew Tyler casually referred to members of the plaintiff class as 'flotsam and jetsam' — as wreckage and discard (*New York Law Journal*, 11 December 1979).[3]

My argument in brief is that those of us who work in public policy arenas are strategically positioned to respond critically to what are proffered as simple matters of fact or as uncontested cultural 'givens'. A considerable portion of our work is thus rhetorical, bent on recomplicating issues that have been flattened or reduced to familiar simplicities. Whether directly recruited as participants in ongoing struggles for change or not, we anthropologists in the wings constitute something of a latent Greek chorus of commentary. As informed citizens, we could play a much more visible role in the debates of civil society than presently is the case.

Native Views and Larger Contexts

Ethnography's project — its 'arrogance', Agar reminds us (1980) — is the double conceit of trying to show what it is like to make one's way in the world 'from the native's point of view' while, at the same time, painstakingly 'attending to context' (Ware *et al.*, 1992). Each has its complement of troubles. Much attention, and no little anxiety, has been directed toward the problems of position, access, engagement, as well as those of bias, understanding, and 'translation' of the native's grasp of the world (e.g., Geertz, 1988; Briggs, 1988; Rosaldo, 1989; Sanjek, 1990; among many others). Less progress, it seems to me, has been made in sorting out the difficulties, interpretive and explanatory, raised in mapping the 'macro-micro' or 'structure/agency' linkages implied in the appeal to context. Although promising leads have been charted,[4] both methodological and conceptual problems remain formidable.[5] Long an anthropological article of faith, the dynamics of such 'place-person' connections — both enacted and passive, applying not only to performance but to 'belief' as well — are yielding to careful ethnographic study,[6] even if work on the epistemological foundations remains unfinished.

The unresolved — or, at best, provisionally reconciled — status of both sets of questions can lead to a quandary that most of us, in practice, dodge. Any half-sentient student of Anthro 101 has puzzled over this conundrum, but it may be worth revisiting if only to remind ourselves of the difficulty outsiders sometimes have in seeing what it is exactly, 'stones and bones' aside, that we anthropologists actually *do*, when working at home.

On the one hand, anthropologists remain committed to viewing the world — or, better, to reconstructing the world as viewed — through native lenses. We do this because any inventory of the causes of the way people act must include their own, locale-specific, meaning-riddled reasons for so acting. Adopting an insider's view of how things work is thus essential. At the same time, we remain acutely alert to the influence of outside factors, factors that limit and bias, pressure and contain, both behavior and feeling in myriad ways. Such influence may be subtle or otherwise, it may be acknowledged or not, and it often occurs entirely 'out of [the] awareness' of the actors themselves (e.g., Hall, 1966, 1968; Karp, 1985). Indeed, part of how we represent culture as working is that it retires a whole host of environmental cues for the conduct of routine action to the status of background noise, unnoticed by, and certainly untroubling to, any but the newly arrived.[7] Just to complicate things further, it turns out that even when the relevant actors are confronted with evidence of such background or structural influences on their everyday speech and behavior, competing beliefs (or commitments) may work to block their recognition of the fact.[8]

An example from fieldnotes taken during an extended stint on an acute psychiatric ward may help to clarify the point. The occasion was a seminar for first-year psychiatric residents, led in this instance by the chief of service. The topic under discussion was Erving Goffman's *Asylums* (1961), a study of 'total institutions' unrivaled in its appreciation of how stage, setting and implicit scripts shape perception and behavior. From commonplace routines of 'batch processing' (all inmates marching lock-step through the daily round) to the 'degradation ceremonials' that mark and mediate the new patient's rite of passage to the ward, this allegedly therapeutic institution[9] exacts a pronounced toll on the familiar self. With acclimation the ward's intrusive presence makes itself felt in the most intimate and private moments of the day as well as in consensually public time and space. Clinical ministrations get inextricably bound up with the trappings of custody and confinement. Much of what transpires in the course of a day for patients, aside from their captive 'convalescence', can involve elaborate stratagems to salvage remnants of a former self and seek space safe from inspection.

That much would seem to be apparent to anyone with even a brief acquaintance with routine ward practice. But as the discussion that day progressed, it became clear that the new psychiatric residents had already donned an alternative perspective that effectively overrode what, a few months earlier, would have been the clear evidence of their common sense. None of them (excepting the wily senior psychiatrist) was prepared to recognize the extent to which her/his own psychiatric practice was substantially moulded by such mundane matters as locked doors, lack of privacy, loss of control, and the salient belief that much patient behavior on the ward (especially troublesome behavior) was illness-driven. Admittedly, these were young physicians, new to the profession and tentative about their own proficiency in the craft. But by that time, they were spending the better part of their working days in the busy commerce of the acute ward and were familiar with even the unwitnessed segments of its day-to-day rounds through evening- and night-shift reports. Yet almost to a person, they were unable to see Goffman's structural analysis as anything but an indictment of intent, an 'outsider's' attack on the personal motivation of beleaguered clinicians 'trying to do the best we can'. For all the time Goffman had logged as a minor player on a similar ward,[10] he simply 'didn't get it'. In their eyes, excruciatingly detailed though it may have been, his account of intrinsic pathologies of place — to which they themselves were routinely subjected — amounted to a kind of freelance sociological assault on the profession.[11]

Preliminary Questions

My own work addresses homelessness in urban areas, especially as it is officially defined, as it intersects with mental illness, and as specific program and policy options for dealing with it are proposed.[12] Most of that work has taken place in New York City. I have carried out basic ethnographic and historical research, helped draft enabling legislation, co-founded a local advocacy organization, and worked in program design and evaluation. In four cases, I have also served as an expert witness in public interest litigation involving the rights of homeless men and women.

Initially, I began by casting these remarks as a rough meditation on questions of rhetoric and access or, equivalently, style and power (Wolf, 1990). I also hoped to deal with the specific circumstances that make ethnographic findings relevant to public debate or presentable as evidence in trials.[13] I want to concentrate here on the bracketing conditions and persuasive contingencies that determine the relevance of

ethnographic work to the problem at hand. In this regard, a few preliminary questions are as unavoidable as they may be familiar.[14]

Before taking the measure of ethnography's potential for advocacy
in a given instance, a number of real world circumstances — some
having to do with policy or program constraints, others with the
nature of ethnography's products — must be delineated. With no claim
to originality, these are:

- *What problem is to be solved and in what context?* As defined by
  whom, for what kind of decision-makers, facing what sort of
  decisions, hemmed in by what boundary conditions? What is
  the stipulated scope of inquiry? How did the specific problem
  at hand emerge?

- *What are the translation difficulties that obtain?* How easily can one
  move from abstract description to concrete application? How
  obscure is the language of the discipline and how, in turn,
  might this hamper applicability or render its relevance indeterminate?

- *How will research findings be used?* Are findings intended to gain
  entrée to an ongoing debate, or to reshape its terms and assumptions? Are findings relevant to the evaluation of programs,
  especially potentially 'orphaned' programs (those with no established constituency) and innovative models? Or are they
  concerned more with laying open new possibilities for programmatic initiatives in what are often data-scarce domains?

A different set of questions arises as a function of the ethnographer's
own position, be it upstart critic, seasoned commentator, or retained
consultant. These may well determine ease of *access* to relevant settings
and material and thus materially affect ethnography's potential to shape
policy or programs (cf. Koegel, 1992):

- *Inside*: as consultant, program advisor or evaluator, etc. Especially in the early stages of problem definition, an ethnographer may find that her work has the enviable status of being
  the only game (or provisional expertise) in town.[15]

- *Outside*: as advocate, assistant in litigation, consultant to dispossessed groups, often undertaking specific problem-driven
  research with immediate utilities.

- *Marginal*: as one with multiple, strategically shifting loyalties, sometimes serving as a member of a shadow administration, sometimes as adviser to out-groups, juggling the question of how best to promote interests that are not the privileged property of any avowed representative.

The following three examples, brief and uncomplicated as they are, will serve to illustrate ethnography's potential as a corrective in public debates concerning the homeless poor.

1. Missed Connections: Labor and Homelessness

In the present instance, 'attending to context' means placing overt homelessness within the larger and framing transformation of American cities that has occurred over the past two decades. Especially in its economic and demographic dimensions, this transformation makes for the distinctive marginality of young African-American men (the largest group of shelter users) in places like New York. I have in mind not only the new service-based labor market with its polarized wage structure and the persistent rise of female-headed households, but also the restructuring of urban space into increasingly segregated residential zones, a more and more contested public space, and a steadily deteriorating, ever more costly housing stock.[16] The account should be situated as well, in an ideological environment that continues to insist that deinstitutionalization itself — and not the radically altered contexts of everyday survival in which the mentally ill and other marginal groups find themselves — is the primary engine behind contemporary homelessness.[17] And, finally, in light of the alarming number of states choosing to close budget gaps by limiting aid to single able-bodied adults,[18] it should be located in the ongoing practical debate over the terms and conditions of public relief to those who cannot find work.

Case in point: the linkage between shelter and the labor market.[19] During what had become the longest newspaper strike in decades, the *Wall Street Journal* ran an Op-Ed piece (November 14, 1990) arguing that the local Coalition for the Homeless was wrong to oppose the efforts of *The Daily News* to recruit replacement vendors from within the public shelters.[20] After all, James Taranto asked, wasn't peddling papers (the term 'scab' was studiously avoided) a preferable 'alternative to panhandling'? Did Mary Brosnahan, the Coalition's Director, really believe she was advocating for the true interests of such men by opposing work opportunities?

The answer, of course, turns on how one frames the issue at hand. Indeed, the history and ethnography of men making use of shelters suggested a radically different tack. For regardless of one's attitudes to specific union demands or positions, it is indisputable that unions have played an indispensable role in bettering working conditions for laboring men and women generally. Equally certain is the fact that business has repeatedly attempted to replenish striking workers by reaching deeper into the ranks of the dispossessed, culling from among those whom want has left desperate, if not yet utterly demoralized. That the linkage between a weak and battered labor movement and the proliferation of soup kitchens in the 1980s is so rarely made[21] only underscores how much ground has been lost.

Neatly enough, New York's own shelter system provides a bracing instance. As early as 1914, Stuart Rice — formerly a homeless client and soon to be superintendent of the Municipal Lodging House — observed that huge numbers of recently unemployed men had joined the ranks of the homeless. Public shelter, he warned, was fast becoming a makeshift camp for the 'reserve army' of unemployed labor.[22] The shelter's function, whether administrators recognized it or not, was not only to sustain those without kin or friends to put them up, but also to discipline those who still had jobs. These 'new poor' were an object lesson in the fruits of 'excessive' demands on the part of labor; they were also a living reminder that there were others who would be only too glad to take even menial, ill-paid work. Marx himself had earlier dismissed what sociologists would one day christen the 'disreputable poor' (Matza, 1971), remarking upon the ease with which the 'lumpen-proletariat' could be recruited by firms as strike-breakers.

The point, of course, is not chapter, verse and authority; it is utility. To defend the right of individual workers to labor for a pittance is to condemn the class (homeless and not) to bitter divisiveness. Unorganized workers are virtually defenseless against the heartless logic of the accountant's ledger. The real challenge of the shelters, to which neither industry nor government has yet risen, is how to stem the destructive effects of enforced idleness, institute effective training programs, and offer such men a genuine alternative — not just to panhandling — but to enforced dependency. Public shelters, no less today than in the early 'thirties, function primarily as 'schools for bums' (Vorse, 1931). And hopelessly myopic as it will seem in retrospect, serious discussion is only now beginning[23] on the prospects or design of 'public works projects', whatever modifications may be needed to re-invent the brave Keynesianism of the 'thirties as a rational program of relief in the 'nineties.

Two weeks after the initial Op Ed piece, the *Journal* saw fit to run a letter making essentially the argument laid out above. What its readers did with it is anyone's surmise, but at least the original charge had not gone unanswered.

2. An Ambiguous Legacy of Success

A different lesson entirely may be read in the story of the successful litigation of a right to shelter. The street homeless population in New York City had begun to surge late in the 1970s, subsequent to the loss of scores of thousands of low-cost residential hotel units. The public shelters for men and women regularly turned homeless applicants away. (At that time, capacity for men was limited to beds in the few remaining Bowery flophouses and the floorspace of the lobby at the intake building; for women, a total of forty-seven beds was available.) In October 1979, Robert Hayes, a young Wall Street attorney, filed a class-action suit, *Callahan v. Carey*, on behalf of three homeless plaintiffs, claiming that the City and State were violating constitutional and statutory obligations to care for the indigent needy. As the case wound on, the preliminary findings of a street and shelter ethnography that Ellen Baxter and I were doing at the time would come to figure prominently (and problematically[24]) as evidence. Trial proceedings were well under way when settlement negotiations began early in the spring of 1981. Six months later, a court-entered consent decree was signed, setting minimal conditions for the provision of shelter and providing for ongoing monitoring of compliance.

New York City currently (April 1992) operates fifteen shelters for men (including one located sixty miles north of the city), and a dozen for women. All but two were opened since December 1979, usually pursuant to court order in the continuing compliance proceedings that have dogged the decree. Occupancy in the shelters tends to peak in late winter; in March 1990, it set a record of over 11,000 individuals. Today, on an average night, some 8000 men and women will be lodged.[25] But note, despite a tenfold increase in shelter capacity, there are still thousands who remain encamped on the streets and in other public spaces, for reasons that, even today, have more to do with the terms and conditions of public shelter than with the impaired capacity of potential clients. Estimates of the numbers of people who regularly sleep on the street, in transportation depots, public parks, shanty structures, on the subways, under highways, or in any of thousands of spots hidden from sight, are notoriously unreliable. The latest attempt — the Census Bureau's 'S-Night' effort in 1990 to enumerate those who were 'visible on the street' in pre-identified locations — faced many difficulties in definition, design and implementation.[26] Even so, the Bureau reports that 10,447 individuals were counted.[27] Seasoned observers, whether they be 'outreach' workers seeking to engage these street dwellers, mobile soup and sandwich teams, or the long-term homeless themselves, are almost uniformly of the opinion that the numbers continue to grow.

What, then, has been won? As has become painfully clear in this case, implementation of judicial redress is subject to compromises and unforeseen exceptions; the scope of its application has been repeatedly contested;[28] and obsessive concern with protecting the decreed particulars of 'adequate shelter' has effectively eclipsed the original goal of offering stranded men and women a decent alternative to the streets. Emergency housing, typically in the form of barrack-like shelters, has mushroomed into a substantial cost center in the city's budget. As evidence mounts of the system's failure — even for those for whom it 'works' as an emergency resource (see Gounis, 1992) — advocates find themselves in the unhappy position of defending a crisis-driven enterprise that nearly everyone agrees is a shambles.

The fault for this mess, of course, cannot be laid at the feet of ethnography; nor, indeed, can it be written off as a lapse in legal judgment. The situation seems much more in keeping with the limits of judicial redress and the restricted range of strategic options available to anti-poverty forces at the time (White, 1990–1). But it does seem fair to say that my own ethnographic endorsement of the 'native's point of view' (from the street and from plaintiffs' counsel) and its translation into targeted remedies took clear precedence over properly 'attending to context'. The immediate interests of reform may have been served, while at the same time a larger opportunity for more lasting change was arguably squandered. Surface remedies were implemented with little concern for the larger institutional apparatus, labor and housing markets, and improvised ways of life[29] within which patterns of shelter use are embedded. Had the later occurred — had 'shelter' in short been interpreted as part of the larger dynamic of coping with poverty — it is conceivable that some of the structural injury may have been averted,[30] some unanticipated consequences of shelter growth might have been detected earlier, and more productive alternatives to an expanding institutional makeshift could have been proposed.

Conceivable, yes; probable, no. 'Only connect' may be a memorable epigram but simply 'making the linkages' won't suffice as the watchword of ethnographically informed policy recommendations, as a third example should show.

3. On the Misuse of Ethnographic Material

Nowhere, perhaps, is the public responsibility of the ethnographer more pointed than in correcting distortions of research findings. Here, again, a recent episode from the local press may prove instructive.

On September 4, 1991, the *New York Times* ran a cover story that strongly suggested that officially homeless families were in fact descendants of that old bugaboo, the crafty poor — in this case, doubled-up families capitalizing upon the city's munificent shelters to escape what were in fact tolerably crowded conditions. It was a dismaying tribute to the ease with which tantalizing fragments of a story can be converted into evidence for a coherent narrative whole. To go from the scanty histories of two sheltered families, endorsed by the say-so of official apologists, to the statement that 'hundreds, if not thousands, of families who could stay elsewhere are flocking to shelters' was a breathtaking feat of deduction.

All but hidden in the story were tokens of an alternative narrative. That more complicated story would have told of the scores of thousands of families displaced every year from their homes who never show up as 'homeless', no matter how dire their need or urgent their circumstances. It would have reckoned with the hundreds of thousands more who have learned simply to make to do in doubled-up conditions, because pride and an enduring sense of kinship make the act of applying for shelter unthinkable. It is one thing to pay tribute to such resiliency; it is quite another to turn it into an indictment of the connivance of those comparative few who do seek official help. The latter comes close to prescribing rigors of doubling up — informal, illicit, and demanding as the practice is — as the 'solution' to homelessness.[31]

Ironically, in constructing such depictions, ethnographers of contemporary urban poverty may be said to have met their nemesis. Regrettably few in number,[32] such studies have nonetheless repeatedly found that bureaucratic categories of need fail to do justice to the survival makeshifts of people who never become 'clients' of state agencies.[33] These researchers have hammered home the structural roots of the problem while insisting upon the inventiveness and strength of the poor they have come to know. They have striven to keep public policy debates from degenerating into yet another sorry round of distinguishing the 'deserving' poor from the decidedly less so, in the face of considerable momentum in the opposite direction.

Now, no doubt to their amazement, they watch as this ethnography of a capable poor and their sustaining networks, of people who defy adjectives like 'abject' and mock the stereotype of 'broken' families, has been put to subversive utility. Newman is certainly correct in arguing that '[o]ne can hold that coping strategies are remarkable examples of human adaptation and, at the same time, insist that society must bend its resources toward the elimination of those conditions that force people to do no more than survive' (1992) — but that is not the only interpretation making the rounds. The rough improvisations, the patchwork supports, the doubling up, the sharing, can instead become evidence — not of shredded safety nets, of need gone unmet, of invention under duress — but of a vibrant tradition of popular relief, of a need that will be met quite well enough if only government can refrain from meddling.

Certain policy implications follow with the force of deliberate mischief. Put simply: if potentially homeless people — far from suffering from 'a condition of disaffiliation, a lack of bonds, a pathology of connectedness' as one analyst has argued (Bahr, 1989) — *do* manage to retain kinship ties, why not oblige them to make use of such ties for emergency lodging, instead of relying on public shelters? Though not likely known to its contemporary champion, a similar provision in 1938 raised the rejection rate of applicants for shelter from 40 per cent to 56 per cent the following year (Herlands, 1940). Indeed, the suggestion that homeless men and women should look to their family and friends for lodging instead of exploiting the 'good housing deal' offered by New York shelters was made nearly a decade ago by Thomas Main, in a lengthy critique of our early homeless research that appeared both in *The Public Interest* and in the *Wall Street Journal* (Main, 1983). The principle was soon seized upon by city officials as well, who wondered aloud about individuals who were not 'truly homeless' misusing the shelter system. It has since been applied to homeless families by other researchers (Filer, 1990), despite strong evidence that when families do show up for shelter, they have generally exhausted alternative sources of support (Weitzman *et al.*, 1990).

Everything turns on the meaning of 'alternatives' and the role that informal support is expected to play within the formal bureaucracy of the welfare state. It can be argued that without the work of such informal networks and the counter-example of the succor they provide,[34] the public apparatus of assistance would neither function nor be critically called to task for its performance. The more fundamental point is that we will never know how many of the officially homeless 'could be living elsewhere' until we dare to take a close, sustained look at such 'elsewheres'. Those costs may not be tallied in official budgets and the toll taken on those families or friends who give shelter and risk their own domestic peace and legal tenancy is not easily amenable to cost-benefit analysis. But to see these stubborn refusals to beg or capitulate as a warrant for maligning the legitimacy of the need of others is, I think, badly to misread the evidence.

Thus does poverty become more noteworthy for what the poor do with it, than for what it does to the poor — precisely the leitmotif of the new conservative 're-moralization' of the issue of dependency.[35]

Conclusion

Any ethnographer who would place herself in the thickets of program and policy debates had better have vast reserves of fortitude stockpiled. As most readers will appreciate, proper technique requires forbearance, self-reflection (on an order that does not come naturally to many of us), and no little humor, if one is to sustain the marginal position that is critical to preserving ethnography's edge as a corrective. No doubt there are times and circumstances when it is useful to work from within while trying to maintain something of an outsider's perspective. I myself have found it tricky to do that: when to settle for (which version of?) 'the possible' and when to press on for a wholesale restructuring of the terms and conditions of the debate and the roster of participants is, not uncommonly, a tough call (cf. Hombs, 1992). Consoling oneself with the longer view — that even successfully prosecuted demands are transitional in nature and thus are to be valued more for their part in advancing the debate than for any intrinsic 'reform' they embody — may help some, but not much.

Still, whether we choose to make our contributions or work our 'covert treacheries' (Rieff, 1973) from within, to fire broadsides from without, or to attempt something ambivalently situated in between — in that muddled, suspect terrain where I expect many of us in fact toil away — the objective is to be taken seriously. Or rather, and what may be a very different thing, the objective is to have the work we do, the principles we stand for, taken seriously. In a word, discretion — rhetorical camouflage, concealment, and other modes of dissembling — may well be the better part of disciplinary valor in certain 'collaborative' endeavors.

In this regard, the anthropologist could find no better mythological model than Azdak, errant hero of Brecht's quasi-Biblical fable, *The Caucasian Chalk Circle*. Azdak, the reader may recall, is the ersatz judge who wreaks a great deal of constructive chaos in his brief dominion on the bench, culminating in his adjudication of competing claims for custody of a child. He is not your run-of-the-mill arbiter, having been introduced by the narrator in the following way: 'At long last the poor and lowly/ Had someone who was not too holy/ To be bribed with empty hands . . .' At the dawning of the new age which his own miscreant activities on the bench have helped to inaugurate, in the midst of festive celebrating to mark the occasion, Azdak weaves in and out of the dancers on the stage, and then disappears before the final curtain falls. Brecht's point, I take it, is the obvious one: individual initiatives, even those enhanced by the mantle of the judiciary, are inherently self-limiting. The work of lasting social change is only beginning when the artful midwifery of reform comes to completion. If so, the role of ethnography as a corrective may best be appreciated in the long run, after the players have retired and the historians have arrived.

Notes

1   I pass over here the embedded issues of what change? in what direction and in which social domains? by whom? and at what pace? — some of which will emerge on their own accord later. For one discursive treatment, see Hammersley, 1992.
2   See, e.g., Rossi, 1989; Sosin *et al.*, 1990; and Wright and Rubin, 1991 for contemporary data on adult General Relief recipients in Chicago — half of whom live with friends or family.
3   Also relevant in this regard: early ethnographic findings on the 'Hogarthian' (as a later trial judge put it) conditions of public shelter in New York, for example, were met with bemused exasperation by local officials — 'What do you expect for such scum?' was the prevailing response.
4   A topic that has recently drawn a great deal of attention from American sociologists as well (see Alexander *et al.*, 1987; Fielding, 1988; Huber, 1991).
5   On the general issue of the 'dilemma of context', see Scharfstein, 1989; cf. Hammersley, 1992. For specific problems that arise in measuring 'neighborhood' effects on behavior, see Tienda, 1991.
6   The cogency of this claim is forcefully demonstrated in Favret-Saada's work on rural witchcraft in the Bocage (1977; 1989) as well in Luhrmann's stunning exploration of the slow process of 'interpretive drift' at work in the case of present-day British witches acquiring new — and, at the outset, utterly alien — modes of perception and thought (1989).

7   One of the striking things about Bateson *et al.*'s 'double bind' theory of schizophrenia (1956) was that it drew attention to just such unspoken and, in the event, contradictory messages in the claustrophobic confines of disturbed families — confines which, even if they were apparent to the victims themselves, were implicitly understood (in a prior, 'framing' maneuver) as belonging to that class of things 'which must *not* be noticed, let alone acknowledged'.

8   Cultural beliefs and practices that are officially disavowed remain especially difficult to document and validate. Explicit documentation and interpretation of others may simply be too much to take in — or highly charged and contestable representations. The issues of ownership, recognition and prospects of collaboration as they arise in illness narratives have recently been addressed by Sue Estroff (1992).

9   This phrasing is not meant to suggest that *only* harm is done, or that sanctuary is impossible to find in formal asylums.

10   He worked as a recreational therapist in St. Elizabeth's Hospital in Washington, D.C.

11   Vainly, the chief of service attempted to distinguish between limits imposed from outside and those for which the staff are immediately accountable, on an interpersonal level, within; '[n]o one pick[ed] up on the notion of external, or structural, in-built limits'. He did no better when rehearsing Goffman's careful presentation of how forceful a pressure the ward 'setting' exerts on behavior — 'the entrance rites, roles ascribed to patients, loss of face-saving mechanisms, presentation of self constantly monitored and corrected by staff'. But the other seminar participants don't get it. One argued that such a perspective 'vastly overrates the degree to which the hospital setting determines behavior'. An attending (more senior) psychiatrist added that Goffman's brand of liberalism holds 'a certain contempt for the individuals', seeing people as hapless victims of circumstances. Still another insisted that Goffman does tend 'to get carried away' with his analysis. And one simply protested: 'I don't feel guilty about what we do . . . trying to help people in the best way we know how'. The defensiveness persisted despite repeated efforts by the chief of service to re-cast the discussion. Later, in private conversation, one resident allowed that it was pretty clear to him that the 'crimes committed by the institution were the same [as those in the old asylums]; only the period in which they can be inflicted has been shortened' (fieldnotes, 13 August 1976).

12   Obviously, this takes me as well into allied issues of hospital admission and release policies, street begging, official 'sweeps' of public spaces and shanty settlements, and neighborhood opposition to housing for poor people, often people of color.

13   I deal elsewhere with the specific issue of taking ethnographic interview material beyond the status of 'hearsay' in another article (Hopper, 1990). On the general subject of 'the rhetoric of the human sciences', see Nelson *et al.*, 1987.

14 Recall Hymes, in an essay written twenty years ago: 'Who is the problem to whom? Whom does one's knowledge help? What responsibility must one take for the outcome of one's work? The questions are inescapable . . .' (1972).
15 This happy circumstance enables one to build up a track record (e.g., on grant review committees), the institutional inertia and good repute (let us assume) of which may well be useful later.
16 See Hopper *et al.*, 1985, for an early assessment of this phenomenon.
17 Though within certain precincts, this may well be changing, not least of all within the official mental health establishments: see the analysis of the problem contained in the Report of the Federal Task Force on Homelessness and Severe Mental Illness, *Outcasts on Main Street* (1992).
18 See Shapiro *et al.*, *The States and the Poor*, Washington, D.C. and Albany: Center on Budget and Policy Priorities and Center for the Study of the States, 1991; a convenient summary is provided in J. Kosterlitz, 'Behavior Modification', *National Journal*, 1 February, 1992, pp. 271–275.
19 This case also illustrates that it isn't just the direct findings but the indirect implications of ethnographic research that may be publicly contested.
20 As reported in the *New York Times*, 10 November 1990, p. 25.
21 For a notable and moving exception, see Geoghegen, 1991; esp. pp. 219, 239–240.
22 See, for discussion, Rice, 1914, 1918, and 1923.
23 See Levitan and Gallo, 1992, and for its application to homelessness, look for a forthcoming report from the Coalition for the Homeless (New York). Senate Bill S.2373, the Community Works Progress Act of 1992 introduced by David Boren and others in March 1992, proposed a new WPA-type program. Cf. *New York Times*, 3 May 1992:E6.
24 See the discussion in Hopper, 1990.
25 New York City Human Resources Administration, nightly shelter statistics for the early months of 1992.
26 For detailed treatment, see Hopper, 1992a, 1992b. The count of those visible in public spaces of projected occupancy of at least 6 occupants is estimated to have fallen short by a factor of over 40 per cent. The national picture was examined in a Hearing before the Senate Committee on Governmental Affairs on May 9, 1991.
27 By comparison in the mid-60s, on a warm summer's night, at most a hundred or so men could be seen sleeping on the street (Nash, 1964).
28 In New York, a right to shelter for women had to be separately litigated.
29 The 'economies of makeshift' that, for example, we have hypothesized as the pragmatic undergirding of shelter use (Hopper *et al.*, 1985).
30 Even this is an ambiguous wager: see Grunberg and Eagle, 1990, on 'shelterization' and the responses of Hopper and Gounis later that year in the same journal.
31 Note, however, the many varieties of shared lodging grouped under the single heading of 'doubling up' — from temporary quarters to

relatively long-standing strategies of saving (see Hamberg and Smolinski, in press).

32 See Wilson 1987, pp. 6–18 and Newman, 1992, for discussions of the reasons for this neglect.

33 Peter Hainer's work on folk versions of kin among African-Americans in Boston is exemplary in this regard (see Hainer, 1985, 1991; Hainer *et al.*, 1988).

34 Precarious, double-edged, grudging as it may be, it is never anonymous. The individual *recognition* (if not regard) that is intrinsically a part of such informal aid, along with its private, unregulated character, set it apart from its state-run counterparts (Ignatieff, 1984).

35 See, for example, the articles by L. Mead and J. Schwartz in the Spring 1991 issue of *The Public Interest*.

Acknowledgments

Thanks to Mary Brosnahan, David Fetterman, Jennifer Gometz and Marg Hainer for helpful comments on earlier drafts. I owe a special debt of gratitude to Sue Estroff for helping me think my way into — if not through — the issues touched on in this chapter.

References

AGAR, M.H. (1980) *The Professional Stranger*, New York, Academic Press.

ALEXANDER, J.C., GIESEN, B., MUNCH, R. and SMELSER, N.J. (Eds) (1987) *The Micro-Macro Link*, Berkeley, University of California.

BAHR, H.M. 'Introduction', in *Homelessness in the United States*, edited by J. MOMENI, pp. xvii–xxv. New York, Greenwood Press, 1989.

BATESON, G., JACKSON, D.D., HALEY, J. and WEAKLAND, J. (1956) 'Toward a Theory of Schizophrenia', *Behavioral Science*, 1, pp. 251–264.

BRIGGS, C.L. (1988) *Learning How to Ask*, New York, Cambridge University Press.

ESTROFF, S. (1992) 'Whose Story Is It Anyway? Authority, Voice and Responsibility in Narratives of Chronic Illness'. Paper delivered at the Conference on Chronic Illness, Institute for Medical Humanities, University of Texas, Galveston, May 1–2.

FAVRET-SAADA, J. (1977) *Deadly Words*, Cambridge, Cambridge University Press.

FAVRET-SAADA, J. (1989) 'Unbewitching as Therapy', *American Ethnologist*, **16**, pp. 40–56.

FEDERAL TASK FORCE ON HOMELESSNESS AND SEVERE MENTAL ILLNESS (1992) *Outcasts on Main Street*, Washington, DC, National Institute of Mental Health.

FIELDING, N.G. (Ed.) (1988) *Actions and Structure*, Beverly Hills, Sage.

FILER, R.K. 'What Really Causes Family Homelessness?' *The City Journal* (Fall, 1990): 31–41.

GEERTZ, C. (1988) *Works and Lives*, Stanford, Stanford University Press.

GEOGHEGEN, T. (1991) *Which Side Are You On?* New York, Farrar, Straus Giroux.

GOFFMAN, E. (1961) *Asylums*, New York, Doubleday.

GOUNIS, K. (1992) 'The Manufacture of Dependency: Shelterization Revisited', *New England Journal of Public Policy*, **8**, pp. 685–693.

GRUNBERG, J. and EAGLE, P. (1990) 'Shelterization: How the Homeless Adapt to Shelter Living', *Hospital and Community Psychiatry*, 41, pp. 521–525.

HAINER, P. (1985) 'Census Definitions and the Politics of Census Information', *Practicing Anthropology*, **7**, **3**, pp. 7–8.

HAINER, P. (1991) *Sharing Kith and Kin: A Study of Kinship Behavior, An Approach to Explanation*, Ph.D. Dissertation, Brandeis University.

HAINER, P., HINES, C., MARTIN, E. and SHAPIRO, G. (1988) 'Research on Improving Coverage in Household Surveys', *Fourth Annul Research Conference Proceedings*, Washington, DC, U.S. Bureau of the Census, pp. 513–539.

HALL, E. (1966) *The Hidden Dimension*, Garden City, NY, Doubleday.

HALL, E. (1968) 'Proxemics', *Current Anthropology*, 9, pp. 83–108.

HAMBERG, J. and SMOLINSKI, C. (In press) *Illegal SROs and Other Illegal Occupancies in New York City: Only One Way Out?*

HAMMERSLEY, M. (1992) *What's Wrong With Ethnography?* New York, Routledge.

HERLANDS, W.B. *Administration of Relief in New York City*, New York Department of Investigation, City of New York, 1940.

HOMBS, M.E. (1992) 'Reversals of Fortune: America's Homeless Poor and their Advocates in the 1990s', *New Formations*, **17**, pp. 109–125, 1992.

HOPPER, K. (1990) 'Research Findings as Testimony: The Ethnographer as Expert Witness', *Human Organization*, 49, pp. 110–113.

HOPPER, K. (1992a) 'Counting the Homeless in New York: An Ethnographic Perspective', *New England Journal of Public Policy*, 8, pp. 771–791.

HOPPER, K. (1992b) 'Counting the Homeless: S-Night in New York City', *Evaluation Review*, 16, pp. 376–388.

HOPPER, K., SUSSER, E. and CONOVER, S. (1985) 'Economies of Makeshift: Deindustrialization and Homelessness in New York City', *Urban Anthropology*, 14, pp. 185–236.

HUBER, J. (Ed.) (1991) *Macro-Micro Linkages in Sociology*, Newbury Park, Sage.

HYMES, D. (1972) 'The Use of Anthropology', in HYMES, D. (Ed.) *Reinventing Anthropology*, New York, Vintage, pp. 3–79.

IGNATIEFF, M. (1984) *The Needs of Strangers*, New York, Viking.

JOSEPHSON, M. (1933) 'The Other Nation', *The New Republic*, 17 May, pp. 14–16.

KARP, I. (1985) 'Deconstructing Culture-Bound Syndromes', *Social Science and Medicine*, 21, pp. 221–228.

KOEGEL, P. (1992) 'Through a Different Lens: An Anthropological Perspective on the Homeless Mentally Ill', *Culture, Medicine and Psychiatry*, 16, pp. 1–22.

LEVITAN, S. and GALLO, F. (1992) *Spending to Save*, Washington, DC, George Washington University.

LUHRMANN, T.M. (1988) *Persuasions of the Witch's Craft*, Cambridge, Harvard University Press.

MATZA, D. (1971) 'Poverty and Disrepute', in MERTON, R.K. and NISBET, R. (Eds) *Contemporary Social Problems*, 3rd. ed., New York, Harcourt, Brace Jovanovich, pp. 601–656.

MEAD, L. (1991) 'The New Politics of the New Poverty', *The Public Interest*, 103, pp. 3–20.

NASH, G. (1964) *The Habitats of Homeless Men in Manhattan*, New York, Columbia University, Bureau of Applied Social Research.

NELSON, J.S., MEGILL, A. and McCLOSKEY, D.N. (Eds) (1987) *The Rhetoric of the Human Sciences*, Madison, University of Wisconsin Press.

NEWMAN, K.S. (1992) 'Culture and Structure in *The Truly Disadvantaged*', *City and Society*, 6, pp. 3–25.

RICE, S.A. (1914) 'Vagrancy', in *Proceedings of the National Conference of Charities and Correction*, Fort Wayne, Fort Wayne Printing Company, pp. 458–465.

RICE, S.A. (1918) 'The Homeless', *American Academy of Political and Social Science*, 77, pp. 140–153.

RICE, S.A. (1922) 'The Failure of the Municipal Lodging House', *National Municipal Review*, 11, pp. 358–362.

RIEFF, P. (1973) *Fellow Teachers*, New York, Harper & Row.

ROSALDO, R. (1989) *Culture and Truth*, Boston, Beacon Press.

ROSSI, P. (1989) *Down and Out in America*, Chicago, University of Chicago Press.

SANJEK, R. (1990) 'On Ethnographic Validity', in SANJEK, R. (Ed.) *Fieldnotes*, Ithaca, Cornell University Press, pp. 385–418.

SCHARFSTEIN, B.-A. (1989) *The Dilemma of Context*, New York, New York University Press.

SCHWARTZ, J. (1991) 'The Moral Environment of the Poor', *The Public Interest*, 103, pp. 21–37.

SHAPIRO *et al.* (1991) *The States and the Poor*, Washington, DC and Albany: Center on Budget and Policy Priorities and Center for the Study of the States.

SINGER, M. (1990) 'Another Perspective on Advocacy', *Current Anthropology*, 31, pp. 548–550.

TIENDA, M. (1991) 'Poor People and Poor Places', in J. HUBER (Ed.) *Macro-Micro Linkages in Sociology*, Newbury Park, Sage, pp. 244–262.

VORSE, H. (1931) 'School for Bums', *The New Republic*, 29 April.

WARE, N., DESJARLAIS, R.B., AVRUSKIN, T.L., BRESLAU, J., GOOD, B.J. and GOLDFINGER, S.M. (1992) 'Empowerment and the Transition to Housing for Homeless Mentally Ill People', *New England Journal of Public Policy*, 8, pp. 297–314.

WEITZMAN, B.C., KNICKMAN, J.R. and SHINN, M. (1990) 'Pathways to Homelessness among New York City Families', *Social Forces*, 46, pp. 125–140.

WHITE, L. (1990–91) 'Representing "The Real Deal" ', *University of Miami Law Review*, 45, pp. 271–313.

WILSON, W.J. (1987) *The Truly Disadvantaged*, Chicago, University of Chicago Press.

WOLF, E. (1990) 'Facing Power — Old Insights, New Questions', *American Anthropologist*, 92, pp. 586–596.

WRIGHT, J. and RUBIN, B.A. (1991) 'Is Homelessness a Housing Problem?' *Housing Policy Debate*, 2, pp. 937–956.

3 Testifying on the Hill: Using Ethnographic Data to Shape Public Policy

G. Alfred Hess, Jr.

During the 1989 annual meeting of the American Anthropological Association, I was invited to present testimony to a subcommittee of the US House of Representatives Committee on Education and Labor. The Elementary, Secondary, and Vocational Education Subcommittee was considering H.R. 3347, a bill to establish a National Demonstration Program for Educational Performance Agreements for School Restructuring. I testified in favor of the bill sponsored by Congressman Peter Smith of Vermont.

I returned from the Hill to attend a discussion in which other anthropologists were complaining that the work of anthropology is generally overlooked, and is specifically ignored as public policy is being formulated. Participants claimed that other disciplines were more frequently sought out to present testimony to legislatures and to give interviews to the media. Some participants were offended by this lack of recognition. Others, particularly those representing the Association itself, appeared defensive that they had not been more effective. What was frustrating was that there was little careful attention given to the role of testimony in the making of public policy and little discussion of what news is, and to whom the media looks for expert comment.

This chapter is a response to the juxtaposition of those two events. I will begin with a fuller description of my experience before the Congress, using that experience as the basis for some personal comments on the role of testimony in the formation of public policy. I will provide some further background on my own experience in forging public policy, primarily in my experiences in the movement which successfully enacted legislation mandating school restructuring in the

Chicago Public Schools. Finally, I consider the implications of the policy formation process for anthropologists.

Testifying on the Hill

Congressman Peter Smith was a freshman Republican representative from Vermont, a state with only one member in the House. As his major initiative in his first term, Smith introduced H.R. 3347, which would enable the Secretary of Education to enter into Educational Performance Agreements with states and local school districts to relax federal regulations on the use of federal funds in exchange for commitments to improve student performance. This legislation was in line with other Republican administration initiatives to deregulate airlines and other industries. It was also in line with recent policy research which was calling into question the long held presumption that educational quality could be assured by regulating the *inputs*, such as certification of teachers and requirements of courses which must be passed before graduating from high school. Instead, reformers were suggesting that more attention should be given to the *outputs*, the measures of student achievement (Elmore *et al.*, 1990). This bill was similar to legislation adopted several years earlier by the State of Washington which granted to specified 'Schools for the 21st Century' waivers from inhibiting state regulations. With this federal legislation, Smith was trying to make his mark in the Congress.

Congressman Smith and his staff had to work hard to line up support for his bill among a number of educational advocacy groups before he could even get a commitment from the Committee Chairman, Gus Hawkins, to hold hearings on his bill. Hawkins had authored many of the bills which created the federal government's support for various initiatives in public education. The regulations Smith wanted to remove were frequently safeguards Hawkins had included in his bills to assure that federal funds were spent on the disadvantaged students he was trying to help. Practically, this meant that Smith had to convince Hawkins, a liberal Democrat, that he was not attacking the *intent* of the earlier bills, but difficulties which were preventing the intent from being successfully realized. Given the political tenor of the Reagan-Bush administrations, it was not surprising that Hawkins was suspicious of the Vermont Republican. Hawkins, about to retire from the Congress, was not going to allow passage of legislation which would gut his life's work.

Thus, the witnesses before the committee had to reflect persons whose commitment to improving education for the disadvantaged could not be questioned. The witness list included Al Shanker (president of the American Federation of Teachers), Governor Kean of New Jersey, the president of RJR Nabisco who had just announced a major education grants program, a teacher from one of the 21st Century Schools in Washington, and myself. I was invited because I was one of the authors of the Chicago School Reform Act which has decentralized authority in the Chicago Public Schools by establishing school-based management at each of the system's 542 local schools. (See Hess, 1991 for more detail on the Chicago School Reform effort). One aspect of the legislation restricts the central administration of the system from imposing program and budget constraints on local schools, a local parallel of Smith's federal proposal.

My testimony[1] explained the major provisions of the reform act, it explained the research, both ethnographic and quantitative, through which we were able to demonstrate the failures of the Chicago Public Schools to adequately educate its disadvantaged students (Hallett and Hess, 1982; Hess and Lauber, 1985; Hess et al., 1986), and it drew the parallels between our efforts in Chicago and the proposed Smith legislation. In the longer written testimony, I was also able to describe more fully the work of the organization which I direct, the Chicago Panel on Public School Policy and Finance.

My testimony was particularly effective with the committee for several reasons. First, it was obvious that our concern was to improve educational opportunities for disadvantaged students, the very students whom the federal government's programs were designed to help. But I was also presenting evidence, based on our own research, that the current efforts were not being successful with those students. Second, the Chicago School Reform Act, discussed more fully below, is the most radical effort to restructure a major urban school system in at least two decades. It is far more dramatic than the shared decision making models underway in Dade County (Miami), Hammond, San Diego, or Rochester. Part of the philosophy underlying that reform act, freeing local schools from bureaucratic control, was the same philosophy behind Smith's proposal. Third, one of the committee chair's prominent allies on the committee was from Chicago, Congressman Charles Hayes. Hayes holds the seat on the committee formerly occupied by his predecessor, Mayor Harold Washington, under whose aegis school reform in Chicago was launched. I had served Washington as a released time consultant for his Education Summit. Many of the provisions of the Reform Act were drawn from the agreement of the Education Summit. Thus, I was a witness to whom at least one of

Hawkins' key allies would be sympathetic. Finally, I am an experienced witness, who has testified frequently before legislative committees of the federal, state, and city government.

What is Public Policy Testimony?

Testimony before legislative committees has several different functions. All the eleventh grade civic books tell you that it provides the basis for legislators to make up their minds whether to support or oppose legislation. In my experience, this is rarely the case. I have provided lots of testimony over the last eight years, most of which was designed to support, and make a public case for, legislation whose fate was already fairly well assured. The exceptions to that situation are the Chicago School Reform Act and my periodic testimony before the Chicago Board of Education in which I was presenting the results of research into the Chicago Public Schools or commenting on the priorities revealed in the budget which the Board was considering adopting (see Fig. 3.1).

Legislation is rarely shaped in legislative hearings, though testimony presented at hearings may be the culmination of a lobbying effort which results in a commitment by committee members to act in certain ways relative to the bill under consideration. So it was on H.R. 3347. At the end of the hearing, during questioning following my testimony, Chairman Hawkins committed himself to work with Representative Smith to perfect the legislation and to see to it that it would be heard by the full committee. It is unlikely that it was anything I or any of my co-witnesses said that changed Hawkins' mind. It was the fact that, given the opportunity of a hearing, Smith could marshal public support for his proposal from big business, from a teachers' union, from a state governor, and from local practitioners. The fact that my testimony was presented by an anthropologist, and that my research was, in part, ethnographic, was not very relevant to this outcome. Yet, I would not have been in a position to present my testimony, were it not for my anthropological training and my ethnographic research.[2]

Providing legislative testimony is a political act. It is not an academic act, regardless of the scholarly effort on which it is based. The Congress is not a place to report on your research, though your testimony may include such a report. Most testimony provided to the Congress or to state legislatures serves a political purpose. Only that research which is directly related to the political purposes being served is likely to be solicited. Thus, only research which is policy relevant,

DATE	TO WHOM	LEVEL	TITLE	TOPIC	WHERE
1983-01-11	Chicago Board of Education	City	Present Study: 'Teacher Transfers & Classroom Disruption'	Research	Chicago
1983-08-16	Chicago Board of Education	City	Testimony on FY 1984 Budget — Potential Savings	Budget	Chicago
1983-11-01	Chicago Board of Education	City	Testimony on Reaching Reasonable Contract Settlement	Budget	Chicago
1983-11-09	Chicago Board of Education	City	Testimony on Paying Prevailing Wage Employees More Than Teachers	Budget	Chicago
1984-03-14	Chicago Board of Education	City	Mismanagement in State Title I Forces Teacher Layoffs	Budget	Chicago
1984-06-24	Chicago Board of Education	City	Testimony on FY 1985 Budget: Scorecard on Proposed Booz-Allen Cuts	Budget	Chicago
1984-09-12	Chicago Board of Education	City	Budgeted Positions and Educational Program Staffing	Budget	Chicago
1985-01-08	Chicago Board of Education	City	Testimony on Amended FY 1985 Budget	Budget	Chicago
1985-01-09	Chicago Board of Education	City	Staff Analysis in Amended FY 1985 Budget	Budget	Chicago
1985-07-10	Chicago Board of Education	City	Testimony on FY 1986 Budget	Budget	Chicago
1985-08-06	Chicago Board of Education	City	Testimony on Amended FY 1986 Budget	Budget	Chicago
1985-09-20	Chicago Board of Education	City	Testimony on Final FY 1986 Budget — Significance of Strike Settlement	Budget	Chicago
1986-05-14	Chicago Board of Education	City	Present Study: 'Who Gets Extra Pay?'	Research	Chicago
1986-07-01	Chicago Board of Education	City	Testimony on FY 1987 Budget — Staff Increases, Supplies Cut	Budget	Chicago
1986-07-08	Chicago Board of Education	City	Testimony on FY 1987 Budget — Revenues Expenditures, Priorities	Budget	Chicago
1986-08-06	Chicago Board of Education	City	Budget Priorities Ignore Wishes of Parents, Community	Budget	Chicago
1987-10-14	Chicago Board of Education	City	Testimony on Strike Settlement: Avoid Cuts for Kids	Budget	Chicago
1987-11-23	Chicago Board of Education	City	Testimony on Revised FY 1988 Budget: Revenues & Expenditures	Budget	Chicago
1987-11-24	Chicago Board of Education	City	Testimony on Revised FY 1988 Budget: Staffing Analysis	Budget	Chicago
1988-07-21	Chicago Board of Education	City	Testimony on Tentative 1989 Chicago Bd of Ed Budget	Budget	Chicago
1988-12-13	Chicago Board of Education	City	Present Study: Pregnant Teens are 'Invisible' in Chicago Schools	Research	Chicago
1989-07-18	Chicago Board of Education	City	Testimony on Interim Board's FY 1990 Budget	Budget	Chicago
1984-06-14	City Council: Education Comm	City	Present Study: 'Revenue Short Falls at Chicago Bd of Ed: 1970–84'	Research	Chicago
1987-11-03	City Council: Education Comm	City	Potential Reform Agenda: School Based Management	Reform	Chicago
1988-06-06	City Council: Education Comm	City	Testimony on School Reform Bill now in House of Reps	Reform	Chicago
1987-11-08	City Council: Ed & Fin Comms	City	Vs: Proposal to Alter Qualifications of Parents on LSCs	Reform	Chicago
1987-10-16	Community Development Comm	City	The Strike Settlement: Administrative Cuts to Avoid Cuts for Kids	Budget	Chicago
1984-03-21	Mayor's World Fair Coord Group	City	Vs: Proposed Tax Increment financing of North Loop Development	Budget	Chicago
1983-08-25		City	Review Costs for Impact on Board of Education Fiscal Crisis	Budget	Chicago
1984-09-10	Ill Senate Comm: Decentralization	State	Questions about Dividing School System into Ten Districts	Reform	Chicago
1984-12-05	Ill State Bd of Education	State	Call for Political Realism in Bd's Proposed Budget & Reform Plan	Reform	Chicago
1986-10-22	Ill House: Appropriations II Comm	State	Estimated Reductions in State Support of School Reform on CPS	Budget	Chicago
1987-02-11	State T/F: Encourage Citiz Involvemt	State	Testimony on CPS Implementation of School Councils & Budgeting	Reform	Chicago
1987-02-19	State T/F: Encourage Citiz Involvemt	State	Failure of Implementation of Budgeting Reforms at Local Schools	Reform	Chicago
1987-03-16	State T/F: Encourage Citiz Involvemt	State	Suggestions to Improve Local Councils and Budget Process	Reform	Chicago
1987-03-30	State T/F: Encourage Citiz Involvemt	State	Proposal to Enhance Local School Autonomy	Reform	Chicago
1987-06-11	Ill Senate: Elem & Sec Ed Comm	State	Pass HB 935, Proposal to Enhance Local School Autonomy	Reform	Springfield
1987-10-13	Ill Joint Elem & Sec Ed Comm	State	CPS Resists Reform: Strike Settlement Should Avoid Cuts for Kids	Reform	Chicago
1988-03-31	Ill Joint Comm on Schl Reform	State	Strengthen Initial Agreements of Mayor's Education Summit	Reform	Chicago
1984-04-27	Natl Bd of Inquiry on Schools	Federal	School Finance and Its Effects on Children At Risk	Reform	Chicago
1989-01-10	Natl Task Force: Next Generation	Federal	Pregnant Teens are 'Invisible' in Chicago Schools	At Risk Yth	Chicago
1987-12-10	US Dist Court: OffCivRts vs CPS	Federal	Expert Testimony on Decrease in Special Ed Staff in CPS	Spec Ed	Chicago
1985-10-30	US Senate: Ed Sub-Comm	Federal	Present: 'Dropouts from CPS' — For Dropout Prevention Bill	Dropouts	Washington
1986-06-23	US Hse: Elem, Sec, Voc Sub-Comm	Federal	Present: 'Dropouts from CPS' — For Dropout Prevention Bill	Dropouts	Chicago
1989-11-16	US Hse: Ed & Labor Comm	Federal	For: Educational Performance Agreements for School Restructuring	Reform	Washington

Figure 3.1   Record of Testimony (Hess, G.A.)

and relevant to the particular political processes embodied in particular legislative hearings, is likely to be presented.

Undoubtedly there is much anthropological research which might be policy relevant. Similarly, there are anthropological theories and understandings which, if generally held among legislators, might change the kind of legislation that is adopted. But legislative hearings are not the place to make that case. Hearings are the culmination of the effort to create a consensus among legislators, not the start of that effort. If anthropologists wish to create a consensus about needed legislative action, they must start by meeting with and convincing a number of key legislators in private sessions. Hearings might be the outcome of such a successful effort; they are not the starting point.

Testimony is more credible if it is presented by persons experienced in the political process. This is quite at odds with frequently articulated professional academic approaches, under which the quality of research is supposed to be the determining factor. Yet, when the tribe known as 'anthropologists' is studied in its annual meetings, it is easily determined that something very similar to the political process is at work. Recognized scholars, those very familiar with the process, are given more credibility in our meetings, and more opportunities to present their research and opinions, than are neophytes. Their words are listened to by more members of the Association and given more significance, even if not based on any recent research, than are the words of newcomers who may be reporting on recently completed and compelling work. Every organizational culture values those whose experience allows them to address the particular aims of the process underway. In that, there is a similarity between our association and the political process.

But legislative hearings are part of the political process, not the academic process. Successful testimony fits into that political process. It is built upon previous efforts to engage in the political process. Anthropologists who have not engaged in the political process at the local and state level should not expect to be invited into the national political process, no matter how well known they are among their own tribe. If they have not gained experience and something of a reputation in the tribe 'body politic' their academic credentials will weigh relatively lightly.

Qualifications for Testifying

I was invited to testify on H.R. 3347 because I do have experience in the body politic. In preparing this paper, I went back through my file of formally presented testimony and found that I have presented formal testimony at least forty-five times. The bulk of that experience (twenty-nine testimonies) is at the local level, most of it presenting research or budget analyses to the Chicago Board of Education. Ten times I have formally testified before state legislative committees or task forces. I have appeared six times before federal bodies, three of these being Congressional committees.

Most of this testimony has been built upon research which I have designed and directed. More of our research has been reported through testimony than has been presented in the academic forum. Because our focus, at the Chicago Panel, is upon improving the educational opportunities for students in our city, only on rare occasions do I have the time to recast our research into a format suitable for publication in academic journals. This is the perennial frustration of scholars who are primarily engaged in policy relevant research. We probably produce more pieces of original research during a given time period than do most academics, but we rarely have the time to relate our work to the research more widely reported in academic journals. However, our research has been more widely reported in the popular press and has had greater impact on public policy than most of the research published in academic anthropological journals. This is not necessarily true in other disciplines, some of whose journals are more directly focused on reporting policy relevant research.

Enacting Chicago School Reform Legislation

The primary reason I was invited to testify before the elementary and secondary education sub-committee was my involvement in enacting the Chicago School Reform Act. Let me describe briefly what kind of local, policy focused efforts were required to enact this legislation (for a fuller account, including a comparison with other school reform efforts across the nation, see Hess, 1991). I was just one among hundreds of persons who were involved in securing the passage of the legislation, but the contribution of my organization was important to the passage of the act, and I did author several sections of it, and helped to shape the consensus to include other important dimensions of this school restructuring effort.

The school reform movement in Chicago has many antecedents in the unique history of the public school system in our city (e.g., in the twenty year desegregation effort, see Hess, 1984). But the present effort can be traced specifically to two research reports released in early 1985.

The first, *The Bottom Line*, released by Designs for Change (1985), showed that only one in three graduating seniors in Chicago could read at the national norm. The second, *Dropouts From The Chicago Public Schools* (Hess and Lauber, 1985) showed that 43 per cent of entering freshmen never graduate at all. Thus, of any five entering freshmen, two will drop out, and only one of the remaining three will graduate reading at the national average.

This failure of education, along with limited job opportunities for minority youth, was seen as a major political vulnerability by the forces of Mayor Harold Washington, who was facing a re-election campaign in the winter of 1987. In the fall of 1986, I was invited to join the mayor's staff as a released time consultant to help organize and support a projected Mayor's Education Summit. During the first year of that summit, the Chicago Panel released a follow-up dropout study, a matched-pairs ethnographic study of eight Chicago high schools designed to discover qualitative variables which might account for differences in dropout rates among schools with similar student bodies (Hess *et al.*, 1986). This research was in the tradition of the effective schools research (Edmonds, 1979; Brookover and Lezotte, 1979). One of our primary findings was that *all Chicago high schools* shortchanged their students of a full school day through the use of non-existent or non-functional study halls at the beginning and end of the school day. This study showed there were things under the control of the school system which were contributing to the educational failure of the system. Administrators could no longer just blame the students for their own failures (Ryan, 1976).

The first year of the mayor's summit ended with an unsuccessful attempt to negotiate an agreement between the city's business community and the school system which would emulate the Boston Compact (Schwartz and Hargroves, 1986). I acted as an adviser to the businessmen during these negotiations. During this same period, at the request of the Speaker of the Illinois House of Representatives, the Panel submitted draft legislation to create a pilot project in school-based management in the Chicago Public Schools. This legislation (H.B. 935) passed the House on a 72 to 38 vote, but died in the Senate Education Committee.

During the summer of 1987, while the summit negotiations were failing, the Superintendent of Schools presented a tentative budget for 1987–88. I presented testimony to the Board of Education showing that this budget would cut employee salaries by two per cent while continuing to expand the administrative bureaucracy. I predicted a strike, if the proposal was not changed, and recommended how the budget could be changed (by cutting the administration rather than expanding it) to give employees a 3.5 per cent raise. My suggestions were ignored and the city suffered its longest teacher strike, nineteen school days, delaying the opening of school by a month. Ironically, the final settlement almost exactly matched my July recommendations.

The strike gave impetus to a reinvigorated Education Summit, now expanded to give added influence to parents and community members incensed by the long strike. The president of my organization was a key actor in the newly appointed Parents' Community Council (PCC), and was one of its representatives on the expanded summit. I presented an updated, phased-in, version of our school autonomy proposal to the PCC. Designs for Change, in concert with a wider coalition of a community groups, presented an even more radical school-based management proposal. After months of indeterminate haggling, during which time Mayor Washington succumbed to a massive heart attack, the summit produced a set of reform agreements which featured nominal school-based management proposals and a number of other more costly programs. Alone among the summit activists, I criticized the agreements as providing little new real power to local schools, an opinion in which I was later joined by Designs for Change, other community-based organizations, and representatives of the business community. A month later we significantly strengthened the agreements through a set of amendments which the summit adopted.

At the same time, the Chicago Panel's updated autonomy plan and Designs for Change's school-based management plan were introduced as separate pieces of legislation in the General Assembly. These bills were combined through the co-operative efforts of our sponsors in the Senate Education Committee. After extensive lobbying and some compromises, the bill passed the Senate by one vote; similar legislation in the House never got out of committee. When the Senate bill was considered in the House, it was obvious a consensus did not exist. The Speaker reconvened the members of the education summit in his office in Springfield, and in four days of line-by-line negotiation, the final consensus bill was drafted. As items were debated, individuals would be sent out of the room to draft language and bring it back to the whole group. On one such trip I wrote the paragraphs reallocating $40 million from the administration to local schools. My colleagues created a cap on the size of the administration and created a vehicle for direct teacher involvement at the school level. The consensus bill easily passed the Democratically dominated House, but again only passed the Senate by one vote on straight party voting. The Governor exercised his amendatory veto powers to rewrite parts of the bill, creating a new confrontation with the legislature. In the fall, after the 1988 elections, a bi-partisan compromise on the minor issues triggering the confrontation resulted in a partially rewritten bill that passed with only one dissenting vote in the Senate and nine 'nays' in the House.

The Chicago School Reform Act established as a goal that Chicago students will achieve at the national norms in five years. It reallocated $40 million in the first year, giving the average elementary school and additional $90,000 in new discretionary funding, which would grow to about $450,000 in the fifth year. It created Local School Councils with the power to adopt school improvement plans, design supporting budgets, and select or fire the principal.

The Chicago Panel secured foundation funding to mount a massive five year monitoring and research project to track the successes and failures of this school restructuring effort. The Panel's monitoring project combines both qualitative and quantitative approaches. It tracks academic achievement data on every child in the system over five years, correlating test scores, retention rates, attendance rates, and graduation rates with changes in programs and budgets at individual schools. This is a massive quantitative study, using the latest statistical techniques of Hierarchical Linear Modeling (Raudenbush and Bryk, 1986). At the same time, Panel staff are qualitatively tracking the development of school-based management and school improvement efforts in a sample of fourteen schools (ten elementary and four high schools) throughout the five year focus of the reform legislation. The Panel produces periodic reports on the status of reform implementation.[3]

Implications for Anthropologists

Another name for this section could be, 'Why don't they call on anthropologists?' To increase the utilization of anthropologists in the process of policy formation, we need to better understand the policy making process and consider how our discipline's current practices undercut or fail to support policy relevant research.

One reason that anthropologists are infrequently consulted on policy formation in America is that anthropology has few vehicles for reporting on policy relevant research which our members undertake. Only a few of our journals focus on policy relevant issues and their policy making readership is very narrow. These journals are focused more towards an academic audience than towards the policy audience. Overwhelmingly, anthropological journals are focused towards abstract knowledge with little relevance for policy making in America. This is in sharp contrast to journals in sociology, political science, and education. Not infrequently, the works of anthropologists who wish to be policy relevant appear in journals in those disciplines, rather than in our own. As I have already suggested, the process of forming public policy gives little value to abstract knowledge.

If we want more anthropologists to testify on the Hill, or to be consulted by the public media, then anthropologists need to be more involved in policy formation at the local level, more engaged in policy relevant research which they report more fully in the local papers than they do in anthropological journals. We need to develop a cohort of anthropologists who understand the constraints of policy setting and who are experienced in the rough and tumble world of getting policies adopted, whether through legislation or through administrative decisions. If we want to be more fully represented in the body politic, we have to be willing to become a part of that culture. When we do, we will be called upon and consulted because of our experience in policy setting, not because we are anthropologists. But in that process, anthropology will have gained a wider voice.

Notes

1 Copies of this testimony, or others listed in this article, are available from the Chicago Panel on Public School Policy and Finance, 220 S. State St. #1212, Chicago, IL 60604.
2 I am sad to relate that while the 'Educational Performance Agreements' bill was successfully incorporated into the omnibus education bill of 1990, that bill was not called for a vote before the end of that session. Unfortunately, Congressman Smith fared little better at home, where he was defeated in his bid for re-election. Perhaps one of his 34 co-sponsors will reintroduce this legislation which may ultimately change the way the federal government provides support for public education.
3 Copies of reports issued as part of the project *Monitoring and Researching Chicago School Reform* may be secured from the Chicago Panel at the previously cited address.

References

BROOKOVER, W.B. and LEZOTTE, L.W. (1979) *Changes in School Characteristics Coincident with Changes in Student Achievement*, East Lansing, Michigan State University.

DESIGNS FOR CHANGE (1985) *The Bottom Line: Chicago's Failing Schools and How to Save Them*, Chicago, Designs for Change.

EDMONDS, R. (1979) 'Effective schools for the urban poor', *Educational Leadership*, 37, pp. 15–18, October.

ELMORE, R.F. *et al.* (1990) *Restructuring Schools: The Next Generation of Educational Reform*, San Francisco, Jossey-Bass, Inc.

HALLETT, A.C. and HESS, G.A. JR. (1982) *Budget Cuts at the Board of Education*, Chicago, Chicago Panel on Public School Finances.

HESS, G.A., JR. (1984) 'Renegotiating a multicultural society: participation in desegregation planning in Chicago', *Journal of Negro Education*, 53, pp. 132–146, Spring.

HESS, G.A., JR. (1991) *School Restructuring: Chicago Style*, Newbury Park, CA, Corwin Press.

HESS, G.A., JR and LAUBER, D. (1985) *Dropouts From The Chicago Public Schools*, Chicago, Chicago Panel on Public School Finances.

HESS, G.A., JR., WELLS, E., PRINDLE, C., KAPLAN, B. and LIFFMAN, P. (1986) ' "Where's Room 1875?" How Schools Can Reduce Their Dropout Problem', Chicago, Chicago Panel on Public School Policy and Finance. Excerpted in *Education and Urban Society*, **19**, 3, pp. 330–355, May, 1987.

RAUDENBUSH, F.W. and BRYK, A.S. (1986) 'A hierarchical model for studying effects', *Sociology of Education*, 59, pp. 1–17.

RYAN, W. (1976) *Blaming the Victim*, New York, Random House.

SCHWARTZ, R.S. and HARGROVES, J. (1986) 'The Boston compact', *Metropolitan EDUCATION*, 3, pp. 14–24.

4 Ethnographic Research on AIDS Risk Behavior and the Making of Policy

Margaret R. Weeks and Jean J. Schensul

'Many of anthropology's past contributions could be classi-
fied as policy related if one defines policy science as helping
decision-makers set guidelines for action' (Weaver, 1985).

Policies are sets of ideas or guidelines for action. It is a common belief
that policy is set by governmental bodies through legislation and regulations. We agree with Weaver, however, that guidelines for action can
be established and regulated in any context within which decisions are
made that affect or influence the lives of community residents. By
this definition, policy is generated in governmental institutions, private organizations, non-profit organizations, public agencies, and the
media. If we accept this definition, policy-makers are actors in these
settings. Thus any citizen, by virtue of employment, voluntary participation on boards, committees, and commissions, or community
activism, may be a policy-maker.

Because the individuals that participate in policy-making in these
arenas hold different ideas or theories about the way these guidelines
should be specified in any setting, we may speak about *alternative
policies* and their implications for action. Often these theories are confused or conflicting, and a policy-maker may simultaneously hold contradictory theories which may make it difficult to make rational decisions
about an issue.

In public decision-making arenas in education, health, law enforce-
ment, and so on, there are generally conflicting sets of policies which
may change with changes in the setting. Furthermore, when multiple
organizations or agencies are involved in, or added to, a debate about
directions, theories of action and policy directions may change through
time. Thus policies are continually changing in relation to particular

events, actors, and settings (Patton, 1979). Especially when theoretical assumptions are not clear, policies may be driven or confused by the values, ideologies, and agendas of policy-makers rather than their constituents.

Policy-making is heavily influenced by the balance of power in the group. Thus an understanding of power relationships and politics is crucial for an understanding of how policies are formulated and the ways in which compromises are reached between opposing interest groups. As such, policy formulation is neither scientific nor unscientific, although at various levels, the findings and writings of scientists may or may not be utilized.

As social scientists, where do anthropologists fit in the interface of research and policy formulation and implementation? Anthropologists do their best work 'close to the community' because they are trained to do ethnography in community settings and they seek employment in organizations that permit or encourage them to do research in communities. Most of the domains of observation and interpretation and the best theoretical developments in anthropology have to do with the ways in which communities or sectors of communities function and the ways in which community residents articulate with wider society institutions. Thus anthropologists are often best placed to articulate policy with reference to the communities in which they are active.

Anthropologists can be useful in these complex social arenas in several ways. First, they can specify and clarify the alternative and competing theories that underpin suggested policy directions. They can also suggest particular policies and theories of action with reference to a specific community problem for which they have data. Anthropologists can provide data to inform policy-makers in different settings about an issue and can create policy-making arenas within which the anthropologists themselves can have direct influence, because they are shaping the debate, guiding the discussion, and promoting the outcomes. Finally, professional anthropologists and other social scientists sometimes seek to affect policy by developing programs or other activities designed to test theory or to establish environments within which new policies can be formulated.

In any of these situations anthropologists may find themselves confronting several central dilemmas. First, they may be asked to represent the research community, which may not be politically feasible, acceptable, or representative; second, they may not be prepared to speak about policy at every level; third, they may not understand the power relationships among sectors involved in the policy debate; and finally, they may not be familiar with the social science or other theoretical frameworks which guide the competing positions of policy-makers.

To counter these problems, and to strengthen the likelihood that anthropology and ethnographic research can play a major role in policy formation, anthropologists must be directly involved in those settings in which policy is made. One important strategy involves the anthropologist in the active creation and administration of programs, consortia, action research networks, and other similar activities that involve community residents and the organizations that represent them in research, action, and policy debate (Schensul, 1985). Schensul has referred to this process as the creation of 'policy clusters' (1985). The policy cluster is an *ad hoc* group that comes 'into existence to work on or advocate for issues of public concern. . . . The policy cluster is a focus of power in the policy process and varies in its degree of influence as well as its involvement in action' (1985) with the composition and scope of its membership and the skill of its facilitator.

The creation of a policy cluster sanctions community survey research and ethnography on sensitive topics. It empowers participants in the consortia to use research as a tool in advocacy and public promotion of platforms or directions in education, health, housing, and other areas of public welfare. It ensures widespread community involvement in the research, the program, and the activities around the promotion of policy change. It avoids the problem faced by the anthropologist who is asked to speak in isolation from the community within which research has been conducted. Unlike research alone, involvement in the administration of action programs offers virtually automatic access to other arenas within which policy is being discussed.

This perspective differentiates between research on policy and policy research. The former attempts to analyze the domains of policy as process. The latter involves the researcher as actor in the policy arena. The following case discussion reviews an ongoing program in which anthropologists are both administrators and ethnographers in a broad based, urban, multi-ethnic consortium which is attempting to change high risk behaviors of injection drug users and their sex partners at risk for HIV infection. At the same time, this program constitutes a policy cluster which is attempting to change community, city, and state policy around programs, services, and service co-ordination to meet the needs of this target population. Members of the program consortium participate in other policy clusters, which also vary in strength and influence, to address service co-ordination and case management needs of injection drug users, state and local policies affecting substance abusing mothers and pregnant women, culturally specific HIV educational needs of urban women, the initiation and monitoring of needle exchange programs, and the promotion of continued funding of outreach demonstration projects at the national level.

The Need for Ethnographic Research on AIDS Behavior

The inability of survey research and experimental and quasi-experimental design to provide fully satisfactory answers to a host of AIDS-related questions has led some health science researchers to propose the 'ethnography' as a critical aspect of evaluation research. The discovery methods of 'ethnography' or 'ethnographic evaluation' may be cited as a solution to health policy, service delivery, or program evaluation problems under specific circumstances. One appropriate condition is when the disease is new and its natural history and social definition are relatively unknown or emerging. Another is when the target population is new, unknown, or unpopular, or when this population is difficult to reach by public health officials, physicians, and so on. Ethnographic methodology is also particularly useful when the health problem is of considerable concern to the public, and when existing research paradigms (that is, experimental design, or epidemiology) do not provide satisfactory answers to questions or problems concerning the environment in which the disease is spread, the vectors or vehicles for its contagion, popular responses to the problem, or unexplained differential or unanticipated effects of the disease or public response to it. Finally, ethnography is particularly valuable when existing interventions have not solved the problem of infection or transmission, as in the case of malaria (Sevilla-Casa, 1989), diarrhea, or acute respiratory infection.

Ethnography offers methods for identifying, observing, documenting, and analyzing culture (patterned beliefs and behaviors) in communities, institutions, and target populations under difficult field circumstances. In addition, the ethnographic perspective insists on identification and interpretation of the meanings behind observed behaviors, for example, responses to disease (Werner and Schoepfle, 1987; Weller and Romney, 1988). Ethnographers assume that patterns of behavior and interpretation vary with ethnicity or cultural identity and, further, that ethnic groups are characterized by intra-ethnic diversity, which must always be taken into consideration. The methods of ethnography are generally utilized to understand how and why systems are constructed, in what ways people interact with them, and how they interpret and explain both the systems and their own interactions with them. The behaviors and ways of thinking of newly affected target populations are relatively unknown to health policy-makers. When these populations do not respond to interventions or services in expected ways, ethnography can offer new interpretations to health decision-makers and members of the target population themselves.

What Is Ethnographic Evaluation?

'The label *ethnographic evaluator* suggests a contradiction in terms to some scholars. . . . First, it is a myth that anthropologists are completely non-judgmental. . . . The aim, however, is to assume a non-judgmental orientation toward different cultural practices. . . . Both traditional ethnographers and ethnographic evaluators attempt to adopt this posture throughout a study and to make explicit their more conscious and obvious biases. A non-judgmental orientation and an evaluative approach are not mutually exclusive. Evaluation simply represents another level of analysis.

The major difference between the traditional ethnographer and the ethnographic evaluator is that the traditional ethnographer *concludes* the study with a description of the culture, whereas an ethnographic evaluator *begins* the evaluative segment of the study with a description of the culture. The ethnographic evaluator describes what is going on and then makes a qualitative leap beyond description to the explicit appraisal and assessment of the cultural system in terms of its own cultural norms (Fetterman, 1986).

As Fetterman suggests, the term ethnographic evaluation poses a contradiction for the following reason. Evaluation refers to judgment against an already defined standard; ethnography poses a theoretical framework to account for or predict the ways in which cultural systems are constructed. Evaluation is prescriptive; ethnography is descriptive (Wolcott, 1984). Evaluation tests outcomes against a theory of action. Explicitly stated as a consequence of theoretical framework is a set of clearly articulated goals and objectives, and an action plan (Rossi and Freeman, 1985; Suchman, 1967). Ethnography, in contrast, is a set of 'discovery procedures' through which theory of action — or program theory — is generated, and goals, objectives, and action can be clearly defined as they are being implemented. Ethnographic evaluations 'begin with the aim of ethnography — to understand. However, they make the next logical step — to assess what is understood' (Fetterman, 1984).

Ethnography works best in evaluation when the model is emerging or developing, that is, in the early stages of program development, or when the program is viewed as constantly having to adapt to changing circumstances. Ethnography is most useful when theory, standards, goals and objectives are viewed as 'fuzzy', 'flexible', 'discoverable', and changeable, in other words, when it can assist in generating or discovering the theory and methods underlying a program approach.

Evaluations based on experimental or quasi-experimental designs and quantitative outcome measures assume clear cut positive or negative outcomes as evidenced by a selected set of outcome measures. Ethnography, on the other hand, works best when there is a stated desire to seek expanded and unanticipated outcomes, a willingness to accept and explore negative outcomes, and a recognition that the target population is diverse and unknown and that the program is likely to affect that population in different, and not fully predictable, ways. Quantitative evaluation of individual outcomes generally compares 'classes' of individuals; ethnography is most useful in examining and explaining differential outcomes and variation in outcomes among individuals or across subgroups within target populations.

In short, ethnography can play a critical role in AIDS program evaluation under several circumstances. The first is when there is a recognized need to understand cultural variations in target populations in order to increase efficacy of outreach and prevention/education efforts. A second is when AIDS prevention programs are in the formative stages and information about the process of the program, the organizational base, the community context of the program, and the target population are critical to shaping the program itself. A third is when the program is ongoing, but theory, goals, objectives, methods, and even desired results are not clearly stated or understood. A fourth is when there is a clear discrepancy between the program standard and program operation and the reasons for this discrepancy, as well as its consequences, are not understood. A fifth is when aspects of a program are not working as anticipated and an explanation is required. A sixth is when outcomes are uneven or not as anticipated and the explanation is believed to lie with as yet unidentified patterns of difference among program participants. Finally, ethnographic evaluation can be critical when there is an interest in describing or demonstrating operational aspects of a program for adaptation by others.

In the remainder of this chapter we will describe the use of ethnographic evaluation in AIDS programs and its importance for defining policy on AIDS issues. We will begin with a description of AIDS prevention programs, using the case of one specific demonstration research project, in which ethnographic evaluation is utilized in combination with quantitative outcome measures within a quasi-experimental design. Following this, we will outline ways that ethnographic documentation and assessment of AIDS intervention programs can be carried out by program staff to complement the collection and analysis of quantitative data. With this, we will indicate some of the advantages and disadvantages of using program staff for ethnographic evaluation, and the training they received in one project in which they contributed to carrying out such data collection. Finally, we will discuss some of the ways this program has used data gathered through its ethnographic and quantitative evaluation methods to affect local and national policy on AIDS prevention among injection drug users and their sex partners.

AIDS Programs

Almost all AIDS programs are prevention oriented. AIDS prevention programs fall into three classes (Fischl, 1988; Hopkins, 1987; Mason, 1988). These include, *AIDS prevention education* intended to change high risk behavior in order to reduce exposure to HIV; *AIDS post-test counseling* for those whose HIV antibody test results are positive and who may be at risk for continuing exposure to HIV or for transmitting the virus to others; and *prevention, education and support programs for people with HIV* and people who anticipate or who are already experiencing symptoms and diseases associated with AIDS.

One AIDS prevention program that includes all of these activities is Project COPE (Community Outreach Prevention Effort), a demonstration research program run by a consortium of community-based research and service agencies in Hartford, Connecticut. The project is funded by the National Institute on Drug Abuse (NIDA) as part of a National AIDS Demonstration Research (NADR) program to develop and evaluate experimental interventions for people at risk of HIV infection through needle use or unprotected sex with needle users. Among these NADR projects, Project COPE is unique in that it is one of only two that are consortia. Project COPE policies are determined by a Steering Committee made up of representatives from each of the six collaborating agencies, including two research and program development agencies (the Institute for Community Research and the Hispanic Health Council), three community-based service agencies (the Urban League of Greater Hartford, Latinos/as Contra SIDA, and the Hartford

Dispensary), and the City of Hartford Health Department. Steering Committee members are generally directors of their agencies or department heads within them and act as co-investigators for the project. These individuals are able to use their positions to insure the link between the project and the community, and to influence community policy using information obtained from the project.

Project COPE targets injection drug users (IDUs) and their sex partners for group and individual education, counseling, service referral, group support, and pre- and post- HIV antibody test counseling. The primary goal of this project is to test and compare the effectiveness of three intervention programs. The first is a culturally appropriate program for African American participants, which is conducted by African American staff at an agency located in the center of Hartford's African American community. The second is a Latino culturally appropriate intervention primarily targeting Hartford's at-risk Puerto Rican IDUs and their partners, which is run by Latino staff and located in the city's Latino community. The third is a non-culturally specific intervention for a randomly assigned mixed group of African Americans, Latinos, Whites, and others in the project, which is located in a drug treatment clinic and is provided by a multi-ethnic staff. The basic hypothesis this project aims to test is that intervention that incorporates elements of ethnic culture in its content and presentation format, is provided by ethnically similar program operators, and is located within the ethnic community to be served, can more effectively bring about behavior change necessary to reduce risks of HIV infection than intervention provided outside the community in mainstream health care institutions.

Preliminary indications of the project's outcomes support this hypothesis. Measures available to date include rates of initiation of participants assigned to each intervention and rates of completion of their assigned programs. Both African American and Latino participants assigned to the culturally appropriate programs preferred to enter those interventions more so than African American and Latino participants assigned to the standard intervention in the drug treatment health clinic (38 per cent of African Americans and 59 per cent of Latinos entered the culturally appropriate interventions; 33 per cent of African Americans and 20 per cent of Latinos entered the standard). Participants were also more likely to remain in the culturally appropriate interventions to completion; 55 per cent of African Americans and 45 per cent of Latinos who entered the culturally appropriate interventions stayed to completion, compared to 23 per cent of African Americans and 35 per cent of Latinos who entered the standard intervention. These data suggest the need to place culturally oriented interventions within specific ethnic communities to provide effective intervention for people at risk there.

AIDS prevention programs, like Project COPE, have multiple target groups and staffs differentiated by ethnicity, gender, HIV status, education, and other factors. They may also provide services in multiple sites. Such programs are susceptible to changes in administration and staff, funding level, the results of new research, and many other factors that impact on program implementation and outcomes.

It is helpful to think of AIDS prevention programs, including Project COPE, as containing the following components, which may influence the ways in which the programs operate:

Institutional base	The base from which the program to be evaluated is operating
Target population	The population in a community setting from which program participants are drawn and against which they may be evaluated
Program standard	Theoretical framework, goals, objectives, and action plan
Inputs or resources	Human, technical/material, economic, informational
Process	Activities, actions, and interactions which may or may not be related to the target population, may or may not be anticipated, intended, expected, or recognized, and may have unintended as well as intended consequences bearing on outcomes
Consequences and outcomes	Short, intermediate, and long term; desired, undesired, and/or unrecognized

A comprehensive evaluation must take all of these program elements and their interactive effects into consideration. Unfortunately, the constraints of program funding generally do not favor comprehensive program documentation. Even programs that include ethnographers on the staff must make choices concerning what the ethnographer will document. One solution is to improve the observation and documentation skills of program staff. This strategy has several benefits. First, program staff become increasingly self-conscious and self-aware in selecting elements of their own interventions, in carrying out street outreach, or in administration. Second, program staff, through active participation, learn to value evaluation. Third, the distinctions among 'researchers' and 'activist', or program staff, are eliminated.

Use of AIDS Prevention Program Staff for Qualitative Data Collection

In the absence of a project ethnographer to conduct ethnographic studies or carry out the collection of qualitative data to supplement quantitative measures and to do process evaluation, it is possible to rely on a variety of project staff to participate in these activities. Several general factors affect the ability of these staff to act as partial ethnographers and collect these kinds of data. First, all staff are already overextended with responsibilities of their positions. They are only minimally available for the time-consuming tasks of collecting and organizing qualitative data. Second, most staff are untrained in the collection of these data. They have not been trained in skills of observation and documentation, in rigor and consistency in data collection, and in developing an analytical framework within which to place the information and questions that develop through the process of ethnographic work.

When considering staff to participate in qualitative data collection, it is important to address the issues deemed important by the staff themselves. It is essential to involve these staff in the planning process to decide what is to be collected and through what means. This insures, first, that their own issues will be addressed by the data collection process. Second, it increases the likelihood that they will find usefulness in the tasks they are performing and that they will understand the inherent need to perform them.

Contributions of Specific Staff to Qualitative Data Collection

In Project COPE, staff in a variety of roles have contributed to the collection of qualitative data from the vantage point of their own positions. Some of the ways people in different roles have participated within the frameworks of their other responsibilities follow.

Project administrators   In the process of organizing and implementing demonstration research, project administrators can participate in a number of activities to pursue questions of interest to the project and can contribute on an ongoing basis to process evaluation. Questions of interest may spring from initial set-up needs of the project; others may develop while carrying out the program.

In Project COPE, project administrators (three out of eight of whom are trained ethnographers) conducted preliminary focus groups with injection drug users and prostitutes to gain a sense of the project target population needs and interests and to provide background information on the city in general. Notes from the focus groups provided information useful in locating and recruiting these targeted groups and in designing interventions that could address their needs appropriately. Additionally, administrative staff played a key role in documenting project set-up and revisions in project design and structure during early implementation of the program.

Additional activities to which administrative staff can contribute include designing and documenting development of appropriate methods to address ongoing problems and issues that arise while implementing the project. These methods often require addressing the issues in a manner that is appropriate within the theoretical framework of the project design. Issues that arise in the NADR projects include such problems as why the project is not reaching certain groups, and how the project can document and then analyze differential participation by clients in the interventions (in order to operationalize project activities to measure and analyze outcomes). Project COPE has an additional set of issues resulting from a research design oriented toward the development of culturally appropriate interventions for specific ethnic groups. Project administrators have been grappling with the problem of creating a common understanding among all project staff of concepts like 'culture' and 'culturally appropriate'. They then have had to find ways to use this common language to document the cultural components of the project's interventions.

In summary, project administrators can participate in the analytical tasks of defining issues and then develop appropriate methods to address them, they can revise the research design or project structure to incorporate new knowledge or conditions in the project's environment, and they can help determine issues that are in need of further inquiry to keep the project up with changes in the city, among target populations, and within their own project.

Aside from these contributions, staff in administrative positions are limited in the degree to which they can contribute to ethnographic data collection and in organization and analysis of qualitative data. In many NADR projects, administrative personnel are not trained in qualitative data collection. Additionally, they do not have time available to do complete and systematic ethnographic work and to exhaust a particular question. Even in the documentation of their own project's activities, because of the difficulty (or impossibility) of being always present when outreach or intervention is taking place, administrative staff must depend on other project staff to provide documentation of these activities.

Outreach workers   In the context of their street, agency, or other outreach AIDS education activities, outreach workers can contribute greatly to the project's knowledge and awareness of activities in the city and issues affecting the project participants. Because they are on the streets, they can pursue specific questions and provide critical information to keep the project in touch with changes in the general environment and those that affect participant needs.

In Project COPE, outreach workers have been asked to pursue several key questions. In the early stages of the project, street outreach workers observed and documented activities in specified areas of the city to look for patterns and new activities. They were also asked to pursue with male participants the question of why these men do not want to bring in their partners. Finally, outreach workers made attempts to find some project participants who had dropped out of the program before their intervention was completed or who never attended any intervention, and to ask why they left.

Outreach workers can also play significant roles in qualitative documentation for the project. Most of the NADR programs have their outreach workers keep quantitative records of street contacts to document who the project is reaching. These data are, in many programs, augmented with log records that provide anecdotal information pointing to relevant questions or answers to questions that come out of doing outreach. In Project COPE, agency outreach workers have also been doing in-depth interviewing with agency staff and service providers on more general issues of the socio-cultural environment for the provision of services to the project's targeted groups. Direct and regular contact that outreach workers have with the streets and social service agencies makes them suitable staff to pursue questions and issues of interest in these areas.

Nevertheless, these staff, in most cases, cannot provide thorough ethnographic or qualitative documentation while they are concurrently recruiting or providing AIDS education and intervention. Their greatest limitations to providing these data are time and training. These limitations make it difficult for outreach workers to be systematic in their collection of data. It is also extremely difficult for them to pursue a question to completion, either through observation or in-depth interviewing. Though anecdotal information in logs and even limited answers to question of interest pursued on the streets and in agencies can be useful and interesting, it is likely to be incomplete (and therefore possibly misleading) and is generally without a theoretical framework from which to assess and analyze these data.

Social workers and other intervention providers   Because of their direct contact with participants to provide intervention and education, several tasks in qualitative data collection and documentation naturally fall to the social workers. In addition to keeping records of their own activities, they can contribute to the collection of other important qualitative data for the project.

In documenting their intervention activities, they are able to provide detailed descriptions of the kinds of intervention they offer, the general outline of their intervention program, and records of how much intervention they have given to each participant. Several NADR projects have found it necessary to develop forms to detail the level of participation and amount of intervention for each participant. These forms often include records of qualitative data, such as participant feedback on the impact of the intervention, including group sessions, one-on-one counseling, and other formal or informal intervention provided them. It is important to note that the original ideas for the content of the forms being used by Project COPE originated from similar forms the social workers were using for their own documentation needs. These forms were then augmented to address research needs of the project with the assistance of and feedback from those who would mainly be using them.

Additionally, social workers are in a strategic position to collect more in-depth information that comes out of the process of providing intervention, within the confines of maintaining information on issues most critical for specific groups, for example female injection drug users, female sex partners, specific ethnic groups, and so on. They can also provide key information on the variation *within* groups of participants, their responses to the intervention, and the issues participants feel are critical.

Limitations social workers face in the collection of qualitative data stem first from their responsibilities to provide intervention. It is not possible for them to observe and document themselves and how they ran a group session while in the process of doing it. Another observer is required to fill this function. They are also not able to do exhaustive documentation of issues that come out of interventions, either for individuals or special groups, nor can they be expected to record all the variations in responses to interventions. The focus of social workers is to provide services, not to pursue research questions. Paperwork is time-consuming and, for them, secondary to implementing intervention. A possible solution to these limitations is to have other project staff regularly interview the social workers about some of the issues that come out of the interventions with groups or for individuals.

The best solution to limitations of project staff to do qualitative data collection is to combine the efforts of people in different positions and have them work in conjunction with each other. For example, in Project COPE, interviewers will be working with social workers to observe and document activities in group sessions at the intervention sites. Sharing the time required to do this kind of documentation and collection of other qualitative data is necessary because all staff are limited by the demands of their various project responsibilities.

Training of Project Staff in Ethnographic Data Collection

Proper training of project staff is critical in preparation for qualitative data collection. This preparation should serve two purposes: a) project improvement by improving inquiry, observation, and interpretation skills to strengthen outreach and capacity; and b) project dissemination by collecting data leading to more accurate description of interventions for project replication.

Project COPE has made a commitment to train interviewers, agency outreach staff, and project social workers in ethnographic data collection and analysis. In Project COPE, interviewers are also assigned to agency outreach and the documentation of the project's culturally targeted interventions. To increase their ability to document agency support systems for injection drug users and their partners, and the intervention process, program administrators who are trained ethnographers developed an ethnographic training curriculum. After reviewing this curriculum, project social workers also saw the advantage of working on observation skills and asked if they could join the training group. The social workers are the central figures in Project COPE's prevention interventions. Their participation in these sessions offered the potential for developing observer/facilitator documentation teams (cf. Erickson, 1977). This was an exciting option for the project.

Observer/facilitator team work offers rich possibilities for raising critical questions, offering multiple perspectives on project activities, deepening ability to understand and interpret participant responses, and expanding explanatory material for use in manuals and guides to interventions.

The first seven ethnographic training sessions of the curriculum designed by project administrators addressed the observer as instrument of observation, observer bias, observation, recording and note-taking, interpretation and analysis, elements of a program, components of Project COPE interventions, and process questions raised by observer/facilitator teams. Additional sessions yet to be conducted will focus on social mapping, activity sequences, ways of measuring risk perception, facilitator/participant interaction, intragroup diversity in participation in interventions, and cultural symbolism in curriculum content.

Curricula from each of the sessions, coupled with exercises, notes, and comments produced by these sessions, are being collected as the basis for an ethnographic/process evaluation training manual for use by staffs of other AIDS prevention programs. The next challenge is to monitor, manage, maintain, and present the ethnographic data obtained through observation, interviewing, pile sorts, maps, and other materials so that its utility is guaranteed.

Ethnographic Data and the AIDS Policy Arena

Various kinds of qualitative data have thus far resulted from the activities of COPE staff trained in basic observation and documentation techniques. These primarily include descriptions of the cultural aspects of the interventions (cf. Weeks *et al.*, 1993; Haughton *et al.*, 1990) and anecdotal information on specific issues, such as needs of project participants, how they prioritize these needs, their attitudes toward needle exchange, and so on. Project staff have used these data in several policy arenas by working through the project or their agencies in a variety of policy clusters. The following outlines some of the uses of project information, including that collected through ethnographic methods, to affect policy locally and nationally.

The Project COPE Steering Committee members have interacted both individually and as a team to affect policy on AIDS prevention for IDUs and their partners. Several members were directly involved in the development and activities of a city-wide AIDS Collaborative. This organization brought together research, health care, and support agencies. It grew out of a need to identify service providers and to review existing services for people with AIDS. The serious lack of services for people with AIDS or with HIV that quickly became evident led the Collaborative to build a prevention component. One of the Project COPE principal investigators participated in shaping the prevention direction of this collaborative. Additionally, the project director participated in the funding committee, whose goal was to look for sources of revenue that could be brought into the city and to direct information on potential funding to appropriate members of the Collaborative. Qualitative data on service needs of Project COPE participants also aided in orienting the direction of the Collaborative.

After two years of activity, the AIDS Collaborative developed a broader, regional focus, and the local efforts to collaborate around AIDS were taken up by the HIV Action Initiative. The Action Initiative was created through a combined effort of a local class of the American Leadership Forum, the City of Hartford Health Department, and other local AIDS organizations. The HIV Action Initiative is an attempt to structure local collaborative efforts through a three-tiered system, with a steering committee, operating committee, and work groups. The goal of the Action Initiative is to identify gaps, prioritize the city's prevention/education, support service, primary care, and research needs, and focus resources accordingly. All members of the Project COPE Steering Committee sit on either the Action Initiative's steering committee or its operating committee. On both levels, COPE co-investigators have played an important role in orienting this committee to serve the needs of African American and Latino people with HIV and AIDS more effectively. Other staff in Project COPE participate in one or more of the work groups, including the Research, Education/Prevention, and Support Services Work Groups. In the Legal Services subcommittee of the Support Services Work Group, Project COPE social workers will present their experiences of trying to access services and supports for COPE participants who are HIV-positive. This information will be used to advocate for better access, and minimizing barriers, to services. Additionally, Project COPE data have been presented at HIV Action Steering Committee and other work group meetings to help assess local service gaps and provide direction for program development.

Another issue of direct interest to Project COPE is needle exchange, whereby injection drug users can exchange used needles for sterile ones in a controlled setting, without risk of police interference and with counseling and support for getting into drug treatment. Connecticut is one of only eleven states in which possession of non-prescription injection equipment is illegal. There is currently a move to establish an experimental needle exchange program in Hartford similar to that in another Connecticut city, New Haven. Proponents of such a program refer to the need to use whatever means available to reduce the number of people potentially at risk of exposure to HIV through sharing of needles and other drug paraphernalia. Opponents see needle exchange as a band-aid solution to a major problem and as ethically questionable because it enables the IDU to continue using. Local African American opponents of such a program also fear a message to people in their community, especially children, that condones drug abuse by virtue of locating a needle exchange program in their neighborhoods. Local advocates of the idea from the same community, however, believe that the potential number of lives saved outweighs the ethical problem of enabling drug users. Project COPE and other local survey data have been utilized in the local debate, first at a public forum in a local university, then at a presentation to the city council (Singer, *et al.*, 1991).

Qualitative and other information gathered through Project COPE have also been used to address local policy issues other than AIDS. Local political efforts by the State Permanent Commission on the Status of Women to promote more liberal legislation to protect the rights of women substance abusers to retain their children, called upon anecdotal and other qualitative data on women in Project COPE. The director of the Commission utilized information on substance-abusing women's multiple issues and needs for services and supports in order to deal with their drug and alcohol problems. This information was also used to counter the emphasis on punitive measures by pressing for more treatment programs for pregnant women and women with children. Efforts to deal with this issue community-wide in Hartford led to the Women's Community Alliance for Recovery, a collaboration of health care, service, and treatment agencies brought together by the Director of Research at the Hispanic Health Council (who is also the principal investigator of Project COPE) around the issue of treatment for pregnant substance abusers.

In addition to policy-related activity on the local level, Project COPE staff have used information collected through the project to advocate for sustaining funding for AIDS prevention programs for IDUs, their partners, and others at risk. COPE directors have been involved with state legislators for continued funding for outreach programs. They have also presented project findings at national conferences at the invitation of NIDA staff in Washington. For example, one of the principal investigators on the project attended the most recent conference on substance abuse policy in Washington to promote continued funding for AIDS prevention, demonstration research, and culturally appropriate programming to reach specific ethnic groups with education and services. Project findings are also presented by staff from all roles in the project at the annual NADR conferences, at which information is shared with other projects like COPE on effective strategies to reach and provide intervention to IDUs and their partners.

Conclusion

Ethnographic documentation of AIDS prevention programs offers unique insight into multiple factors that impact on individuals at risk of HIV infection. Likewise, ethnographic evaluation of such programs can provide an assessment tool to determine the most effective ways to guide at-risk individuals toward changes in behavior to protect themselves. Data collected through ethnographic techniques complement quantitative outcome data by providing information on how interventions 'work', factors influencing levels of participation in interventions, intra-cultural variations in participation and outcomes, and inter-site variations in process and outcome. Effective documentation is invaluable because it is the best means by which the rich detail of intervention activities can be captured as examples for others of what can be expected through time and across ethnic and other cultural groupings. Such detail is most valuable when it can be used to bring greater understanding to policy makers and players in any arena in which policy is created and affected.

AIDS prevention project staff, given basic training in ethnographic data collection skills, can contribute greatly to the collection of these data and their utilization in a variety of policy spheres within the community. The most effective mode for documentation and interpretation is the observer/facilitator team model, in which the observer (who may or may not be a formally trained ethnographer) works closely with facilitators on site as a participant-observer. This relationship is especially critical for project ethnographers, who frequently find themselves outside the project mainstream, because it gives them a central role in relation to interveners. But it is equally important for any observer to enhance understanding, eliminate the hierarchical and disciplinary distinction between research and action, and ensure the utility of *research process* and *research results* for facilitators and adaptors. It provides a valuable connection between research, documentation, and evaluation and the community or beyond, where decisions are made that impact upon the ability to implement needed programs to address specific needs.

Such a link is critical to AIDS prevention for IDUs and their partners, in light of the social, economic, and political difficulties many face as a result of stigmatization by mainstream class and ethnic groups. Collaboration between researchers and service providers to collect and disseminate information on project processes and outcomes insures a greater capacity of the project to advocate for programs that are appropriate to people of different class and ethnic backgrounds and that are better designed to address their needs. Mutual commitment of all project staff to collect and disseminate in-depth information on the project and its participants brings a powerful force to bear on policy-making bodies.

References

ERICKSON, F. (1977) 'Some Approaches to Inquiry in School-Community Ethnography', *Anthropology and Education*, Q. 8, pp. 58–69.

FETTERMAN, D. (1984) *Ethnography in Educational Evaluation*, Beverly Hills, CA, Sage.

FETTERMAN, D. (1986) *Educational Evaluation: Ethnography in Theory, Practice, and Politics*, Beverly Hills, CA, Sage.

FISCHL, M.A. (1988) 'Prevention of Transmission of AIDS During Sexual Intercourse', in PEVITA, V.T., HELLMAN, S. and ROSENBERG, S.A. (Eds), *AIDS: Etiology, Diagnosis, Treatment and Prevention*, Second edition, Philadelphia, Pa, J.B. Lippincott Co., pp. 369–74.

HAUGHTON, C., SANKS, M., PEREZ, W., HUNTE-MARROW, J. and SINGER, M. (1990) 'Culturally Appropriate Intervention: Doin' the Right Thang', (unpublished manuscript) presented at the Second Annual NADR Conference, Washington, DC.

HOPKINS, D.R., MD, MPH (1987) 'Public Health Measures for Prevention and Control of AIDS', *Measures/Outcomes*, Sept.–Oct., 1987, **102**, 5, pp. 463–7.

MASON, J.O., *et al.* (1988) 'Current CDC Efforts to Prevent and Control Human Immunodeficiency Virus Infection and AIDS in the United States Through Information and Education', National AIDS Information/Education Program, May–June, 1988, **103**, 3, pp. 255–260.

PATTON, M.Q. (1979) 'Evaluation of Program Implementation', in SECHREST, L. *et al.* (Eds) *Evaluation Studies Review Annual*, Vol. 4, Beverly Hills, CA, Sage.

ROSSI, P. and FREEMAN, H. (1985) *Evaluation: A Systematic Approach*, Beverly Hills, CA, Sage.

SCHENSUL, J. (1985) 'Systems Consistency in Field Research, Dissemination, and Social Change', *American Behavioral Scientist*, **29**, 2, pp. 164–204.

SEVILLA-CASA, E. (1989) 'Malaria and Anthropology: Towards a Treatment of Malaric Communities as Human Ecosystems', Draft for Restricted Circulation, June.

SINGER, M., IRIZARRY, R. and SCHENSUL, J. (1991) 'Needle Access as an AIDS Prevention Strategy for IV Drug Users: A Research Perspective', *Human Organization*, **50**, 2, pp. 142–153.

SUCHMAN, E. (1967) *Evaluative Research: Principles and Practice in Public Service and Social Action Programs*, New York, Russell Sage.

WEAVER, T. (1985) 'Anthropology as a Policy Science: Part I, A Critique', *Human Organization*, 44, pp. 97–105.

WEEKS, M., SINGER, M., GRIER, M., HUNTE-MARROW, J. and HAUGHTON, C. (1993) 'AIDS Prevention and the African American Injection Drug User', *Transforming Anthropology* (in press).

WELLER, S.C. and KIMBALL ROMNEY, A. (1988) *Systematic Data Collection*, Vol. 10, *Qualitative Research Methods*, Sage University.

WERNER, O. and SCHOEPFLE, G.M. (1987) *Systematic Fieldwork*, Vol. 1: *Foundations of Ethnography and Interviewing*, and Vol. 2: *Ethnographic Analysis and Data Management*, Sage Publications.

WOLOCOTT, H. (1984) 'Ethnographers sans Ethnography: The Evaluation Compromise', *Ethnography in Educational Evaluation*, edited by FETTERMAN, D. Beverly Hills, CA, Sage Publications, pp. 177–210.

5 Protocol and Policy-making Systems in American Indian Tribes

Linda Parker and Bertney Langley

When I was a graduate student, sitting in lectures or seminars, I often used to find myself frustrated, and I would ask my professors, 'But once I have collected all that data, what do I actually *DO* with it? How do I really get it back to the people who I am working with?'. I don't think that I was alone; anthropologists are rarely taught strategies for turning their ethnographic data into action plans. Since working with my co-author, and swallowing enough of my anthropologist's pride to listen to his advice and follow his suggestions about how to work with his own and other tribes, I have found a door that had always been closed seemingly 'magically' opened to me. This chapter is a way of sharing some of the lessons I have learned about protocol and policy-making systems within American Indian tribes, and some of the lessons that we believe to be necessary for anthropologists to learn if they want their research to be useful to Indian tribes, as well as other communities and organizations.

The Tribe that I have worked most closely with in the last two years is the Coushatta Tribe of Louisiana. They are a small, tightly integrated tribe located in the rural areas around Allen Parish, about four hours west of New Orleans. The tribal reservation is small, with trust land of under 200 acres, though tribal members own some 1400 acres adjacent to the reservation. The tribe has maintained a high degree of their traditional culture; the majority of the over 650 tribal members are still full-blooded Indians who speak the Koasati language as their first language. There are still many tribal members who know how to make the traditional crafts, such as the blowgun and bow and arrow, and most young Coushatta girls learn to weave the long-leaf pine needle baskets that the Coushatta are renowned for. The Coushatta Tribe was 'terminated' by the federal government in the 1950s, and then re-recognized in the early 1970s, although they, of course, have existed throughout. One of the possible origins of the name Coushatta, or 'Koasati' in Indian, is 'lost tribe', which is very appropriate, because few people have heard of the Tribe, and the very few references I have seen refer to the Tribe as having been literally wiped out, or as having lost their language and traditions some time ago. At one point I told the Tribal Chairman, 'Look, you people are going to have to face the fact that you simply don't exist. I am an expert, and if you existed, I would know where to find you in the literature or in some records', to which he replied, 'We have always been here, but we didn't want to be found. Now we want to be found, and it's up to you to let people know that'.

This last statement sums up what I began working, and now work full-time, with the Tribe to accomplish. When the present Chairman, Lovelin Poncho, came into office in 1988, he began looking for ways to build programs in all areas, and especially in economic development. When I began working with him shortly after he took office, he asked for my help to work with the tribal programs, talk to tribal members, come down to the reservation and see the surrounding area, look at their convenience store, anything I needed to do to become familiar with the Tribe and what they wanted to achieve, then use my knowledge of the government grant systems to help them figure out what they could achieve and how to do it. The coming down, looking around, talking to tribal members, and 'figuring out', was the ethnographic research, out of which came some ten grant proposals for different programs (several of which have already gotten funded), my current full-time position as the Grants Manager for the Tribe, and several more proposals and program designs that are in process. Along the way I learned some invaluable lessons about how to go from the 'figuring out' stage to the 'doing it' stage, which are as follows:

1 It's important to explain who you are and what you are there to do. You'd be surprised how many people over look this step, but it's especially important for anthropologists working with Indian tribes to explain that you're not there simply to 'study them'. In my first meeting with the Tribal Chairman I assumed that he had been briefed by the person I'd already been working with, and because we only had about ten minutes, I walked in and said, 'look, here's the tentative proposal. What do you think?'. He of course, said nothing, and only months later told me that he had no idea who I was or what I did. My colleague, who is a Coushatta Indian, had followed the practice of saying nothing, thereby giving me the opportunity to

explain my work myself, so for that whole first meeting, we were all in the dark. A sense of humor on all of our parts was the only thing that saved the day so that I could later make the explanation I should have made in the first place. But beware that an overly rehearsed explanation won't work either, in fact, I have often been advised to leave the word 'anthropologist' out in initial meetings and just explain the nature of ethnographic work, such as 'meet and talk to some people about what they might like to see happen'.

2   It is very important to figure out *who* makes the rules and sets the standards that other people follow. As in any organization, there will always be a formal authority chain, and then an informal power hierarchy. In the case of Indian tribes, anthropologists should work closely with the elected government, of whom the elected leader (variously called Chairman, Chief, President, Governor, etc.) is the head, roughly comparable to the CEO of a corporation, and the Tribal Council, who assist the Chief in making decisions. At the same time, it's essential to find out who in the community is respected and who others turn to for advice. It's a good idea to start with the tribal elders, but there will usually be a key person who is a leader in each of the major age groups within the tribe.

3   Once you figure out who the leaders and decision makers are, you must follow the protocol appropriate to each, which translates to meeting each and interacting with them on their own turf and in their own terms. This means working with Indian tribes, attending community meetings and tribal council meetings (to which you must be invited by the Chairman or receive that person's permission to attend), and also going to people's homes, attending church services, playing in volleyball games, asking teenagers to wash your car — in short, 'blending in' and according respect. Anthropologists are accustomed to doing this in the course of research, but too often assume that when the research phase ends this kind of participation ends as well. In order to see our research turned into recommendations, this according of respect really begins in earnest when the research phase ends.

4   One of the pitfalls I see people from outside the Tribe fall into most readily comes from not understanding that there are

always factions or differences of opinion within Indian tribes, but they are all part of one community and word gets around. It is important to be impartial and keep your story consistent, no matter how many people try to pull you aside and tell you the 'real' truth. Once the elected tribal leader has made a decision or statement, that is what the researcher has to go with, and that decision is usually based on a more complete understanding of a situation than a given individual's perspective. In our current project to establish a restaurant, gift shop, and printing and sewing facility on the reservation so that the tribe can begin to manufacture and market clothing, crafts, and the special Coushatta rice they grow, there are so many decisions to be made about where the facility should be located, who should be employed, and so on, that I could easily be swamped by individual desires and differences of opinion. As a researcher, I can never afford to be careless in making personal statements or in listening to statements made about individuals and giving any kind of tacit compliance. I can listen, but I always remain neutral!

5　The manner of presenting data, conclusions, and recommendations is essential. All material must be clear, concise, jargon-free, and easy to understand. I find that my academic training is almost a hindrance to these kind of presentations, and I have taken to asking tribal members with the *least* formal schooling if they understand what I'm saying before I make the report or presentation. Now that they believe that I'm sincerely asking for their opinion, they often tell me to 'take it down a grade'. I make frequent use of memoranda and always include summaries of past events, decisions, and examples to make my points. I also like to use graphs or other illustrations to show the 'big picture', such as how different grants can overlap within tribal programs and departments. These graphs or pictures have also to be kept simple and non-academic. A good rule-of-thumb I use is that the graph can be drawn in the air or on a piece of paper without using any fancy equipment or tools.

6　One of the most important steps that I believe we all have difficulty with is presenting a detailed and concrete action plan for implementation of recommendations. No matter how much people want to follow your suggestions, they usually won't be able to unless you provide them with some kind of a road map.

I learned this lesson, like so many others, the hard way. After a team of people, myself included, managed to secure a large contribution of computer equipment for the Tribe, had a building, created a position and hired someone to fill it, and had gone through all the steps of setting up a computer learning center on the reservation and taught over 200 lessons to tribal members, I assumed we were finished with that project. I explained that the computer learning center could be self-sustaining by securing contracts from the state and federal government for such services as word-processing, and by offering classes to people in the surrounding community for a small fee. What I neglected to realize was that I had not provided or assisted in any plan to teach tribal members the next level of computer skills once they had learned the basics, so of course interest dropped off, and that 'getting state or federal contracts' and 'opening the center to people from the surrounding area' were not simple, one-step tasks either. What seemed like an action plan to me was actually just a vague long-range goal to the Tribe, and the project was stalled until this misunderstanding could be resolved.

7   Perhaps the most important lesson I have been taught is that *above all, never try to take over*! As anthropologists, we are so well trained not to interfere that it's hard to see that we can easily end up doing just that. Frustrations, misunderstandings, time pressures, deadlines, and even a strong sense of wanting to help can result in a desire to do it ourselves or do it our own way. But in order to make your results useful to decision-makers, it is essential that you remain the researcher and they remain the decision-maker. I have learned to make sure each step of the way that I am presenting my ideas and actively soliciting feedback and suggestions, and that I go no more than two or three rounds at the most to present my point of view before going with the communities' suggestions. After all, it is their program or development project or whatever, they have to live with it long after I am gone, and nine times out of ten I will later learn that they had a very good reason for doing it that way which was incomprehensible to me at the time. No matter what, the Tribal Chairman is the elected Chief of the tribe, and the buck stops with him just as it does with the CEO of a corporation. I can present my ideas carefully and thoroughly, but when I am outvoted, or overruled, I have

learned to accept it with good grace. This is no longer theoretical, or the domain of my research alone, but their world, and when all is said and done, I am there making recommendations at their request.

The steps that we have outlined are ones that I have learned in the course of my work, some by being told, and others by making sometimes costly mistakes. Learning the system of protocol and policy-making in American Indian Tribes is essential to making ethnographic data applicable to real world concerns, as we believe is necessary in all communities and organizations.

6 Communicating Evaluation Findings as a Process: The Case for Delayed Gratification

Jolley Christman and Elaine Simon

Introduction

The purpose of this chapter is to discuss two aspects of ethnographic evaluation which we have found essential to establishing an evaluation process which engages program stakeholders in considering what they are doing and why they are doing it. We use a case example to illustrate how we: (1) collaborate with stakeholders *over time* to design and carry out a study which is credible and useful and (2) derive standards for evaluative judgments which are informed by *emic* perspectives. These are obviously interrelated topics. Both have implications for interpretation and validity; both are centrally related to communicating findings; and both bear on issues of utilization and impact.

Ethnographic evaluation involves extended time in the field setting. It also requires a holistic perspective on the research problem. As our title indicates, our experience with ethnographic evaluation argues for patience, as well as a broader and longer view. Holistic research which enlightens by raising questions, creating agendas of concern, reorienting perspectives, reconceptualizing issues, and challenging taken for granted assumptions may, in many instances, be of greater use than more focused research which is directly, but narrowly applied. (Finch, 1986.) However, clients do not often share this perspective, at least not initially. In this chapter, we discuss the strategies we used to 'sell' the broader and longer view and how these strategies ultimately enhanced the credibility of the study.

Our engagement with program stakeholders over time included the following aspects:

— negotiating evaluation purposes
— using a series of small pilot studies to increase knowledge about the program as well as understanding of what might be learned from an ethnographic approach
— involving stakeholders in decisions about evaluation design (e.g., identifying the evaluation focus, choosing the unit of analysis, and developing the sample)
— involving stakeholders in interpreting data.

We will show how these activities built validity into the evaluation and helped to insure that stakeholders would value and use findings.

We also describe how we developed our judgments of the program. Schwandt has observed that evaluators have been much more likely to 'focus our evaluation practice on the procurement of scientific evidence of program effectiveness while avoiding any attempt to examine the nature and character of evaluative judgments'. (Schwandt, 1989.) Here we discuss our process of taking an evaluative stance and describe how working with program stakeholders (program staff and participants) over time invites their sustained engagement in data analysis and interpretation which informs the criteria or standards used to judge program worth.

Our process for taking an evaluative stance involved:

— recognizing the need to evaluate the program by not only documenting its impact through a cataloguing of program effects on teachers, students, and schools, but also by examining the worth of its purposes
— identifying and understanding emic perspectives on the program's goals, activities, and impact
— making visible the tacit values underlying these various perspectives
— examining our own values and beliefs about curriculum and pedagogy and their relationships to educational reform.

The Program

Since 1984, The Alliance, a collaboration involving the School District of Columbia[1] and local corporations and institutions of higher education, has worked to revitalize public education and improve the academic achievement of Columbia children. The Alliance has sponsored a wide range of programs aimed at the professional development of teachers and the enrichment of curriculum. The Alliance receives funding from a variety of sources which include: corporate donations, grants from private foundations and governmental agencies, and fees from the School District of Columbia.

The following types of programs are representative of Alliance efforts.

Teacher Institutes

The Alliance offers a variety of summer institutes in which teachers learn new subject matter. Institutes are taught by university faculty and teachers receive a stipend and/or graduate credit for their participation.

Teacher Grants

Teachers submit proposals requesting funds for classroom curriculum projects. Minigrants fund small projects written by one teacher (up to $300.00); collaborative grants written by two or more teachers fund larger projects (up to $1,500.00).

Curriculum Renewal Projects

These projects bring teachers and outside experts (usually university faculty) together to develop new curricula.

In 1988, the Executive Director of The Alliance approached the Dean of the University of Pennsylvania's Graduate School of Education to conduct an evaluation of the project's accomplishments. We participated in these discussions in our roles as co-instructors for the course, Qualitative Methods of Program Evaluation at the Graduate School of Education.

Working with Stakeholders Over Time

Evaluation Purposes

In our early meetings with The Alliance staff, we learned what they believed about the organization's purposes and how the many and varied programs the organization provided were operating. We also learned about their perspectives on program evaluation; what they hoped an evaluation would offer them and their Board of Directors. Staff told us that this Board (which is composed of local CEOs, university presidents, education advocates, as well as School District staff) desired information about The Alliance's impact. Program staff interpreted this request as an evaluation which would provide quantifiable data about student achievement outcomes and wanted to accommodate their Board's wishes.

Program staff also said that they wanted a 'comprehensive' evaluation, one that addressed all of their activities. In most cases, staff members had job responsibilities in only one or two program areas, and their knowledge about what other programs did and how they operated was limited. For this reason, staff could only imagine that a comprehensive evaluation would essentially address each program separately, but also include some general findings that might cut across all programs.

As staff talked with us and each other, they articulated two program goals which they saw as integral to The Alliance's mission and educational reform: enriching the School District's Standardized Curriculum and supporting the professionalization of teaching. They hoped that the program promoted such curriculum innovations as multidisciplinary studies, the use of literature in the teaching of reading and primary documents in social studies. They also hoped that institutes which increased teachers' subject matter knowledge would promote teachers' development of rigorous classroom curriculum. In terms of professionalization, The Alliance staff perceived that their programs developed and supported formal and informal teacher networks in schools and across the district and encouraged teachers to assume leadership roles.

As staff members offered different hypotheses and hopes for The Alliance's effects on teachers, they talked at length about certain 'star' teachers whom they considered to be extraordinarily gifted classroom instructors. These were teachers who had usually participated in several programs; they had quickly assumed leadership roles in The Alliance by making presentations at Alliance colloquia. Program staff often consulted with these teachers in developing new activities, and they had played an important role in the evolution of the organization. It was clear that The Alliance staff felt a deep appreciation and respect for such teachers. Many of these teachers were also known to us through our own involvement in the School District since the early 1970s.

As we listened to program staff, we had several concerns about the kind of evaluation that they were proposing. We believed that an evaluation which focused on student achievement outcomes measured by existing quantitative data (report card marks and standardized tests) would not be valid. We thought that a deeper understanding of how The Alliance's many programs worked was needed before a valid evaluation design which looked at student outcomes could be developed.

We also hypothesized that the various Alliance programs interacted within schools and believed that we needed a broad conceptual frame to capture these interactions. Our ethnographic perspective encouraged us to consider carefully how we might take a holistic look across programs at cumulative impact.

Pilot Studies

We suggested to Alliance staff that we engage in several activities through which we could get to know more about their programs. During this process we also hoped to expand The Alliance's vision of what an ethnographic approach might offer them, to suggest some other ways to think about program impact, and to demonstrate how we might look across programs at cumulative effects.

As a preliminary effort, we began small scale studies of several programs. We conducted focus group interviews of teachers and principals about Writing Across the Curriculum to discern their perceptions of how this program had strengthened the instruction of writing in their schools; we examined how teachers were using the Franklin Institute Museum-To-Go Science Kits, hands-on science materials keyed to the School District's standardized science curriculum, in their classrooms; we looked at how teachers' participation in two summer institutes run by university faculty (American history and 'Heat, Light, and Motion') influenced how and what they taught in their classrooms.

Findings from these preliminary evaluations proved to be an effective tool for expanding Alliance staff's conceptions of what they might learn from an evaluation which was ethnographic in its approach. They also served to sharpen our understanding of what The Alliance was about, keep staff interested in the evaluative process, and build our credibility. For example, the evaluation of the Museum-To-Go Science Kits project provided The Alliance with a picture of what was happening in classrooms, a picture that had previously been inaccessible to them and which they valued. We described the great variety of ways in which teachers were using the kits. Some teachers were not using the kits at all and one reason was that they did not know how to manage the small group learning activities which the hands-on kits materials demanded. This was a simple and obvious finding, but one that staff had not considered because of The Alliance's emphasis on enriching the curriculum and upgrading teachers' content knowledge as the means to improving student achievement. The Alliance did not perceive instructional strategies as a central concern and, in fact, had most often avoided explicit discussion of pedagogy because in the interest of respecting teachers as professionals, it did not want to violate the strong professional norms of teacher as expert in areas of classroom practice.

Another way that we collaborated with Alliance staff was to develop a conceptual model to guide the evaluation approach. This model emerged from the research on the Museum-To-Go Science Kits Project. In that study, we had provided some analysis of why the classrooms looked the way that they did. We identified and discussed numerous kinds of influences on science teaching and learning and described how those influences interacted. During the discussions, we collaboratively refined the evaluation question from: *Are the Museum-to-Go Science Kits improving student achievement in science?* to: *How have the Museum-To-Go Science Kits strengthened science teaching and learning in the classroom?* We then engaged staff in a discussion of criteria for judging the quality of science instruction that we identified through integrating our observations with a review of the literature. Thus, Alliance staff came to see what teachers and students were now doing in their classrooms as a kind of program impact.

We also involved Alliance staff in thinking about what the purposes and possibilities of ethnographic evaluation were through our graduate course, 'Qualitative Methods of Program Evaluation'. In the course, students become program evaluators and, for three years, The Alliance graciously agreed to serve as a 'laboratory'. In one year, students looked at The Alliance overall; in another, they examined the Teacher Grants Program; and in a third, they looked at the Writing Across the Curriculum Program. Throughout the course, students talk to Alliance staff about their programs and evaluation needs. They also interviewed a participating teacher or principal, observed at a school, and interviewed Alliance staff. The goal of these assignments is for students to generate three or four broad questions which will then guide their development of an evaluation design. Each year we shared our students' work with Alliance staff. This interaction further expanded The Alliance's vision of what an ethnographic approach might offer by providing examples of questions which cut across programs. Staff, who had been wedded to their individual programs, began to see new connections among programs and to talk about them. The questions piqued staff's curiosity, provided opportunities for them to critique different kinds of questions, and involved us all in a discussion of how an evaluation design might pursue specific questions. All the while, The Alliance was becoming familiar with an ethnographic approach.

Involving Stakeholders in Evaluation Design and Data Analysis

In the fall of 1989, we joined with Carla Asher of the Institute for Literacy Studies at Lehman College to begin work with The Alliance on a design for a holistic ethnographic evaluation which would look at cumulative impact across all programs. Many Alliance projects (all of the teacher institutes) seek to encourage and support educational reform through activities which occur *outside* of the school; most projects also view the individual teacher as the target and agent of change. However, our previous evaluation work with The Alliance, the literature on educational change, and our knowledge of current School District reorganization efforts to support change at the level of the individual school encouraged us to consider the school as our unit of analysis. Teachers who attend institutes return to their schools and classrooms and it is in these settings that they wrestle with how to transform ideas into new ways of working with students and colleagues. It seemed that case studies of schools would offer The Alliance the opportunity to see its efforts at the point of enactment, *inside* classrooms and schools. Case studies of schools would also reveal the ways in which many influences and pressures converge at the school level to shape what happens in classrooms.

As our discussions with The Alliance proceeded, we recognized that the salient evaluation issues would be quite different in the three types of school organization: elementary, middle, and high school. Our sampling strategy involved creating three pairs of schools, so that we would have contrasting cases at each organizational level. We continued to work with program people, this time to choose school pairs which would illuminate the issues which seemed most central at each school level. We constructed a purposive sample so that we could learn about the influence of various contextual factors including the role of the principal, the number of Alliance programs and participants within a school, and interactions with other programs and initiatives in the school. In these discussions, we began to develop the initial working hypotheses which would guide our work.

The Alliance invited a teacher in each school to serve as a liaison to the research team. The research team met with the six teachers and talked at length with these liaisons about their involvement in Alliance programs and about their colleagues' perceptions of and participation in Alliance activities. We asked them to help us consider what we might look for as evidence of Alliance impact in their schools, and we also talked to them about how we might assess the degree of teacher involvement. We had decided that at each school we would interview and observe teachers who had been 'highly involved' in Alliance programs, teachers who had had no involvement, and teachers who had been moderately involved. The six liaison teachers worked with us to define the attributes of these three categories. They also talked about their perceptions of why individual Alliance programs had or had not taken hold in their buildings. Unlike many teachers we spoke with during the course of the study, these teachers were quite knowledgeable about things going on across the school district and articulate about where their colleagues and their schools fit into this larger scheme of things.

The liaisons helped to negotiate our entry into the schools. They explained the study to their principals, helped us to decide whom to interview and observe, scheduled our visits. Their help in defining who fit the sample categories meant that the selection of informants represented the different levels of involvement *from the perspective of that school*, contributing to validity.

After six months of fieldwork in the schools and numerous analytic meetings of the research team, we met with Alliance staff to discuss the case descriptions. Present at the meeting were the two directors with whom we had negotiated the evaluation, as well as a new Executive Director, who had arrived over the summer after a year long search. We were, of course, eager for their responses to the cases; we were humanly curious about their reactions to telling vignettes and we wanted to know if our portraits of the schools rang true. But most of all, we wanted to hear them discuss our descriptions of what teachers were doing in classrooms; how schools were making use of Alliance resources. Did they see the portraits that we painted as evidence of strong and effective Alliance impact on schools and classrooms or were they disappointed in the images we presented? In hindsight, we realize that these questions reveal our continuing efforts to help Alliance staff to articulate more clearly the kinds of impact they wanted their programs to have on schools.

The interaction was lively as staff told us the ways in which their perceptions of the six schools were confirmed or shaken by our accounts. We discussed individual teachers, many of whom they recognized despite the pseudonyms, and they underscored the fine work that a number of teachers were doing. This discussion gave us more information about the characteristics of teachers and classrooms Alliance staff valued. It served to involve staff in analyzing data and thus strengthened the validity of our findings as well as contributing to the development of emically derived standards of judgment. We agreed that we would write a cross-site summary of findings and recommendations.

We went to work on preparing a summary which identified the kinds of impact Alliance programs had on classroom teaching and learning and students. We discussed:

— the increased use of teaching strategies that actively involve students (for example, small group work, hands-on materials in science, etc.)
— the increased use of educational resources outside the school (for example, museums, community organizations, etc.) for the purpose of connecting students' educational experience to their community
— the involvement of students in a greater variety of writing activities which emphasized writing as a process
— the incorporation of innovative subject matter, particularly an emphasis on the arts, an expansion of inter-disciplinary teaching, an increased emphasis on science, and the addition of a multi-cultural perspective.

Based on teachers' perceptions and classroom observation, we also identified a number of student outcomes which resulted from teachers' involvement with The Alliance:

— an increased interest and involvement in learning due to teaching strategies and materials which more actively involved them, and curriculum topics which were more relevant to their own lives
— an expanded awareness of and experience with the world around them because of exposure to additional school and community resources (for example, Afro-American community leaders who were involved in a 'Return to Roots' curriculum project; violins provided through a school collaborative grant, etc.)
— a greater comfort with writing and an improved quality of writing
— increased self-esteem and pride in their racial and ethnic identity and in themselves as competent learners
— an expanded understanding of multi-disciplinary concepts.

Taking an Evaluative Stance

A Value Position

As we developed and discussed our findings, we grew increasingly uneasy with the report that we seemed to be writing. Although this summary of findings captured the variety of educational innovations we had observed and teachers had reported, it did not account for the variability in the degree to which teachers and schools were involved in substantive change efforts which utilized Alliance resources and were clearly linked to Alliance program activities. The findings offered these changes as separate puzzle pieces with no explanation of what their relationship to one another might be.

For example, at the classroom level, we identified the use of certain kinds of materials (e.g., primary sources in social studies, literature in language arts, hands-on math and science materials) and strategies that actively involved students as evidence of Alliance impact. We realized that we were not addressing the nature of the learning tasks themselves and how those learning activities fit into an overall pedagogical approach. We recognized that, with a few notable exceptions, teachers and Alliance staff were also failing to connect these puzzle pieces into a conceptual framework that joined curriculum with pedagogy. One of those exceptions was Marilyn Foster, a middle school reading teacher highly regarded by Alliance staff and one of our teacher liaisons. Her explanation of how her earliest participation in The Alliance affected her stood out for us.

> The Writing Project's summer institute (an institute sponsored, in part, by The Alliance) changed my life. Right before the institute, I had taken a course in learning styles and had realized that I am a global learner. The way I was taught had always been hierarchical, fragmented, and sequential. Then I became a teacher, and they wanted lesson plans with these very specific objectives. I always rebelled against thinking about what I was going to do in forty minute segments.

> In a way, the Writing Project was a vindication for me. It showed me that I was right to think that the greater whole is more than all those parts. It makes more sense for me as a teacher to think about an overall approach and then to figure out what I'm going to plug in with this particular class or this particular piece of literature.

The lack of an overall pedagogical framework also represented what we were coming to see as the absence of an evaluative stance in our work. The question for us became: 'How are we going to look authentically and critically at what we have described in the case studies?'.

Making Tacit Values Visible

We re-examined our data, looking carefully at what we believed to be the notable exceptions — classrooms like Marilyn Foster's where various pieces of the puzzle fit within the larger framework of a teacher's vision of teaching and learning. As it turned out, these classrooms belonged to teachers whom Alliance staff had frequently identified as outstanding teachers and personifying Alliance ideals; in a number of cases, they were also our research liaisons. The following excerpts from the evaluation report are illustrative of the kinds of things these 'ideal' teachers said about their teaching and what they did in their classrooms.

Steve Bolan, high school math teacher:

As he outlined it, he spent the first month 'without touching books'. Instead, students used manipulatives and pattern blocks, made observations, and built theories. Then they began to make arguments to defend statements about what they were observing. Eventually, they would build up theory in geometry, which they would use as they progressed through the geometric concepts.

We observed the class at the point in the year where the students were able to draw on the body of theory they themselves had built for geometry.

Joe Crawford, high school history teacher:

Asked how his participation in The Alliance has influenced him, Mr Crawford responded, 'In every way . . . content and method . . . I think that The Alliance encourages a shift in the way we teach — that we become less purveyors of knowledge and more willing to be co-questioners. . . . Mr Crawford described his educational philosophy as a belief that questions are more important than answers. 'I don't think that the teacher has to have the last word. I want to ask, what do we need to ask, and what kinds of responses can be counted as good answers?'

Expanding on this, he said 'Several people have the belief that they are the possessors of revealed truth, that their knowledge is unassailable. Kids become discipline problems when they challenge that'.

We triangulated this data with our observations of the pedagogy used and promoted in the summer institutes for teachers and with our conversations with program staff. We also discussed our own pedagogical values. From this analysis and self-examination we constructed a standard for our judgments about the impact of The Alliance. In the introduction to the report we wrote that

> . . . the fundamental criterion for an excellent learning environment used in this study was the use of inquiry-based learning processes which are embedded in students' exploration of their own and others' questions and concerns about subject matter. Thus, we looked for examples of classrooms where knowledge is not only transmitted from teacher to student, but where it is created by teachers and students together as they pose and pursue problems about the stages of the moon, about the life of a black boy in South Africa, about geometry, and so forth. We looked for the development of skills (reading, writing, computation, etc.) within the context of learning about subject matter. We looked for the use of materials which support experiential learning and for ways that teachers and students are exploring lines of inquiry that cut across the disciplines. We also looked for students who were using writing to make connections between new material and their previous experience and for teachers who build their lessons from the questions and issues raised by students in their writing.

In introducing our recommendations, we elaborated how the concept of coherence was important to understanding the variability in The Alliance's ability to build and sustain teachers' capacity to enact an inquiry-based pedagogical approach. We wrote:

> Teachers highly involved in The Alliance are likely to have an existing philosophy of pedagogy and practice consonant with an inquiry approach. Teachers with beliefs that are inconsistent with The Alliance's philosophy tend not to participate. Those teachers whose pedagogical philosophies are partially consistent with The Alliance's approach present the greatest challenge

and opportunity for change. It is in their classrooms that we most often saw the adoption of features without the supporting framework.

We went on to explain that teachers in this last group, who are experimenting with new instructional strategies on the way to constructing an overall pedagogical approach, are also most vulnerable to factors in the school and district context which are philosophically and/or structurally inconsistent with an inquiry-based approach. For example, a teacher using a process-oriented approach to explore a science topic in depth, may abandon this innovation in the face of standardized tests which emphasize curriculum breadth and factual recall.

Two of our most important recommendations included:

— The Alliance should make its beliefs about teaching and learning more explicit and these beliefs should be incorporated in its mission statement and serve as a set of guiding principles for all of its program activities.

— The Alliance should collaborate with members of the immediate school community as well as the larger setting in which it operates to promote a coherent school context which supports an inquiry-based approach to teaching and learning.

Evaluation Impact

The Alliance circulated the report to its staff and its board. Staff appreciated the close look at schools which had previously been unavailable to them. One long time staff member, who had responsibility for a variety of programs, told us,

> The concept of the overall pedagogical framework was extremely helpful to me. It really helped me to understand my reaction to visiting classrooms all these years. Yes, I would see a number of things going on that were encouraging, but there were also things missing.

In contrast, the former Executive Director wrote a response to the evaluation which voiced concerns shared by other staff members. The following are excerpts from that letter:

> I have read the Evaluation of The Alliance with very great interest, as you can imagine, and found much of it to provide a

useful set of indicators as to where the focus in future years would be most productive. As such, I am sure you have also found this a highly productive piece of research for your planning. . . . There is one aspect of the study, however, that truly puzzles me. The researcher's entire study is based on a statement that the central mission of The Alliance is inquiry-based learning. Inquiry-based learning is certainly one of the by-products of the arts and science focus of The Alliance, but not a necessary goal.

For you, the question being posed [by the evaluation] is whether you wish to shift that goal from subject matter to pedagogy, and to advocate for a particular pedagogy as your central mission. That would be a major shift in purpose, and one which you and your board need to make consciously and not simply as a result of an assumption made by the evaluators . . . then you must decide if The Alliance is now going to go into the business of changing that (the way teachers teach), which probably entails an entirely different set of activities from those that The Alliance has ever undertaken. Is The Alliance equipped to do so? Does it wish to do so? . . . Your next steps will be most interesting to observe.

These comments represent any evaluator's fondest hope in the sense that they testify to program stakeholders' engagement with substantive issues. They clearly connect evaluation findings to future program direction and therefore increase the potential impact of the evaluation. However, they also raise critical questions about the evaluation: its validity and its evaluative stance. They are illustrative of the challenges that confront program evaluators and stakeholders when they examine the relationship between explicit and implicit values and reveal the ways in which program activities and program context may undermine and/ or contradict those values.

The letter was one impetus for a meeting in which teachers, principals and other school district administrators, program staff, and the evaluation team discussed the evaluation and its implications for future program activities. Teachers and principals were appreciative of the 'rich portraits' of schools and agreed with the accuracy of the accounts. Program staff again raised questions about the value and appropriateness of The Alliance taking an overt stance in regard to instructional approach. There was a discussion of the connections between curriculum and pedagogy. The meeting was inconclusive in terms of charting program direction, but it did generate serious consideration of the critical issues raised by the evaluation as evidenced by one teacher's written comment:

> Although the World History Project is based on inquiry-based teaching and learning, I did not know that inquiry-based teaching and learning was a fundamental tenet of The Alliance . . . I think that I saw The Alliance as having less of a philosophical or ideological center. I thought that it might support and encourage competing views of education. I am not sure what I mean by this . . .

Several months later, the Board revised The Alliance's mission statement as part of a strategic planning process and included pedagogy as a focus for program efforts. While the statement does not incorporate 'inquiry-based pedagogy' as part of its language, it does identify the support of teachers in their development of instructional strategies which 'actively engage students in learning' as a major purpose of Alliance programs.

In presenting this case example, we have argued that our criteria for evaluative judgments were informed by emic perspectives revealed not only in the data collected during fieldwork in the schools, but also in our collaborative interactions with program staff and participants during the evaluation process. The teachers who exemplified The Alliance's values viewed curriculum and pedagogy as inextricably connected and they incorporated this view in their development of a coherent conceptual framework for teaching. They explicitly articulated this connection to us and their classrooms reflected it.

But if the criteria for our judgments were informed by emic perspectives, why did the former Executive Director and some staff question them as appropriate for judging program worth and effectiveness? Why did teachers seem to believe that The Alliance had been (and perhaps ought to remain) pedagogically 'neutral'? Why did the Board, when it chose to address instruction in its mission statement, use the language of 'active learning' rather than 'inquiry-based teaching and learning'?

We believe that the former Executive Director recognized that the evaluation recommendations challenged The Alliance to redefine its mission and its relationship to teachers, schools, and the school district. In the words of a teacher, The Alliance did not have a 'philosophical or ideological center'. Because it did not advocate for a particular pedagogical approach, The Alliance did not overtly challenge teachers' philosophical orientation nor threaten their roles as instructional experts.

In addition, The Alliance's stated purposes of curriculum enrichment and the professionalization of teaching more delicately positioned it as a complement and support to the school district. A commitment to inquiry-based teaching and learning would require that The Alliance become activist in its advocacy for school district policies and structures which promote a consistent and coherent context for inquiry teaching and learning at the school level.

The Board's focus on instruction which encourages 'active learning' is congruent with The Alliance's historical emphasis on engaging students with hands-on materials. It offers teachers a concrete image of what they might do in their classrooms and seems compatible with a variety of educational philosophies.

We have continued to work with The Alliance as it has restructured its organization, renegotiated its partnership with the School District, and its relationships with schools through such efforts as:

— providing programs which develop the capacity of middle school science teachers to involve their students in extended scientific investigations and to serve as resources and consultants to colleagues in their schools

— facilitating and supporting whole school change efforts through direct involvement of Alliance staff in program planning, implementation, and assessment at the school level

— implementing an alternative assessment initiative which involves schools in pilot projects to integrate alternative assessment processes with the development of new curricula.

In all of these efforts we, in partnership with Alliance staff and school people, are continuing to engage with the issues generated in the evaluation discussed here. Understandings deepen and dilemmas continue in this unfolding story. We have tried to understand and be more sensitive to stakeholders' perspectives on the political context in which they operate, but this remains a continuing challenge in a large urban school district. We have appreciated the opportunity to continue our collaboration as program planners develop ways to enact recommendations and new understandings.

In this chapter, we have described the ways in which we collaborated over time with stakeholders to design and carry out a program evaluation. This collaboration occurred during conceptualization of the evaluation focus, design of the study, data collection, analysis, and interpretation. It occurred with two groups of stakeholders: program staff and program participants. We believe that this case illustrates how an ethnographic evaluation approach, which reveals and scrutinizes taken for granted assumptions and tacit values, helps to engage program stakeholders in critically examining what they are doing and why they are doing it.

Note

1 'The Alliance' is a pseudonym, as is 'Columbia', which is a large urban school district serving more than 200,000 students in the north-eastern United States.

References

FINCH, J. (1986) *Research and Policy: The Uses of Qualitative Methods in Social and Educational Research*, London, Falmer Press.
SCHWANDT, T.S. (1989) 'Recapturing Moral Discourse in Evaluation', *Educational Researcher*, **18**, 8, pp. 11–16.

7   Massaging Soft Data, or Making the Skeptical More Supple

Mary Jo McGee Brown

The practical effect of a belief is the real test of its soundness.
— Froude

Introduction

Many of my evaluation efforts are targeted toward educational innovation projects and my contacts with policy-makers in educational reform. I am currently conducting an ethnography of an educational project in which sub-groups of participating public school teachers are writing position papers on a variety of topics related to curriculum development and implementation of the project. A few weeks ago I was observing the 'Children's Ways of Learning' group as they negotiated their philosophy of how children learn. After reading a number of scholarly articles and philosophy statements from previous innovation projects, the teachers rejected all suggestions except what they felt they 'knew' as a result of their collective years of teaching experience: children learn by doing. One teacher said, 'They come to us with many correct understandings and many misconceptions that they've acquired in their experiences in the world prior to formal schooling. We correct their misconceptions and teach them new concepts best through demonstrations and letting them experience things'.

As I observed and listened, I remembered an assertion by Rosalind Driver in a speech at the University of Georgia in Spring, 1990, that even when children are presented with clear evidence and learning experiences, they frequently refuse to change long held beliefs about the way things function in the natural world. She presented two or three examples of this in science with students with whom she works. Individuals give meaning to their world; they construct their understanding in a way so that the world makes sense to them. Beliefs are concerned with the acceptance or rejection of propositions and may vary within and across individuals and events depending on factors such as context, evidence, and the system of rules one has developed to process doubt.

Research Belief System

Many stakeholders in educational innovation projects have constructed understandings about the nature of naturalistic research and evaluation prior to any formal learning or experience with it. Although they know neither the types of questions which can be best answered using naturalistic evaluation nor the methodology of naturalistic inquiry, they form very strong beliefs about the nature and value of the approach to knowing. As the group of teachers felt that children learn best through experience, I suggest that the only way to change individual's beliefs and constructions is through some type of experience with naturalistic inquiry rather than simply being told that it is a valuable process. I further feel that changing the nature of reporting of findings from narrative to numeric does not serve us well as naturalistic evaluators, nor does it aid in changing policy-makers' beliefs about naturalistic research and evaluation data. Mary Black (1973) notes that the construct 'belief system' has been used to connote anything from a major unifying philosophical structuring of the universe to the conceptual structuring of the most minute and 'trivial' domains of cultural knowledge. The notion of belief system is useful in helping us explain some of the issues in naturalistic evaluation relative to the translation of knowledge into action.

Hudson (1973) suggests that while belief systems of preliterate people seem complex, that it is a complexity which is based on a system and that the complexities can often be accounted for in terms of a few basic categories and principles. He further suggests that the categories and principles fit together in a complete and ordered way where everything relates to everything else in explaining the world. In a similar fashion, educators' beliefs about the nature of naturalistic inquiry are neatly interwoven into their individual belief systems about the world of research and the value of different research methodologies. Kluckhohn (1964) asserted that Navaho categories and native language referential systems are a reasonable means to present the values and thought system of the Navaho. He also added to this values model a classification by a series of binary oppositions. The concept of binary oppositions is used frequently in our culture to help account for segments of our belief systems.

I recently heard a very interesting commentary on National Public Radio on public perceptions on the nature of journalistic reporting. The journalist described readers' perceptions about types of newspaper articles using a binary opposition format: soft data and hard data. The speaker described soft data as being news that 'does not matter'. Examples of this were women's sections, data which are factual but not perceived as essential, opinion pieces, etc. Hard data were defined as 'news that matters'. Examples of hard news were 'state of the world' articles, articles relating statistical data, articles for decision-making in major issues. The speaker suggested that there was a value judgment attached to the two labels: hard data are valuable and soft data are not. She further asserted that journalists use 'hard data terms' in article titles to attempt to transform readers' perceptions about the nature of articles. The example shared was something like changing the title of an article entitled 'Parents' Concerns about Drug Use Among Teenagers' to 'The War on Teenage Drug Use: Our Plan of Attack'. Somehow the use of the terms 'war' and 'plan of attack' make the article seem to matter more than simply reporting parents' concerns about their teenagers' use of drugs. As ethnographic evaluators, we often attempt to transform policy-makers' perceptions about the nature of our data and interpretations by using 'hard data' titles and including numerical data with the justification that 'We will never change them if we don't present our findings in their language'. The speaker's substantive argument for the value of 'soft data' news articles was based on the notion that real life news reporting of issues central to the public which are personalized by stories and opinions that they offer, are as informative and often more informative than highly theoretical, statistical, or coldly 'factual' articles. It is this latter point which speaks most directly to the issue of sharing of knowledge from naturalistic evaluation with policy-makers. How can practitioners of naturalistic evaluation help policy-makers expand their belief system and change their value system to recognize the value of shared experiences of participants in innovative project endeavors?

Like preliterate peoples, evaluators have used linguistic categories and category labels quite effectively to reflect values, specifically here, the value of different inquiry modes. The binary oppositions are 'hard data', the results of quantitative inquiry and 'soft data', the results of naturalistic inquiry. Hard data are good, can be trusted, are numeric (and therefore true), are based on valid and reliable instruments administered in ideal conditions, and are not subject to researcher interpretation.

Statistics can't lie. Soft data, on the other hand, are questionable at best, cannot be trusted, are easily manipulated (or massaged), are not representative, are simply narrative accounts from participants in the setting or a researcher immersed in the setting, and are highly subjective. Participants' opinions can be massaged and twisted to say anything the researcher wants to say. The two beliefs merged together form a neat belief system about research. If an evaluator or consumer of evaluation results is schooled only in one area but holds strong beliefs about both, it is highly likely that some of those beliefs will be based on misconceptions. Since statistics courses are required in most graduate academic programs, it is most likely that naturalistic inquiry will be the area in which students have no training and, therefore, hold the most uninformed constructions. As a strategy to change perceptions of current policy-makers, I feel it is critical for us to promote required naturalistic research and evaluation methods courses for all research oriented students in our institutions now. They are the policy-makers of the future in one way or another.

At the American Evaluation Association meeting in 1990, I was in one session where an evaluator said, 'I asked them whether they felt the program was effective, but that's just their opinions. What the hard data tell us, however . . .' and went on to present analysis of test score data.

Many policy-makers in higher education, however, even display a feeling of mistrust and concern about qualitative and naturalistic approaches and practitioners. The following excerpts from a recent exchange of memos between Deans and curriculum committee members at a major American university reflect the beliefs held about naturalistic inquiry:

> Memo (5/7/90): . . . Qualitative research uses empirical methods such as case study, document analysis, interviewing, etc., but it stops short of statistical analysis. . . .
>
> Memo (5/23/90): . . . Dean (X) has thus been alerted to the increase in the numbers of these qualitative courses. He suggested that the Curriculum Committee continue to monitor these numbers and ask him to look into the matter further during the 1990–91 year, if warranted. . . .

One wonders if the qualitative approach was not perceived to 'stop short of statistical analysis' whether the parties involved would be so interested in monitoring the increases in qualitative courses to determine if further investigation might be 'warranted'. While the memos indicated additional concern about quality control of the courses and potential overlapping of courses, the tone set by the descriptions was quite negative, and I believe is rooted in the belief that anything that 'stops short of statistical analysis' cannot be worthwhile research. Fortunately, in order to find out more about the approach, the policy-makers involved in the above exchange have recently accepted invitations to be involved in sessions where methods, approaches, and findings in naturalistic research and evaluation will be presented.

In an introductory qualitative research methods course that I am teaching this quarter, one of the doctoral students gave the following reflection on the second night of class relative to an assigned article: 'I never doubted that the study was qualitative because it was so vague and I couldn't tell where they got any of the data. Isn't that what qualitative reports are?' Of course I suggested that given the grade she would get in the course as a result of that remark, she might as well drop the course at that point! Sadly, this construction is far too common among students, faculty, and policy-makers.

The key question here is why are stakeholders in projects so reluctant to pay close attention to the opinions of the persons closest to the project implementation about the effectiveness of the project? I would suggest that the belief system about research which is prevalent in the academic community, including the nature of knowledge, the nature of reality, and the nature of truth perpetuates the notion that anything which cannot be measured with valid and reliable instruments is simply 'news that does not matter'. Just as real men don't eat quiche, real educators and policy-makers don't consume and use data which are reflections of real life, personalized by project participants' opinions. We become inflated with our own knowledge and assumptions about phenomena and tend to negate the experience and perceptions of the persons living it.

Scholars have argued the issue of art versus science in naturalistic inquiry literature for the past decade (Ball, 1990; Carrithers, 1990; Grumet, 1990; Smith, 1987). One reaction is that naturalistic evaluators have developed criteria for 'trustworthiness' of process and product in qualitative research and evaluation (Guba and Lincoln, 1989; Marshall, 1985). We negotiate meaning about validity, subjectivity, and objectivity (Peshkin, 1988; Phillips, 1990; Wolcott, 1990). The problem with this kind of approach to these issues is that the debates and attempts to persuade readers of the value and rigor of the naturalistic approach seem primarily to be generated and read by naturalistic researchers and evaluators, not quantitatively oriented researchers and policy-makers. I decided to conduct an informal poll of some of the quantitative faculty of my department about this issue. The reaction of one scholar of multivariate analysis is representative of the rest: 'No, we don't talk about it at our meetings, it's not in our literature, well, except for the *Educational Researcher*, and, well simply, it's just not an issue for us'. The most common reflection my new doctoral students have each quarter as they read the qualitative methodological literature for the first time is, 'These authors all take such a defensive posture like they're trying to defend what they are doing and at the same time convince the reader that it's worthwhile, rather than simply describing the philosophical and methodological basis of the approaches'. The result is that others question the value we place on our own work.

If naturalistic evaluators were interacting solely with one individual who hires them to conduct evaluation, then this consideration of how to help consumers of naturalistic evaluation results would be a moot point. One would assume that if an individual hires a naturalistic evaluator, that she values the types of data that will be generated by that inquiry approach. But the reality is that we are often hired by a person who expresses a desire for a naturalistic evaluation approach and then evaluation results are presented to a variety of levels of persons. In educational evaluation, for example, data are shared across levels from the participants in the schools to parents, central office personnel, external project evaluation teams hired to evaluate the evaluation results, and others. Because all persons in this multi-tiered scenario are not equally knowledgeable about naturalistic inquiry, and they do not equally value naturalistic findings, narrative evaluation data are frequently dismissed in favor of more familiar numerical data. Therefore, as naturalistic evaluators, we must move beyond the concern of how to present narrative data in a more acceptable numerical format, to the real issue of how to change the research belief system of the consumers of evaluation results.

I would suggest that this can best be accomplished by naturalistic evaluators providing specific opportunities for non-naturalistic and anti-naturalistic educators and policy-makers to observe us conducting our evaluations. This seems as if it would be more productive than continuing the paradigm debate among ourselves of qualitative versus quantitative or positivism versus constructivism, as titles of many recent articles and books suggest. If we provide opportunities which are not threatening or combative, we may be able to make policy-makers more supple from the perspective of being more adaptable or responsive to new situations and approaches. If policy-makers understand the nature of the data we are generating about projects and believe that the data are valuable, then increased use of these data to make changes will be enhanced.

Approaches to Expanding Belief Systems

I would like to share variations on two approaches I have used to try to expand belief systems of policy-makers and evaluators with whom I have worked: 1) longitudinal instruction and experience and 2) brief information sharing.

Longitudinal

One variation of the longitudinal approach is that I invite colleagues from other departments, universities or projects who are either antagonistic toward or express an interest in naturalistic research to sit in my graduate introductory course in qualitative research methods. I generally have at least one faculty member or professional person per quarter to audit the course, but most quarters I have a small group of faculty auditing (e.g., one quarter it was the department head and all new faculty from Science Education). I attempt to establish an informal interactive seminar atmosphere where both students and faculty read, discuss, debate, and apply what they learn about naturalistic inquiry. While my goal is not to convert them, many of the professionals who are involved in evaluation projects, begin reading examples of naturalistic evaluation and research and frequently incorporate naturalistic components in their own evaluations. While some have reported after the experience that they have 'always been naturalistic researchers and just did not know it', others remain solidly quantitative in orientation but express an appreciation of the ability to read naturalistic evaluation and research reports with understanding. A very common reflection is that faculty believe in the value of naturalistic studies after understanding the goals, different approaches, and methodology.

A longitudinal experience based method I have used to try and expand beliefs and values of quantitatively oriented evaluators and policy-makers is to invite them to observe me conducting naturalistic inquiry in the field. This process was quite successful in one evaluation project where the head of the Educational Research Lab at the University of Georgia whose area of expertise is tests and measurement, followed me around in an elementary school asking why I was doing the things I did, looking at fieldnotes I took, and discussing issues with me. He did this periodically throughout the year. He was jolted at the end of the year by teacher comments that the open-ended questionnaire that I had administered had provided them an opportunity to write what had 'really' happened in the project as opposed to those 'stupid' attitude scales where 'the questions didn't relate to use and we couldn't fit our answers into any of those numbers'. We talked at length about the difference in the types of data produced by each evaluation approach. He then discussed the approach further with a graduate student who had taken my methods course and who was collecting data in an on-going naturalistic evaluation in a system-wide project that he and I were conducting. He began conducting interviews at the site using constant comparative analysis of data and discussing analysis and interpretation with the other data collector and me. After these experiences, this individual presented a paper at the Georgia Educational Research Association in Fall, 1990 in which he characterized his introduction to naturalistic inquiry as an 'out of body experience where I began to see the light on the other side of the tunnel'. A concrete indication of his change in beliefs about the value of naturalistic inquiry is his participation in the Qualitative Research Methods Conference in January of 1991. I believe that this type of collaboration between qualitative and quantitative evaluators is the beginning of the elimination of the oppositions of soft and hard data as the categories which represent evaluation and research belief systems. While this approach takes longer than having professionals audit a qualitative methodology course, the positive aspect of this is that the people can actually *experience* naturalistic evaluation with us and we can dialogue about various components and issues within the context of an evaluation project. We can have no stronger advocates for our approach than formerly totally quantitative evaluators and policy-makers whose belief systems and activities are expanded to include naturalistic inquiry.

There are two critical common characteristics of different variations of longitudinal approaches. One is that the persons have to have a genuine interest in finding out about naturalistic inquiry since it is a self-selected process. Because of this, many ardent opponents to naturalistic evaluation never select the opportunity for learning. To date, I have only had one faculty member begin a course and not complete it. Initialiy he seemed very open to learning, but seemed to be unable to move beyond the generalizability issue. After some strong statements about not seeing the value of anything like a case study where data could not be generalized beyond the context, he quit coming to class. Faculty members have shared a wide range of reasons with me for wanting to audit the course: a need to understand the approach to more effectively serve on graduate students' committees; a desire to use naturalistic inquiry in evaluation; a desire to expand understanding of scholarly literature in educational research and evaluation; a desire to learn how to analyze interview and observation data; and a desire to 'see what this soft data stuff is all about'. Whatever the reason, everyone expresses a genuine internal motivation.

Another common characteristic of longitudinal experiences with naturalistic instruction or activities, is that of time commitment. Whether a professional audits a class or follows you around as you evaluate a project, a large time commitment is required. Frequently, professional educators and policy-makers have the interest, but cannot or do not want to make the time commitment required for systematic study or watching someone else do their job as a project evaluator. In this case, we might indicate essential classes, topics, or site visits to them which would provide a basis for continuing dialog.

Information Sharing

Lack of genuine interest or lack of time leads to the second major approach, brief information sharing. One variation of this approach which I have taken, is to try to informally inform persons at different levels of policy-making in a project about the value and the nature of the naturalistic data. This is different from negotiating the nature of the evaluation findings and report format of a specific project with the project manager or funding agency at the beginning of a study. I have done this with school superintendents who are antagonistic toward 'soft data' and with evaluation and validation team members (usually university or college professors) who assess evaluation efforts at specific project sites. What I generally do is to briefly describe the philosophy, types of questions that can be answered by naturalistic inquiry, the nature of the data, and inquiry process. Even more essential than these, I then try to persuade them of the value of 'hearing the voices' of the participants who are implementing change. The underlying key assumption is that conducting holistic evaluation of projects in context with an emic perspective is essential. I try to point out that I have no interest in 'manipulating' or 'massaging' the data to demonstrate that a project is either working or not, but rather want to hear perspectives of the participants. The focus of my discussion is on the importance of moving beyond simply hearing what participants at the site are saying to why they are saying what they do about the causes for things being effective or not. It is educating policy-makers about the issue of power through giving voice to participants. Because policy-makers at different levels do not experience the data collection themselves and because they are not studying the approach totally, they often either say that they see the value in it when they really do not or they say that they see the value in it, but want the data transformed into numbers and frequencies so that it would be 'more meaningful' to persons at other sites. While responses like these indicate my lack of total success with this approach, I have not abandoned it. I feel that an introduction to naturalistic inquiry from an informed person can (and has at two sites for me) open the way to later exploration by the listener.

A more effective variation of the information sharing approach which bridges the systematic and longitudinal approaches and the informal brief approaches is to combine informal discussion and some instruction with policy-makers. I am the naturalistic evaluator for a sub-group of a national educational curriculum change project. A local director approached me and asked if I would conduct the evaluation of the local group. The national directors did not have any input into the decision to have an ethnography written at this level. While the national directors were very skeptical at first about the value of such an effort and unsure of the nature of the data, one of the directors, after some discussions with me about my methods and after sitting in on a five-hour class session in my qualitative methods course, has become quite open to what I am doing. After sitting in on my class she remarked, 'I really feel a lot better about what you are doing now because I see what it is all about'. On a number of occasions subsequently, she has requested to read my field notes and discuss them with me and now understands that it is only with the approval of all participants that I am willing to do that. She seems no longer threatened by what I am doing because she now understands the philosophy and the process. More important, she now understands that my focus is to present the perspectives of the project participants, not to judge them or the national effort. One of the other directors has continuously questioned the value of the 'soft data' I am collecting and the methodology of naturalistic inquiry in general. Rather than inquiring about the nature of what I am doing, he continues to attack it from a quantitatively oriented perspective and does not seem to have any value for the 'non-scientific' naturalistic approach. On the one hand, beliefs and values relative to naturalistic inquiry seem to have been positively changed with increased knowledge; on the other, beliefs and values do not seem to have been changed where there has been no knowledge acquisition.

Conclusions

In conclusion, I would like to suggest that as a group of naturalistic evaluators and researchers, we begin to explore and identify methods in addition to those shared here so that we can begin changing the belief system of seasoned quantitative evaluators and policy makers who may be on the receiving end of our 'soft data'. My goal in each case is not to change policy-makers and quantitative evaluators into naturalistic evaluators, but rather it is to make them informed and open consumers of the types of data that we produce — persons who value the insights we gain by being in the project sites with the participants. Perhaps the real indication that we have been successful in this effort will be when the complex belief system about research and evaluation is no longer accounted for in terms of the categories 'soft data' and 'hard data'. It is time for us to take what we have learned from the paradigm debate and move beyond. 'The practical effect of a belief is the real test of its soundness'.

References

BALL, S.J. (1990) 'Self-doubt and soft data: Social and technical trajectories in ethnographic fieldwork', *Qualitative Studies in Education*, **3**, 2, pp. 157–171.

BLACK, M. (1973) 'Belief systems', in HONIGMANN, J.J. (Ed.), *Handbook of social and cultural anthropology*, Chicago, Rand McNally.

CARRITHERS, M. (1990) 'Is anthropology art or science?', *Current Anthropology*, **31**, 3, pp. 263–282.

GRUMET, M.R. (1990) 'On daffodils that come before the swallow dares', in EISNER, E.W. and PESHKIN, A. (Eds) *Qualitative inquiry in education: The continuing debate*, New York, Teachers College Press.

GUBA, E.G. and LINCOLN, Y.S. (1989) *Fourth generation evaluation*, Newbury Park, SAGE.

HUDSON, C. (1973) 'The historical approach in anthropology', in HONIGMANN, J.J. (Ed.), *Handbook of social and cultural anthropology*, Chicago, Rand McNally.

KLUCKHOHN, C. (1964) 'Navaho categories', in DIAMOND, S. (Ed.) *Primitive views of the world*, New York, Columbia Univ. Press.

MARSHALL, C. (1985) 'Appropriate criteria of trustworthiness and goodness for qualitative research on education organizations', *Quality and Quantity*, **19**, pp. 353–373.

PESHKIN, A. (1988) 'In search of subjectivity — one's own', *Educational Researcher*, **17**, pp. 7, 17–21.

Mary Jo McGee Brown

PHILLIPS, D.C. (1990) 'Subjectivity and objectivity: An objective inquiry', in EISNER, E.W. and PESHKIN, A. (Eds) *Qualitative Inquiry in Education: The Continuing Debate*, New York, Teachers College Press.

SMITH, M.L. (1987) 'Publishing qualitative research', *American Educational Research Journal*, **24**, 2, pp. 173–183.

WOLCOTT, H.F. (1990) 'On seeking-and rejecting-validity in qualitative research', in EISNER, E.W. and PESHKIN, A. (Eds), *Qualitative inquiry in education: the continuing debate* (pp. 121–152). New York, Teachers College Press.

8 Gaining Acceptance from Participants, Clients, and Policy-makers for Qualitative Research

Joseph A. Maxwell

Despite the increasing adoption and acceptance of qualitative approaches and methods, qualitative researchers still encounter misunderstandings, prejudice, and even hostility to their work from people whom they deal with. Unfortunately, courses and books on qualitative research methods rarely contain much advice on how to communicate and justify qualitative research to such people.

A recent exception to this pattern of neglect is Patton (1990), who deals at some length with problems of credibility that qualitative researchers face. Patton focuses on three issues that affect the credibility of a qualitative study: the methods used to ensure the validity of the findings, the personal and professional qualifications of the researcher, and the paradigm orientation that informs the study. He discusses the specific ways that qualitative researchers ensure the integrity and accuracy of their findings, and the philosophic issues that underlie many of the questions and misunderstandings that qualitative researchers confront.

I see no point in covering the same issues that Patton has so well analyzed; in addition, the purpose of my chapter is rather different from Patton's. I think that many of the problems researchers encounter in trying to gain acceptance for qualitative methods have little to do with the specific arguments for the validity of qualitative research that Patton discusses. I am also assuming that readers of this chapter already have some understanding of the particular strengths and advantages of qualitative methods. What I want to do here is to raise some larger, strategic issues that affect a qualitative researcher's success in dealing with people who have some stake in the research in question, but who are not convinced that a qualitative approach is appropriate, legitimate, or helpful.

I am basing what I have to say mainly on two kinds of experience. First, I spent seven years working in the education department of a major teaching hospital, doing in-house evaluations and writing proposals for qualitative studies that were reviewed by people trained in medical research. Second, I have taught qualitative research methods in a graduate school of education for six years, and have dealt both with the lack of understanding or acceptance of qualitative research by students who have been educators, administrators, and policy-makers, and with students' difficulties in negotiating entry for their research projects and communicating their results.

Rather than present an academically impressive paper, what I will try to do here is to say something *useful*. Much of this chapter may seem like obvious, commonsense advice once it's been stated, but I think that the issues that I describe are ones that we often lose sight of under the pressure of negotiating entry, doing research, and reporting our results. I have seen or been told of numerous instances where ignoring these points has led to serious difficulties or even the failure of a qualitative study; I have committed a number of these mistakes myself, and will draw my illustrations from my own errors as well as those of others. I hope to provide here some concepts and approaches that may help qualitative researchers to convey a clearer appreciation of the value and legitimacy of qualitative methods to the people they work with.

I see a number of useful frameworks and approaches that can help accomplish this goal. I think of these as metaphors (Lakoff and Johnson, 1980) for the problem of how to justify qualitative methods to people who are not familiar with this approach. I will discuss five of these metaphors: political persuasion, cross-cultural communication, the adoption of innovations, negotiation, and solidarity. The issues highlighted by the different metaphors overlap substantially, but I think that each metaphor makes a unique contribution to understanding these issues.

Political Persuasion

One of the basic principles of political persuasion is that the credibility and trustworthiness of your views and arguments are inseparable from your credibility and trustworthiness as a person. Thus, it is important to be aware of how you are perceived by the people you are working with. I have seen people whose ostensible purpose was to persuade others of the value of qualitative research, but who in fact seemed to be motivated mainly by a desire to reinforce their own conviction that they were right and that others were wrong. A political consultant whom I know, Michael Emerling, has described a phenomenon that I will call the 'ideological exhibitionist' — someone whose statements and behavior clearly express a desire to proclaim truth and denounce error, rather than to get someone else to understand or accept his position.

Positivist-bashing is probably the most common form of this among qualitative researchers; it may be an attractive strategy in preaching to the converted, as a way of confirming and deepening our own faith, but engaging in this to an audience of positivists will almost certainly undermine any possibility of mutual communication and understanding. The 'debate' mentality that encourages a frontal assault on the beliefs of those who disagree with you is not a productive model for justifying qualitative methods.

More subtly, however, similar motives can infect even a sincere attempt to communicate with others. Using particular types of rhetoric and terminology as a way (consciously or unconsciously) of establishing your superior expertise is a strategy that can easily backfire; instead of impressing others, it can offend and alienate them. Rogers (1983) argues that a change agent whose status is similar to that of her clients may have less *competence* credibility than someone of superior status, but greater *safety* credibility, or trustworthiness, leading to greater success. In order to maximize your chances for effective communication, you need to be aware of, and control, your need to feel superior to those whom you're talking to. This is particularly difficult when they are obviously trying to express their superiority to you; however, responding in kind will usually polarize the situation rather than resolve the problem.

Cross-Cultural Communication

If you want to communicate with someone, you have to speak their language and have at least a minimal understanding of their culture; to use John Holt's phrase, 'If you want to rescue someone who's lost in the woods, you have to get to where they are'. Ironically, one of the most common mistakes that qualitative researchers make in negotiating entry and in presenting their findings is that they fail to understand or use the natives' language and belief system. Sometimes this is largely an issue of terminology: of using words like 'participant observation',

'multiple realities', and 'paradigm' to people who either don't understand them, or worse, attach meanings or connotations to them that
are quite different from those intended by the researcher. I was told of
one researcher who presented a proposed study to a multiracial group
of teachers using the word 'ethnography' with no further explanation.
A Black teacher, not understanding the term, looked it up in her dic-
tionary, which defined it as 'the study of primitive peoples'. It is a
tribute to the researcher's skill that the study successfully survived this
disastrous beginning.

Even the term 'qualitative' can be problematic. I was once invited
to be on a committee to plan a hospital-wide course in research methods, mostly composed of people I didn't know. At the first meeting,
after a discussion devoted almost entirely to fairly advanced statistical
techniques, I proposed devoting one class session to qualitative methods. Others on the committee thought that would be worthwhile, and
asked me to develop a more detailed outline for what should be included. At the next meeting, I gave a short presentation of the important characteristics and methods of qualitative research that I
thought ought to be covered. When I finished, there was a dead silence,
and then one physician said, with some embarrassment, 'I thought
you meant chi-square tests'. The issue was dropped without further
discussion.

More often, the problem is a broader one of conveying the nature
of qualitative research in ways that make sense to the audience. What
may seem to you to be a crystal-clear explanation may be incomprehensible to them. For example, a recent dissertation describing a qualitative
research project quotes one of the key participants in the setting studied:

> The program was introduced in the most vague terms I have
> ever heard. It was called a 'collaboration' involving 'inquiry'
> and a 'process' and an 'evolving' idea and was absolutely un-
> clear to me . . . I hate educational jargon especially if it is vague
> (Gray, 1991).

Qualitative methods can be applied directly to this problem of understanding the concepts and values of the people you are trying to
communicate with. Don't assume that you already know where they
are coming from. Really *listen* to the questions people ask and the
comments they make. Try to grasp their world view, and address
their issues in a way that they will understand. Their concerns about,
for example, the absence of prior hypotheses in qualitative research
are legitimate and important within a quantitative framework; in

responding, you need to show how qualitative research handles, in different ways from quantitative research, the validity problems they raise, rather than attacking or dismissing these concerns as symptoms of benighted positivism.

In one ethnographic study in which I was involved, the funding agency initially requested that the researchers establish a control group of equal size to the group of families studied, and that neither the observers nor the subjects be aware of which group the subjects had been assigned to. An initial appeal by the researchers that was presented in 'qualitative' language only produced a greater insistence that the study be 'double-blind'. However, a second appeal that framed the problems that this requirement would create in terms more familiar to experimental and quantitative researchers, addressing such issues as statistical power, was successful in getting the original design restored.

Finally, it is important to *convey* to people that you are interested in how they understand the issues involved in the research, and what problems they want the research to address. There is an aphorism that nicely captures this point: people don't care what you know until they know that you care. Establishing that you are not coming in as the outside expert with all the answers, but instead are interested in learning how *they* see the situation, may be a prerequisite to any further communication and understanding.

Adoption of Innovations

Even complete communication, however, won't persuade everyone, and no amount of argument is likely to change the views of someone who doesn't *want* to change. I think that it is productive to see this problem as one of gaining acceptance by members of a community (the clients) of an innovation (qualitative research) that is being promoted by someone outside of that community. This is the third metaphor mentioned above: the adoption of innovations.

A vast literature on the adoption of innovations (cf. Rogers, 1983) has shown that people usually will not adopt an innovations simply on the basis of awareness and understanding of it. Two key criteria must also be met: first, the innovation must meet a perceived need, and second (except in rare cases of 'conversion') the innovation must be compatible with the adopter's culture and social situation. According to Rogers, the major factor in successful implementation of change is understanding the clients' perspective and situation.

Thus, a crucial issue in persuading someone to 'adopt' qualitative research is seeing how this approach can meet this person's perceived needs. Some of the things that qualitative methods have to offer other researchers and practitioners are the following:

a) identifying unanticipated factors influencing the situations and issues they are concerned with.
b) providing insight into the *process* by which things happen — getting inside the 'black box' of experimental and survey designs.
c) enabling researchers to study things (social context, meaning, life experience) that are much less amenable to other methods.
d) giving a holistic, 'real-life' picture of the phenomenon studied, rather than reducing it to numbers.
e) incorporating the perspective of the people studied into the research results.

One study I was involved in, a evaluation of teaching rounds in a hospital residency program (Maxwell, Cohen, and Reinhard, 1983; Medio *et al.*, 1984), was successful largely for three reasons. First, the study was initiated by the department responsible for the residency program, as a result of perceived problems with the program. Second, the initial, qualitative phase of the study incorporated the residents' and teaching physicians' perspectives on the program, giving it a verisimilitude that was lacking in the quantitative studies they had previously seen, and increasing the credibility of the researchers. It also created a sense of 'ownership' of the study that led to their collaboration in changes in the program and in subsequent phases of the research. Third, the qualitative study identified and clarified a number of problems with teaching rounds that the physicians had previously been aware of, but for which they had lacked a clear understanding of their scope and implications. The initial study thus led to a commitment by the department to initiate changes that would improve the quality of the teaching program, and to continue the evaluation to assess the results of these changes.

From this perspective, justifying qualitative methods by how they address particular problems recognized by your audience is far more productive than a philosophical argument for their legitimacy or superiority. In my own work as a consultant, I try to think in terms of what my clients' major concerns are, and how they might make use of qualitative methods or the results of qualitative research to address these. The more concrete and specific your discussion is, the more understandable and credible it will be.

Many of the issues that could be included under the second point mentioned above, the compatibility of the innovation with the potential adopters' culture and social situation, have already been discussed under the heading of cross-cultural communication. The compatibility of qualitative methods with the clients' culture and social structure is rarely raised in the qualitative methods literature, and consequently is often neglected by qualitative researchers, yet the innovation literature suggests that the absence of such compatibility is a major reason for the failure of innovations. I am aware of very few explicit discussions of this compatibility issue in qualitative research; two worth mentioning are Howard Becker's 'Studying Urban Schools' (1983), which analyzes why ethnographic research has often been regarded with suspicion by educational practitioners, and Judith Kleinfeld's explication (1983) of the message, written on a blackboard in the Alaska Department of Education, 'We don't need any more anthropological explanations of school failure'. Qualitative researchers often naively see their approach as inherently beneficial to their clients; more attention needs to be given to the reasons why people, given their goals and social situation, might rationally reject particular qualitative approaches and results.

One particular compatibility issue is often important, and deserves specific mention. If your audience relies on quantitative research or evaluation methods, the likelihood that they will accept qualitative approaches is increased if they believe that the two are compatible. Thus, if you feel that the two approaches *can* be usefully combined, this could be a valuable point to emphasize and explain. In my opinion, there is a growing acceptance among both qualitative and quantitative researchers of the view that the two approaches are compatible, and that there are significant advantages to integrating them. Arguments for this view, and discussions of ways to combine the two approaches, are presented by Light and Pillemer (1982), Cook (1985), Howe (1988), Patton (1990), and Maxwell (1990). This doesn't mean that combining them is always easy or productive (see, for example, Trend, 1979), only that there is no inherent conflict and that important potential benefits exist.

Negotiation

It is also useful to think about the process of justifying qualitative methods as negotiation, the fourth of the metaphors I want to discuss. The best work on negotiation that I know of is Fisher and Ury, *Getting to Yes* (1981). Fisher and Ury emphasize several of the points I've already discussed, including being aware of your own emotions and goals, not seeing your critics as 'the enemy', understanding the other side's point of view, and identifying and figuring out how to meet their perceived needs. However, their approach goes well beyond a few rules of thumb; they present an insightful and systematic strategy for resolving differences, dealing with specific problems, and creating mutually beneficial agreements. Most important, in my opinion, is their rejection of the 'Zero-sum' perspective that sees negotiation as positional bargaining, in which the only options are being hard-nosed and demanding or being nice and giving in to what the other side wants. They propose an alternative view that they call 'principled negotiation', which incorporates a separation of the problem at issue from your relationship with the people on the other side, a focus on interests (what I have called 'needs') rather than positions, and a variety of strategies for developing 'win-win' solutions.

I have seen many of my students fall into the positional perspective in attempting to negotiate entry for their qualitative research projects. One student, who wanted to study how a particular subject was taught, proposed to the teacher to whom she'd been referred by the school administration that she conduct observations in his classroom and interview him and some of his students. He refused, and told her that if she really wanted to understand this topic she should teach some of his classes dealing with her subject. She came to me in some distress, feeling that she had no choice but to give in and abandon her original goals or to seek another teacher, which would put her far behind schedule. From our discussion, two things seemed apparent: first, that his demand was probably a way of 'testing' her willingness to provide something in return, and that for her to teach a few classes would be a way of repaying the teacher for his time; second, that such teaching would not necessarily interfere with her planned research, and on the contrary could be valuable in establishing rapport with both the teacher and his students. She returned to the teacher with this new perspective, negotiated a mutually satisfactory arrangement, and completed her research, finding not only that the teacher was far more open and cooperative following her teaching, but that her insights from teaching complemented her results from the interviews and observations.

Solidarity

Much of what I've been describing can also be seen as the problem of how solidarity with others is created and maintained, the last metaphor I want to present. Despite the widespread assumption that solidarity is essentially a matter of similarity — that the way to relate successfully to others is to be (or to be seen as) like them, to have things in common — there are good reasons, both theoretical and practical, to doubt that this is the whole story. While similarity is one way that solidarity can be established (for one example, see the argument made above, that similarity in status between change agent and clients leads to greater perceived trustworthiness), another way is through interaction and complementarity — doing things for the people you're working with that they cannot or prefer not to do themselves. Both are valuable strategies, but the second is often more relevant for qualitative researchers, because they are initially seen by clients as different from themselves. One of the errors we made in the study of teaching rounds, described above, was that we did not establish frequent interaction with the members of the department, and throughout the study were seen as consultants rather than collaborators.

One of the main theoretical rationales for this approach to solidarity comes from the French sociologist Emile Durkheim (1933 [1893]). Durkheim argued that there are two types of solidarity in society: mechanical solidarity, based on likeness and homogeneity, and organic solidarity, based on diversity, complementarity, and the division of labor. A popular version of the same idea is expressed by Coleman and Edwards (1979), who claim that there are two reasons that people choose to interact with others: either they see them as like themselves, or they see ways that these others can meet their needs. Their practical advice is that if you are in a group of people unlike yourself, the best way to become accepted is to find ways to meet their needs. (This is related to the point made above, that meeting a client's perceived need is a key factor in the successful adoption of an innovation.)

Fisher and Ury (citing Jack Sprat and his wife) make a similar argument: that *differences* in beliefs, values, and interests can often form the basis for productive relationships, because of the complementarity that these differences create (1981). They refer to this strategy as 'dovetailing': avoiding the assumption that the negotiation is a zero-sum game, while looking for arrangements that are of high benefit to the other side and low cost to you, and vice versa. They state that 'shared interests and differing but complementary interests can both serve as the building blocks for a wise agreement' (1981).

The five metaphors I have described are best seen as conceptual tools rather than as guidelines or formulas for success. They are ways of viewing qualitative researchers' problems in gaining credibility and acceptance that highlight some issues that often are obscured by conventional ways of seeing these situations. However, much of what I've advocated here can also be seen more broadly as turning the theories, approaches, and methods of qualitative research itself onto these problems. Issues of communication, rapport, sensitivity to clients' needs, and negotiation of the research relationship are part of the fabric of qualitative research. If we can adapt these concepts, values, and strategies to the larger issue of the perception of the credibility and worth of our approach, I think we can be more effective in justifying this approach to others.

References

BECKER, H.S. (1983) 'Studying Urban Schools', *Anthropology and Education Quarterly*, **14**, 3, pp. 99–108.

COLEMAN, E. and EDWARDS, B. (1979) *Brief Encounters: How to Make the Most of Relationships That May Not Last Forever*, Garden City NY, Anchor Books.

COOK T.D. (1985) 'Postpositivist Critical Multiplism', in SHOTLAND, R.L. and MARKS, M.M. (Eds), *Social science and social policy*, Beverly Hills, Sage, pp. 21–62.

DURKHEIM, EMILE (1933) *The Division of Labor in Society*, New York, The Free Press.

FISHER, R. and URY, W. (1981) *Getting to Yes: Negotiating Agreement Without Giving In*, Boston, Houghton Mifflin.

GRAY, C. (1991) 'The Use of Video as a Tool of Communication in an Urban High School', Unpublished doctoral dissertation, Harvard Graduate School of Education.

HOWE, K. (1988) 'Against the Qualitative-Quantitative Incompatibility Thesis or Dogmas Die Hard', *Educational Researcher*, **17**, 8, pp. 10–16.

KLEINFELD, J. (1983) 'First Do No Harm: A Reply to Courtney Cazden', *Anthropology and Education Quarterly*, **14**, 4, pp. 282–287.

LAKOFF, G. and JOHNSON, M. (1980) *Metaphors We Live By*, Chicago, University of Chicago Press.

LIGHT, R.J. and PILLEMER, D.B. (1982) Numbers and Narrative: Combining their Strengths in Research Reviews, *Harvard Educational Review*, 52, pp. 1–26.

MAXWELL, J.A., COHEN, R.M. and REINHARD, J.D. (1983) 'A Qualitative Study of Teaching Rounds in a Department of Medicine', Proceedings of the Twenty-second Annual Conference on Research in Medical Education.

MAXWELL, J.A. (1990) 'Up From Positivism: A Review of Donald T. Campbell, Methodology and Epistemology for Social Science.' *Harvard Educational Review*, pp. 497–501.

MEDIO, F.J., WILKERSON, L., MAXWELL, J.A., COHEN, R.M. and REINHARD, J.D. (1984) Proceedings of the Twenty-third Annual Conference on Research in Medical Education.

PATTON, M.Q. (1990) *Qualitative Research and Evaluation Methods*, Newbury Park CA, Sage Publications.

ROGERS, E.M. (1983) *Diffusion of Innovations* (3rd ed.) New York, The Free Press.

TREND, M. (1979) 'On the Reconciliation of Qualitative and Quantitative Analyses: A Case Study', in COOK, T.D. and REICHARDT, C.S. (Eds), *Combining Quantitative and Qualitative Methods in Evaluation Research*, Newbury Park CA, Sage.

9 An Evaluation Fable: The Animals of United Farms

Ronald E. Mertz

Many factors must work together in order for an evaluation to be successful. Defining its purpose, formulating key questions, careful data collection and analysis, and clear jargon-free writing are all critical. The one aspect of carrying out an evaluation that I have found to be most intriguing, however, is the act of communication between evaluators and program managers.

There are similarities in factors related to communication between traditional ethnographic research and qualitative evaluation. The evaluator, like the traditional ethnographer may be a stranger to members of this 'society', and must attempt to establish rapport. The traditional ethnographer and evaluator may both be perceived with a certain amount of suspicion. The nature of this suspicion, however, is likely to be dissimilar. Members of a traditional society may not understand the ethnographer's purpose, and may have unrealistic notions regarding the ethnographer's culture.

On the other hand, the purpose of the evaluator's presence is usually quite clear to program personnel. They know that the evaluator is not simply interested in learning about their program. Evaluations are likely to be characterized by such central questions as: 'is the program working', 'what factors are contributing to or detracting from the program's success', and perhaps, most threatening of all, 'do outcomes justify program continuation'?

The contrast in cultural background between evaluators and program managers is likely to be much less pronounced than between an ethnographer and members of a traditional group being studied. Nevertheless, while coming from the same national culture, the communication gulf between the evaluator and program manager may be as great due to differences in roles and personality.

Perhaps the clearest delineation of these differences between evaluators and program managers was provided by Gurel (1975), almost two decades ago. The following are several of the major ways in which they were seen to contrast.

1   While managers identify with program survival and preserving the status quo, evaluators identify with innovation and changing the status quo.
2   Managers approach analysis and evaluation in terms of their potential for program defense, while evaluators approach analysis and evaluation in terms of program assessment and appraisal.
3   The manager is likely to be a 'company man' (or woman), while the evaluator identifies as a 'scientist' and individualist.

To illustrate these differences as they affect communication, I would like to tell you the following fable.

The Animals of United Farms

You are likely to be familiar with George Orwell's Animal Farm *(1946) in which he provided a chilling account of totalitarianism. As you may recall, the animals of Manor Farm rebelled against their human owners, drove them away, and attempted to establish a democracy at the newly named 'Animal Farm' based on the credo that 'all animals are created equal'. However, the farm became increasingly totalitarian as the pigs, under the leadership of the boar, Napoleon, subjugated the other animals.*

Animal Farm was not the only experiment in which animals established their own social and economic system. Years before, and far to the west, rebellions similar to the one at Manor Farm took place. The animals, tired of the yoke of oppression imposed by their owners, and yearning to be the masters of their own destiny rebelled. Starting at one farm, the rebellion spread rapidly to neighboring estates until the animals gained control of a vast, though largely undeveloped expanse of land.

Given the richness of the land and the industriousness of the animals, the farms prospered. In fact, the animals were so successful that they expanded well beyond their initial holdings and laid claim to large tracks of virgin land inhabited by non-domesticated animals or 'Forest Dwellers' as they were called.

Unlike Animal Farm, where tyranny under the pigs had quickly replaced any incipient democracy, the animals of United Farms (the name given to this new republic) had been successful in establishing a system which gave a voice to all regardless of species or farm of origin. Of course, this democracy wasn't perfect. Most notable was the inequality that existed between the descendants of the original founders and the Forest Dwellers. The displacement of the humans by the animals of United Farms put new demands on their non-domesticated neighbors. Initially, many of these wild animals died of diseases for which they lacked immunity. Those that did not die were often forced from the woods and meadows of their ancestors so that the farms could be expanded. Some, like the elk and deer tried to follow the ways of the domestic animals, but with little success.

Many changes took place over time as the farms expanded. The techno-economic structure as well as the social structure of the farms became more complex. Additionally, the few simple credos that formed the ideological basis for United Farms society had expanded into a complex code of beliefs and rituals.

While a few tasks were still accomplished through instinct, and many others could be learned through imitating adults during work activities, the leaders of United Farms became increasingly convinced that there was a need for a formal place of learning. This center of learning would be open to all species and would ensure that all young learned to do the tasks they would need to do as adults. It would also ensure that all young understood the history of United Farms and their ancestors' struggle for freedom from human control as well as ensure that youth, regardless of species, learned the expected behavior of all.

A location for this place of learning was carefully selected to ensure it would reflect a 'typical farm' in terms of soil and topography. Each farm sent animals to help in the construction of buildings that would house 'rooms of learning' and quarters for staff. These efforts required a great deal of time, but despite grumbling by some, the majority of the animals were convinced that this place of learning was a key to the continuing success of United Farms.

The staff for this 'Knowing Center' were recruited from among those animals that combined the traits of knowing and caring. Prominent among the staff were several Great Pyrenees, huge white dogs whose ancestors had origin-ally been brought to the region by humans to protect sheep. The canines, while not skilled in most of the practical tasks needed to be taught, were among the most intelligent and empathetic staff members. Their concern for loyalty and obedience made them ideal for instructing others in the ethical code of United Farms, and for important leadership roles at the Knowing Center.

The eldest of the Great Pyrenees was appointed headmaster. Even before his appointment, he had earned widespread respect for his dedication to the welfare and safety of youths. Parents sent their young to the Center knowing that they were in caring paws.

The staff included a variety of other species including several each of swine, horses, cattle, and sheep. The swine, like the canines were among the *brightest citizens of United Farms. Though they often lacked the empathy that characterized many of the canines, they, along with the canines, had mastered the ability to read without any formal schooling. At the Knowing Center they were responsible for teaching this skill to all students.*

Most of the other staff members concentrated on teaching subject areas associated with their species. The horses, for instance, taught practical ways of transporting materials and crop production. Cattle provided classes in milk production and the utilization of dairy products, while sheep taught skills in textile production and applications.

The Knowing Center was generally hailed as a success. The Center's attempt to bring about change among the Forest Dwellers, however, had not been meeting with much success. Although these animals appeared to learn many of the tasks they were taught at the Center, they did not show much interest in learning the ways of the domesticated animals. Many of them left the Center before completing their course of study, and the few who did graduate soon returned to the forests and untilled fields.

Due to the lack of success in educating the non-domesticated animals, the United Farms Counsel (its governing body) decided there was a need to examine the Knowing Center's program.

Who was to be responsible for carrying out this task? The leaders chose two German Shepherds. They seemed ideally suited since they were noted for their alertness and analytic ability. Although some leaders had expressed concern about the extreme self confidence and apparent aloofness that these individuals projected, in the end they too agreed to appoint them to carry out the evaluation.

And so it was that the two German Shepherds entered the office of the Great Pyrenees.

'Good morning', greeted the headmaster, wagging his huge white tail, 'Welcome to the Knowing Center.'

'Good morning', responded the two German Shepherds, almost in unison.

'I understand you have come to observe the operation of the center,' the headmaster continued.

'That's right,' stated the team leader, an almost pure black male with dark piercing eyes. 'As we informed you in the letter, the committee has asked us to conduct a study of the Center and prepare a report.'

'As you probably already know,' the headmaster went on, 'we are very proud of the Center. I and all the staff feel it is the key to the future of United Farms.'

'Yes, I'm sure we all agree that the Center can play a key role in the education of our youth,' the second shepherd, a white female, responded. 'We are confident our report will provide information that can be used to strengthen the program here at the Center.'

'Perhaps,' replied the headmaster, 'but I'm sure you will find that our dedicated staff is doing all it can to make the program a success. I hope your report will contain all the accomplishments of the Center. We are especially proud of some of our outstanding readers that have left the Center. There was one Landrace (a breed of pig) who learned to read even the most difficult materials, and I'm sure you have heard of the progress many of the horses have made. Before the Center, most thought that the horses were simply unable to read. But now even the Clydesdales are reading simple stories.'

'We are most interested in the success of your program with the Forest Dwellers. Based on the figures you have provided the counsel, most of the Forest Dwellers are not finishing the program,' the second shepherd continued.

'Why are they only interested in our problems with the Forest Dwellers? It's as though they want to make the Center appear to be a failure,' the headmaster thought to himself, as he responded. 'Yes, it is unfortunate, but it is not because our staff hasn't tried. They just don't seem interested in learning. In fact, I doubt if they are as capable of learning as our other students.'

'Perhaps, they prefer their traditional life,' suggested the first evaluator.

'Possibly,' responded the headmaster. 'But it is difficult to understand why any animal would rather sleep outside on cold nights than in a warm stall, or why they would rather spend winters seeking adequate browse when they could share food that had been stored during the summer. Frankly, most of the staff have concluded that the Forest Dwellers are not capable of learning without some extensive remedial efforts. Hopefully, your evaluation will conclude that more staff are needed to provide special services for them.'

And so, for the next month, the German Shepherds spent their days visiting classes, and talking to staff and students. In some instances they would simply enter a classroom, find a comfortable location and curl up, appearing to be only vaguely aware of events around them. In other instances, they would join in activities. In addition to these formal settings, the evaluators spent time visiting informally with students and staff.

At first, the non-domesticated students were reluctant to talk with the evaluators, but after a while, they began to confide in them.

By the end of the month the evaluators had completed data gathering, summarized their findings, and developed recommendations. They met again with the headmaster before finalizing their report for the Council.

'I trust your stay at the Knowing Center has been productive,' greeted the Pyrenees as he welcomed the evaluators into his office.

'Yes, we feel it has been productive,' replied the first evaluator, 'We have come to share our findings and recommendations with you before we present them to the Council.'

'And have you found the staff to be dedicated to the success of the Center?' the headmaster asked with apparent confidence.

'Yes, they all seemed dedicated to the Center and its goals,' replied the second team member, 'but we have identified some aspects of program implementation that must be modified if the Center is going to accomplish its goals more effectively with the Forest Dwellers.'

'Do you understand now why I said we need to hire staff for remedial classes?' asked the headmaster.

'Remedial classes will not be the answer,' the male Shepherd returned.

'What then?' responded the headmaster.

'There must be some real changes in the way the Forest Dwellers are educated at the Center,' continued the second evaluator.

'What do you mean?' asked the Great Pyrenees.

'First, they must be appreciated for their uniqueness, just as are all the other citizens of United Farms,' the second evaluator went on.

'But we offer them the same opportunities as the others, we should be able to set the same level of expectations,' countered the headmaster defensively.

'Requiring the young bucks and bull elk to have their antlers cut back in the fall after they have matured instills in them a sense that they are guilty of some wrong doing. Also, it was apparent in the many classes we visited that there was little respect for the ways of the Forest Dwellers. We never heard mention, for instance, of the many plants they introduced to the United Farms, or how their ancestors had helped in the revolution. The only mention we could find in the history books was an account of how they abandoned lands that could then be turned into farms,' the first evaluator explained as he went over the summary he had prepared. 'Furthermore, the deer and elk made it quite clear to us that their families seldom went hungry during the winter or found the cold outdoors less comfortable than the arrangements they would have to share with others in the farm buildings.'

'What are you recommending then?' asked the headmaster.

The first evaluator reviewed the recommendations.

'First, there should be no more trimming of antlers in the fall.

Second, your staff should elicit the help of some older elk and deer to assist in integrating the history of the non-domesticated and domesticated.

Third, since the Knowing Center presently has no non-domesticated staff members it should recruit some as soon as possible to help instruct all students in Forest Dweller practical arts.'

'I'm not sure these changes are really needed,' the headmaster replied wearily, 'but if your findings and recommendations are accepted by the counsel I will do my best to see that they are carried out.'

'We are certain you will,' the second evaluator said reassuringly as they prepared to leave.

With that, they bid farewell to the headmaster and trotted down the campus road toward the distant United Farms capital.

'*What do you plan to do after we have finished the report?*' *asked the first evaluator.*

'*I've thought of returning to the Knowing Center to work with the young,*' *replied the white German Shepherd. 'How about you?*'

'*I think I will leave United Farms for a while and take a trip into some of the unsettled territories to the north. I want to know more about what it is like to be a Forest Dweller.*'

As we have seen in this fable, while program managers and evaluators may share similar programmatic goals, they are likely to bring contrasting world views and values to the evaluation setting. These differences reflect their personal and cultural background, training, and perhaps most importantly, their contrasting roles. Our success as evaluators in communicating with policy decision makers and power brokers will be largely determined by our ability to recognize the force that these underlying world views and values play in shaping behavior.

References

GUREL, L. (1975) 'The Human Side of Evaluating Human Services Programs: Problems and Prospects', in GUTTENTAG, M. and STRUENING, E.L. (Eds) *Handbook of Evaluation Research*, Vol. 2, Sage, Beverly Hills.

ORWELL, GEORGE (1946) *Animal Farm*, Harcourt Brace Jovanovich, New York.

10 A School Board's Response to an Ethnographic Evaluation: Or, Whose Evaluation is this Anyway?

Mary Lopez de Abascal-Hildebrand

Introduction

This chapter explores the politics surrounding the rejection of an ethnographic evaluation I presented to a school board. As the evaluator, I address the ethical questions that emerged because of both the political context and the report's ethnographic character. I discuss the context of the evaluation and some of the contemporary social and political issues in ethnographic evaluation. I offer a combination of social critique and interpretive anthropology as a way to understand the philosophical issues inherent in ethnographic evaluation ethics.

Questioning social and political conditions, while interpreting human action in its cultural context, promotes the ethics which are inherent in any form of social action. Engaging in critique with participants can remind ethnographers of the need to raise questions continually — both while conducting ethnographic activities and afterward. Questioning is important so that ethnographic practices do not become routine and thereby mask the social and political conditions found in evaluation contexts. Examining ethics illuminates those conditions which may deny the rights of evaluation participants and evaluators to protect the evaluation contexts under study. Engaging in critique promotes ethnography and philosophy as a way to understand more about ethics. Therefore, greater understanding makes it possible for ethnographers to act more fruitfully to alter such conditions.

Since this is a confessional tale in Van Maanen's terms (1988), I talk about the ethical context for the solutions I chose in response to the board's initial rejection of my evaluation. My choices concern the way I ultimately communicated my ethnographic insights to the school board. My primary purpose in this chapter is to promote the ethical dimension of ethnographic evaluation because conscious application of ethics extends evaluation. It extends evaluation first because it enables ethnographic evaluators to see that ethics are already implicit in what they do. Further, a conscious ethical stance enables evaluators to be aware that the more they understand ethical implications, the more they can make them explicit for everyone involved. My aim is to show that explicating ethical issues can promote among contracting entities the suitability, and indeed the critical need to engage participants in evaluations. Such engagement can make it more likely that participants will be able to help implement the program development work that evaluations suggest. Thus, evaluation can become a part of program development, not an appendage to it.

Moreover, in explicating ethics, evaluators can educate policy-makers more readily about the possibilities in ethnographic evaluation when they understand the need themselves to anticipate more fully the ways in which typical contracting entities view evaluation. The ultimate advantage is that policy-makers who know more about the kind of knowledge that can be generated through ethnography can support ethnography as an additional approach to educational development and reform.

Ethnography that blends critique with interpretation of data fore-grounds both evaluators and their participants; it promotes and protects ethnographic insights and criticisms as they are presented to outsiders. Participants' views become the substance of the evaluator's analysis. Since their views are at the center, an ethical approach requires that ethnographers communicate them to outsiders so that they can use them to promote appropriate educational reform and develop suitable education policy.

Evaluation Context

Contextualizing this ethnographic evaluation helps point out the complexity in political and ethical questions. Specifically, I evaluated the first year of the implementation of a Title VII grant in a large, metropolitan, county schools program on the West Coast. The grant spanned nearly two academic years — from January 1988 to June 1989. The funding provided inservice education for classroom parapro-fessionals (teacher aides) who work with students with limited English language abilities, primarily those students who speak Asian languages.

The respective county schools office provided the administration, implementation, and evaluation functions. Twelve of twenty-two co-operating local districts were the source of the fifty-five volunteer participants who remained throughout the project, though some of the participants also worked in community service settings as translators and tutors. Most of the participants were Asian-bilingual, others were Hispanic-bilingual, some were not bilingual. The grant also provided for stipends for the aides' Saturday participation and for funds to repay their school districts for substitute costs while the aides attended the workshops on school days.

Further, the project community represents a widely varying racial, ethnic, cultural, and linguistic character in terms of students and citizens: in 1986 (the last census year for which figures were available during the term of the project) more than 14 per cent of the total ADA consisted of Asian students (10,386), while there were only twelve certificated staff who spoke any of the many Asian languages represented. Therefore, those aides who were Asian-language speaking were overwhelmingly the major source of both language and cultural knowledge concerning the educational and cultural needs of Asian students. Moreover, these aides were the primary source for teachers and other educators in implementing educational programs, and for communicating students' progress to parents and other family members. Data suggest that there were 328 aides needed in Asian bilingual classroms, based upon a ratio of one aide for every thirty-five Asian students, while there were only a handful working in those classrooms at the time of this evaluation.

A central issue in any educational setting where paraprofessionals work, and even more so in bilingual, multicultural, or special education contexts, is that their educational understandings and commitment are central to three major educational activities: teachers' work, students' success, and families' participation. However, most inservice programs do not consider the importance of aides' participation in serving these purposes (Robin and Wagenfeld, 1981). Further, inservice programs that are provided are very sparse, technical in nature, and ignore ways in which inservice might engage aides and encourage them to become teachers themselves in programs which serve limited English-speaking students — an area already grossly underserved.

Therefore, the purpose of this project was to provide inservice that might more likely enable the aides to serve these activities more effectively, encourage their retention in education (to offset their desirability in other work places by virtue of their race, ethnicity, and bilingualism), and recruit them into higher education as aspiring teachers.

Overall, the purpose was to encourage them to believe that they are important contributors to educational programs and to their communities.

The more specific goals proposed included developing knowledge about education, particularly bilingual, multicultural, and special education, so aides could add to the quality of student life. An overall goal was that the paraprofessionals would become empowered to begin influencing educational contexts where they typically have little influence.

The project modules, while not designed or implemented with any particular theoretical perspective in mind, except to promote a sense of community among the participants, included a range of topics: instructional strategies and classroom management, second language acquisition, multicultural education, special education assessment and service, the organization of US school systems, and career counseling/ planning. The project staff included the director of bilingual education programs, the director of this project, the module presenters, and me as the project evaluator.

Ethnographic Orientation

The project director and I believed we could engage the participants in an ethnographic evaluation in addition to the series of brief surveys they would complete for each module. She pointed out there were no stated requirements in the grant proposal or in the funding requirements for any particular orientation or format. Since the average length of classroom service was ten years, we discussed the importance of an evaluation perspective that would capture the rich, nuanced world of the aides' educational and cultural experience, point more vividly to this lived experience, and encourage them to become teachers themselves. Therefore, I conducted a series of interviews over the course of the several months from February to June of 1988 during which I interviewed twelve of the fifty-five participants; the project director also conducted several ethnographic interviews. In addition, I attended and participated in some of the workshops and sessions so that I could add observation data to my report.

I spoke at length with the project director as to which form to use to conduct the evaluation. The form of ethnographic evaluation I selected is referred to as phenomenological ethnography (see Tesch, 1988). Principally, phenomenological ethnographic evaluation focuses on the language participants use to describe their experience. Further, phenomenological ethnography considers persons as participants rather than as informants. This approach, like traditional ethnography, also uses interviews in addition to observations as data sources and focuses on the meanings ascribed by the participants to their experience.

An important addition I made to Tesch's phenomenology is that I used critique and interpretation to create the research context, to guide the questioning and the conversations, to interpret the data, and to keep the aides' language as the focal point for the analysis (Abascal-Hildebrand, in press). As such, the means within this approach (promoting participants' thinking through conversational interviews) match the ends (promoting participants' new views of themselves through conversation).

Moreover, integrating a critical and interpretive perspective on the project phenomena into the ethnographic evaluation made it a particular kind of ethnographic evaluation. I conducted the interviews by asking questions that could provoke thinking and further questioning. For example, provoking participants' own insights in conversations can guide them in thinking more broadly about what had been limiting their potential in education. Conversations can promote participants' engagement in critiquing and solving educational problems. Participants can be encouraged to think about the problems and interpret their views about them. Moreover, conversations can encourage a sense of commitment to interpreting and solving the problems they uncover. Conversations are different from straightforward, question-and-answer sessions because they encourage critical interpretation for both researchers and participants.

Hermeneutics refers to interpretation. The origin of the word hermeneutics is Hermes, the name of the Greek God whose task it was to interpret the god's messages among them and mortals. To perform this interpretation, Hermes had to 'bring them forth', or educate them about one another's messages. *Educare* means 'to bring forth'; it is the root of the word, educate. As Hermes carried their messages among them, he interpreted the messages, educating them, 'bringing them forth' into understanding the meanings.

A critical interpretive approach to conversation in ethnographic evaluation illuminates the aides' language, as well as demonstrates how they used their language; they both described their experience and learned to view themselves in new ways, to 'bring themselves forth'. As they became aware of the importance with which I as an evaluator valued their words and ideas, they began believing that they were capable of significant thinking. Moreover, as our conversations linked their experience with their new knowledge, they began believing that they were able to understand and apply what they learn. One aide comments on what she learned about herself in the project's sessions, 'what I did by rote was (actually) from theory'.

Many aides were able to think in new ways about what they had taken for granted, as this woman points out, 'it (the project) linked to what I already did'. They were able to reflect more consciously on their own experience in teaching students and the relationship of their experience to educational theory. One notes, 'that we do here what they are teaching us to do — it's one in the same'.

They took on a new sense of competence and belonging, as this woman exclaims, 'this project brought us up as part of teaching!' Many commented about the project and about the way it promoted new confidence and new relationships back in their classrooms, 'we were treated like first class citizens, not second class . . . the teachers use our questions now'. Moreover, by the end of the first full year of the project, twelve had begun college coursework for teacher certification.

The evaluation report included a variety of ethnographic data: discussions on the overall project and a detailed profile of the participant group, the participants' views about each of the curriculum modules, a data analysis of the written evaluations they completed for each module, comparisons they had made of the modules, observations I made during my participation, extensive interview data analysis, and ethnographic data collected also by the project director (Harper, 1989). The language of the report was ordinary language, I was careful to avoid particular academic references and vocabularies. Conclusions were drawn using these analyses and relating them to the project's purpose, goals, and objectives. Because of the complexity of the data, the report ended with a summary for easier reference. The insights were ethnographic, and specifically critical and interpretive of the language generated in the conversations. As such, I believed the insights could more 'thickly' describe (Geertz, 1983) to the school board the project's success in meeting its stated purpose and goals: changing the paraprofessionals' thinking about themselves and their participation in school life.

The Board's Responses to My Ethnographic Insights

However, the county school board refused to accept my evaluation. The director of bilingual programs referred the evaluation back to me for revision by directing it to me through the project director. I was told that the board believed there was 'no data in it' and that the board would not accept it until I included in it data the board members found suitable. Further inquiry enabled me to understand that the board members were primarily interested in attendance data and numerical representations of the participants' evaluation of the overall project. I had to decide what to do with the ethnographic data that I had already reported and how to respond to the board's request that I 'get some real data'.

While this is a confessional tale (Van Maanen, 1988), it is not at all a confessional in the sense of wrong-doing. Rather it is, as Van Maanen would write, a tale of the dilemmas and insights that the ethnography generated for me as the scribe. I was aware certainly that we as ethnographers live in a world that is dominated by positivism — and, indeed, many forms of ethnography are positivistic — but that is for another discussion. I was aware that most program evaluation has some connection to government sponsored evaluation. Therefore, I knew that positivism and government sponsorship were often interdependent. I knew there was a chance that my orientation might conflict with a school board's expectations, particularly in a contract and policy environment 'in which the problem, and often the research design, has been defined in advance' (Fetterman, 1986). But I thought I had taken care of that possibility earlier through my discussions and interactions with the project director; she collected some of the ethnographic data for the evaluation. Apparently we both had the wrong impression of the landscape; we had not been aware of the need to inform the board of our evaluation plans.

Further, the project director was just resigning from the project to take another position, making matters more difficult. In any case, I had a tome of a report, and I was faced with what to do with it in light of the changing staff conditions, and my unwavering belief that my report must serve the voices of these participants — their tales of the field.

It was my firm conviction that their narratives (Richardson, 1990; Ricoeur, 1987), presented in a 'literary Geertzian tradition' (Fetterman, 1986) were potent evidence that educational inservice programs that consider persons as acting subjects (Freire, 1986) are those most likely to accomplish goals which are based on promoting participation. In particular, since this project sought to create among the participants new beliefs about themselves, I believed that our ethnographic evaluation illustrated how the participants had become educated both about education and about themselves as participants in it.

Continuing my tale, the timing was all wrong for me to rewrite the evaluation. I was already immersed in another major evaluation — this time I was chairing an accreditation self-study for a university. But I believed in the data and wanted to protect its integrity and that of the participants whose efforts created the data. In practical terms, I needed to move on, and I needed to get paid for my work. Even more than that I wanted the program director and the board members to see the evaluation as more than suitable and to support its acceptance. I reflected at length as to how I could communicate the visions within the data to the school board.

Philosophy and the Politics and Ethics of Ethnographic Evaluation

As such, my discussion with the project director and my reflections concentrated on the ethics involved in communicating my vision and the participants' insights. I felt supported by the work in contemporary ethnography that emerges out of ethical questions in social inquiry (Fetterman, 1984, 1986, 1989; Van Maanen, 1988). Fetterman refers to an ethnographer as a new kind of culture broker. Culture brokering, because it is a human enterprise, necessarily requires ethical awareness. Considering the politics and ethics of evaluation are not new issues in ethnography — actions that engage others require an awareness of the ethics inherent in engaging them. But conscious understandings of ethics must pervade every aspect of ethnographic work so they can guide the changes the data suggest.

A critical, interpretive philosophy of the ethics in ethnography can promote a more conscious application of ethics. John Van Maanen (1988) exorts us to understand the need to blur the disciplines that make up social inquiry. Clifford Geertz posits in his essay, 'Blurred Genres', that such blurring reduces fragmentation in social inquiry (Geertz, 1978). David Fetterman writes that ethnographers must be able to 'communicate cultural knowledge across disciplinary boundaries' (1986). Together, these writers point to the need for ethnographers, educators, and policy makers to consider combining perspectives in sociology, literature, and philosophy to enliven modes of social inquiry. They suggest it is appropriate to examine the ethical and philosophical dimensions of protecting conversations that emerge from ethnographic evaluation. I propose that protecting ethnographic data philosophically is central to protecting the potential in the relationship of ethnography to educational development (Abascal-Hildebrand, in press).

Paying close attention to the language generated in ethnographic evaluation avoids separating the process of understanding from what is understood. We as inquirers likewise cannot be separated from the process of inquiry. Neither can we separate participants from the data they generate. Such separation limits social inquiry to a form of individual action one person performs on another and thereby ignores the relational enterprise. An ethnography that focuses on language can portray conversational data in a very different light. It can illuminate understanding as the essence of interaction and social action. It can demonstrate that language and understanding are inseparable. Such a language-centered ethnography can point out why evaluations must be presented in participants' voices.

As social inquirers, we can promote social action more consciously when we are aware that social action emerges naturally when participants feel their voices are valued. In interpreting and protecting their voices, we as inquirers become participants also. We thereby demonstrate that we all have the ability not only to think and talk about what we need to do to solve our problems, but we all have the ability to make changes come about (Abascal-Hildebrand, 1993).

It is appropriate to think in philosophical terms about conversation for social action. Gadamer, a critical social philosopher, writes, 'the human word is potential' (1975). When we understand this potential in ethnography, we can more readily see how our words — those spoken in interviews, and those written in evaluation reports — are themselves the very seeds for school reform (Abascal-Hildebrand, in press).

Numbers alone could not represent the personal triumphs that many of the aides achieved in this project. Numbers alone could not explain how school district personnel can think about aides' work as they plan inservices that promote aides' participation and commitment. Numbers alone could not portray how a project such as this can integrate ethnographic evaluation as one of the means for promoting the project's purpose, and numbers alone could not have represented how the evaluation conversations which promoted their talking about their experiences in the project enabled them to create new views of themselves. Gathering numbers alone could not have generated among the paraprofessionals the seeds for changing their classroom lives along with those of the students and teachers with whom they work, nor could it have portrayed how the project, and the form of evaluation, 'brought forth' the participants (Abascal-Hildebrand, in press).

The Snare of Positivism

This is certainly not meant to serve as a discussion on the distinction between the benefits of qualitative research over quantitative research. Scholars already agree that there is a distinction between quantitative and qualitative paradigms in research. Therefore, we need to get beyond these paradigm wars. To do this, we need to understand how positivism can invade qualitative work. Because positivism is a very powerful tradition it can mask the internal conflict within a qualitative approach that ignores the centrality of language in both creating and analyzing data — and in thinking about and protecting the ethical dimension of ethnographic data.

Positivism can trick us into believing that understanding can be separated from the language that created it. It posits a false sense of data in social inquiry and suggests that it is possible to substitute context-stripping, numerical data, or even well-intentioned question-and-answer interviews for critical conversation. Conversational interviews promote engagement, critique, and commitment through the interpretive process. Evaluations which guard the interpretive process in the data collection, evaluation, and presentation of data are more likely to encourage and present the commitment that is sought in projects such as this. Guarding the interpretive process in ethnography can enable us as evaluators to avoid positivistic traps when we think we are embracing qualitative in social inquiry.

A major problem in a positivistic stance is that it is uninformed by communicative ethics. It ignores the way in which interaction forms understanding. Paul Ricoeur, a philosopher of language, points this out. He writes, 'the hermeneutical idea of subjectivity as a dialectic between the self and mediated social meanings has deep moral and political implications. It shows there is an *ethic* of the word' (emphasis in original; Ricoeur in Kearney, 1984). This ethic means we have to fulfill our moral obligation by being responsible for what we say and the way we say it when participating in and interpreting data in social inquiry, and when presenting it to policy boards.

The way we participate and what we say about our participation has implications not only for how we act as ethnographers, but it has implications for all of us — our participants and ourselves — concerning our ability to act in the world encouraged by the conversations we have together. Overall, it has major implications for how useful ethnographic evaluations will be in actually making changes in the social and political dimensions of education. It has major implications for the way in which we go about reform. In other words, how we respond to demands to relinquish our emphasis on our ethnographic data will portray our belief in the primacy of the data. It will portray our belief in ethnography as a suitable means for portraying and changing the social and political dimensions of schooling. It will portray our belief in the power of ethnography to bring forth participants' lives and meanings. The way we respond as ethnographic evaluators to positivistic traps is critical when our work is intended for use by policy-makers and others whose decisions largely determine the structure within which participants' educational lives can emerge.

My Solutions and Recommendations: Or, Which Way to Education?

What decisions did I make to solve my dilemma? I struggled to meet the needs of all involved, given the new knowledge I had about the school board's preference. I changed none of the ethnographic evaluation. I added data about attendance. I added data from a survey we created and distributed in the beginning of the second year of the project. I rewrote the introduction and summary to legitimate more strongly the ethnographic data. I pointed out that while the newer data may promote similar conclusions, they were very different data because they did not offer nearly the richness of the ethnographic data, nor did they show the aides' new meanings and commitments — or sense of community they developed together.

The newer, quantitative data forms largely displayed agreement on all the points I had already made in the ethnographic report. Indeed, I was not holding out for agreement among the data forms because of the different directions from which survey data forms emerge. Had they been different, I would have used interpretive processes to explain any differences that might have emerged. For the reasoning to support this I look to Ricoeur (1987), who writes that the hermeneutic project is not one that requires agreement, but one which requires that we point out and celebrate differences when we see them, much as literary theorists would in a dialogic.

Quantitative and qualitative sources may point us in the same direction on the way to education. However, both cannot, by virtue of their emerging out of different structures, promote social action in the same way. Both cannot enable us to imagine ourselves as able to make the changes we learn are necessary. We are more likely to find our way toward improving educational programs and participants' educational lives when we conduct ethnographic evaluations that give voice to participants, and 'bring them forth'. But this is only the beginning of what we need to do as ethnographers who see our work as fundamentally that of promoting change.

Therefore, a philosophical view of ethics in ethnographic evaluation, I believe, is what we need to alter the socio-cultural systems within education contexts. We need to engage in ethnographic evaluation approaches that themselves have the potential to change education contexts. In other words, we need to understand that the way in which we participate as ethnographers will be significant in promoting appropriate change. An ethics perspective on ethnographic evaluation can put a whole new light on the way in which we can conceive of our educational evaluations and their relationship to program development and school reform policies.

Our efforts have the potential to change the context out of which the need for problem solving arose initially. Instead of conceiving of reform as something that can be legislated or imposed at worst, or manipulated technically at best, reform can be understood as what ethnographic evaluators and participants can create together that will engage them in making whatever changes they find necessary. They can create this kind of reform as a result of the new views they develop through engaging students, parents, citizens, and one another in evaluations which value conversation and the voices that emerge from it. Then all of us, as inquirers and as subjects, can engage more actively in questioning what we do and why we do it, and the policies which underlie our educational activities.

Just as importantly, we need to 'bring forth' policy-makers in legislative and contracting entities in the early stages of our ethnographies — even if we imagine that an ethnographic evaluation would be acceptable. Then if, or when, we differ with them over the purpose of ethnography or the data we present then at least it will be a somewhat more enlightened disagreement. Further, when we discuss the data together, we are more likely to engage in policy-making which will more immediately descend from our evaluation activities, giving ourselves and our participants a sense that their views of their educational lives have meaning for those in policy positions.

Moreover, promoting an ethnographic view of data can enlarge the sphere of policy-making away from a reliance on positivism and its technical manifestations that tend to restrict understanding. Ethnography can encourage policy-making that re-envisions the way in which knowledge about educational programs can be assessed, presented, and understood. As Fetterman (1990) points out, we evaluators cannot afford to be pawns in the research or policy-making process. We need to work within the evaluation and policy process so that we can get reports into action.

Perhaps this dilemma can point out the ethics in promoting and preserving relationships through ethnography. Perhaps it can widen our discussions about what we who are ethnographers and we who are policy-makers both can and need to do to reform education. This is especially critical in urban education contexts because of the accentuated asymmetry generally found in social relationships in those contexts. Perhaps this dilemma can widen our horizons about the possibilities within ethnographic evaluation for portraying education itself, and our work in it, as vehicles for making more deliberate change within our evaluation efforts. In this way we might more truly bring forth participants, students, colleagues, other citizens, policy makers, and ourselves whose lives are directly and indirectly influenced by the kind of educational system we create through our evaluation efforts; my report, as resubmitted, was accepted.

References

ABASCAL-HILDEBRAND, M. (in Press) 'Understanding Education, Democracy, and Economic Development in Thailand: Applying Gadamer's Concept of "Play" Through Critical Hermeneutic Research' in HERDA, E.A. *Research and Language: A Critical Hermeneutic Approach in the Study of Culture.*

ABASCAL-HILDEBRAND, M. (1993) 'Tutor and student relations: Applying Gadamer's notion of translation', in WALLACE, R. and MULLIN, J.A. (Eds) *Essays on Theory From The Writing Center*, National Council for Teachers of English.

FETTERMAN, D.M. (1990) 'Remarks', American Anthropological Association, New Orleans. November 30.

FETTERMAN, D.M. (1989) *Ethnography: Step by Step*. Newbury Park, CA, Sage Publications.

FETTERMAN, D.M. (1986) 'Beyond the Status Quo in Ethnographic Evaluation', in FETTERMAN, D.M. and PITMAN, M.A. (Eds) *Evaluation: Ethnography in Theory, Practice, and Politics*, Beverly Hills, CA, Sage, pp. 13–20.

FETTERMAN, D.M. (1986) 'The Ethnographic Evaluator', in FETTERMAN, D.M. and PITMAN, M.A. (Eds) '*Educational Evaluation: Ethnography in Theory, Practice and Politics*', Beverly Hills, CA, Sage, pp. 21–47.

FETTERMAN, D.M. (1984) *Ethnography in Educational Evaluation*, Beverly Hills, CA, Sage.

FETTERMAN, D.M. and PITMAN, M.A. (Eds) (1986) *Educational Evaluation: Ethnography in Theory, Practice, and Politics*. Beverly Hills, CA, Sage.

FREIRE, P. (1986) *The Pedagogy of the Oppressed*, New York, Continuum.

GADAMER, H.G. (1976) *Philosophical Hermeneutics*, Translated and Edited by LINGE, D., Berkeley, University of California Press.

GADAMER, H.-G. (1975) *Truth and Method*, New York, Seabury Press.

GEERTZ, C. (1983) *Interpretation of Cultures*, New York, Basic Books.

GEERTZ, C. (1978) 'Blurred Genres', *American Scholar*, Winter.

HABERMAS, J. (1979) *Communication and the Evolution of Society*, Boston, Beacon Press.

HARPER, V. (1989) 'A Critical Approach to Paraprofessional Multicultural Education', *Teacher Education Quarterly*, **16**, 3.

HERDA, E.A. (in Press) *Research and Language: A Critical Hermeneutic Approach in the Study of Culture*, Westport, CT: Greenwood Press.

HEIDEGGER, M. (1962) *Time and Being*, New York, Harper & Row.

KEARNEY, R. (1984) *Dialogues With Contemporary Continental Thinkers*, London, University of Manchester Press.

RICHARDSON, L. (1990) 'Narrative and Sociology'. *Journal of Contemporary Ethnography*, May, pp. 116–134.

RICOEUR, P. (1987) *Time and Narrative, Vol. III*, Univ. of Chicago Press.

ROBIN, S.S. and WAGENFELD, M.O. (1981) 'Paraprofessionals in the Human Services', New York, *Human Sciences Press*.

TESCH, R. (1988) 'Phenomenological Ethnography in Social Inquiry', A Paper presented to the American Educational Research Association, New Orleans.

VAN MAANEN, J. (1988) *Tales of the Field*, Chicago, University of Chicago Press.

11 A Framework for Conducting Utilization-focused Policy Research in Anthropology

Barbara Rylko-Bauer and John van Willigen

The underutilization of social science research in policy is a frequently noted problem, and one that has also been recognized in anthropology. The increasing involvement of anthropologists in various aspects of the policy process underlines the importance of looking at this issue in a systematic manner. Understanding the means by which knowledge is converted into action is critical not only for the development of applied anthropology as a discipline, but also for improving the potential for practising effective social science (Chambers, 1977). One way of addressing this issue is to identify what characterizes those successful cases where anthropological knowledge is used and has an impact on policy.

In this chapter we provide one step toward such an analysis by presenting a framework that focuses attention on factors which have been found to influence knowledge utilization. This framework can serve as a guide for developing methods and strategies which will increase the potential for getting research findings and recommendations used. We then examine its applicability to fourteen anthropological case studies, which are treated as data that contribute to the development of a theory of practice.[1]

Knowledge Utilization Framework

This framework includes propositions that apply to many research situations, as well as specific factors that may vary in relevance depending on the context of a particular case. These general propositions concern how use is defined and measured, and the importance of developing a comprehensive plan for utilization.

Broad Definition of Knowledge Utilization

The general negative assessment of social science contributions to public policy may partly result from an overly narrow definition of use that emphasizes immediate, direct, and concrete impact on decision making.

> When people discuss the use of social research for policymaking, the usual meaning involves a direct and instrumental application. . . . A problem exists; information or understanding is lacking either to generate a solution to the problem or to select among alternative solutions; research provides the missing knowledge; a solution is reached (Weiss, 1977, pp. 11–12).

Weiss (along with other researchers) points out that such a narrow definition not only overlooks the complexity of policy-making, but also fails to recognize that reducing uncertainty, clarifying issues, and providing new understanding of how programs work are also real impacts (Beyer and Trice, 1982; Caplan, 1977; Patton, 1986; Weiss, 1977, 1981).

It has been shown that diffuse, conceptual use, which serves to enlighten policymakers and influence action in less specific ways (Pelz 1978), may be more common than direct, instrumental use (Caplan *et al.*, 1975; Patton *et al.*, 1977; Rich, 1977; Weiss and Weiss, 1981). More significantly, conceptual use 'can gradually bring about major shifts in awareness and reorientation of basic perspectives' (Weiss, 1981, p. 23).

A large number of empirical studies have measured or analyzed the extent to which social science research has had an impact,[2] although few of these concern anthropology (van Willigen *et al.*, 1989). Given the contexts within which anthropological research often occurs, it is important to keep in mind the following points concerning realistic utilization expectations.[3]

The nature and assessment of knowledge use in short term single case research may differ from that which is due to the effect of a series of related studies over an extended period of time. There is a well established history in anthropology of such long term involvement with a specific problem and/or cultural group, and the impact of such cumulative research should not be underestimated (Chambers, 1987). Perhaps the ultimate measure of utilization is sustainability of change over time.

It is also important to make a careful distinction between programs and policy (Chambers, 1987). It may be easier to detect use at the program level (where impacts are often specific and targeted) than at the policy level (where change may be incremental and diffuse).

Our understanding of the knowledge utilization process would be enhanced by the development of more systematic measures of impact and use that could be applicable in a wide variety of cases of anthropological research. A recent example is the use of network analysis by Boone (1989) to assess the impact of a set of related research and advocacy activities on public policy concerning infant mortality in Washington, D.C.

Importance of a Utilization Design

Utilization methods need to be incorporated into all phases of a particular applied or policy research project, from the early planning to the final dissemination of results (Glaser *et al.*, 1983, Patton, 1986). A useful way of conceptualizing this is to develop a systematic *utilization design* — a set of steps one plans to follow that is akin to the research design. This requires, in turn, that the desired use or impact be thought through, recognizing that this may change to some extent as the project evolves.

There are a number of scholars who have developed models for such a comprehensive approach in other disciplines (Alkin, 1985; Beyer and Trice, 1982; Burry, 1984; Davis and Salasin, 1975; Glaser *et al.*, 1983; Weiss, 1977). For example, Michael Quinn Patton's strategy for 'utilization-focused evaluation' is summarized in a systematic flowchart that provides guidelines for decisions and actions at various points in the research process so as to enhance the potential for use of evaluation study findings (Patton, 1986). Within organizational research, there is Jack Rothman's *Using Research in Organizations: A Guide to Successful Application* (1980), which contains a comprehensive checklist of factors that influence utilization, based largely on his study of social service agencies in greater London.

Knowledge Utilization Factors

The framework also includes a number of factors, distilled from the knowledge utilization literature, that must be kept in mind when developing a utilization design (see Figure 11.1). The context of the particular research situation will determine, to some extent, which factors have more relevance (e.g., community or political factors may be important to consider if the research findings are to have an impact on a policy

- Collaboration with potential users
- Communication factors
- Agency factors
- Community and political factors
- Research process factors
- Time factors
- Advocacy for research findings

Figure 11.1   Knowledge Utilization Factors

decision concerning a proposed community project). Each factor can be addressed using a variety of strategies, depending on the specific context of the case.

While these factors are considered separately for purposes of discussion, in reality they overlap and are often dependent on each other. Finally, potential for use is enhanced when several key strategies are integrated into the utilization design.

Collaboration Factors

Current literature suggests that the most significant factor in getting research findings used is the development of a collaborative relationship between researcher and clients (Alkin, 1985; Burry, 1984; Glaser *et al.*, 1983; Leviton and Hughes, 1981; Patton, 1986; Rich, 1975; Rothman, 1980). Collaboration means involving decision makers and other potential stakeholders[4] (e.g., community members) in the research process, so as to identify their information needs, develop relevant research design and methods that have face validity, identify ways in which clients can use the research and increase their interest and commitment to doing so. Patton (1986) refers to this as the 'personal factor', having an identifiable individual or group that personally cares about the project and the information it generates.

User participation may present some potential ethical dilemmas, especially when collaborating with the client agency. Most frequently noted is co-optation of the researcher, which may occur if decision makers shape the research so as to provide results that support preferred or already existing policies and actions, and that do not challenge their own role within the organization (Ballard and James, 1983; Beyer and Trice, 1982; Dawson and D'Amico, 1985).

Mark and Shotland (1985) point out that selecting stakeholders for participation involves a value judgment as to *whose questions* will guide the research. They also note the potential for a different sort of co-optation, the pre-empting of criticism of the project by the inclusion of stakeholders who might have been likely to do so. Finally, if the researcher does not provide stakeholders with the necessary information for effective and knowledgeable collaboration, then user participation can become a form of 'pseudoempowerment' (Mark and Shotland, 1985, pp. 143–44).

Models of collaborative research are fairly well developed in anthropology (e.g., Stull and Schensul, 1987) and have arisen, at least partly, out of a value orientation that recognizes the validity of self-determination as a major force in sociocultural change. Only recently has the idea of user participation been explicitly suggested as a strategy for increasing the use of anthropological knowledge (Davidson, 1987; Schensul, 1987; Stern, 1985; Whiteford, 1987).

For example, Scheinfeld (1987) suggests that collaboration should occur in all phases of an applied project, and presents four research principles that he considers essential for knowledge utilization to occur:

- Develop ongoing working relationships with the people of power and influence in the situation.
- Work collaboratively with an established body for planning and problem solving.
- Build the research around strongly felt problems and issues of decision makers, information users, and other participants.
- Involve members of the organization or community in as many phases of the research as possible.

Communication Factors

Communication of research findings is often limited to the writing of a final report; however, this is not a very effective way of passing on information, and often results in too much (reflecting the tendency for lengthy data presentation and analysis), too late. Perhaps the most important strategy is to communicate preliminary findings throughout the research process and maintain an ongoing dialogue with feedback between researcher and information users (Glaser *et al.*, 1983; Rich, 1975). This is much easier to do if decision makers are collaborating in the research process (Dawson and D'Amico, 1985; Patton, 1986). Other communication strategies include:

- Using multifaceted and appropriate means of communication, such as workshops, conferences, publication in trade magazines as well as journals in other disciplines, and widespread distribution of short draft reports (Ballard and James, 1983; Beyer and Trice, 1982; O'Reilly and Dalmat, 1987; Patton, 1986; Schensul, 1987).

- Presenting findings in the language and style of users. This includes avoiding social science jargon, keeping reports brief, and packaging the findings and recommendations in a manner familiar to the audience you are trying to reach (Ballard and James, 1983; DeLoria and Brookins, 1982; Rothman, 1980).
- Communicating findings directly to relevant decision makers.
- Providing concrete, specific recommendations as to what is to be done, by whom, and when (Patton, 1986; Rothman, 1980). Policy-makers do not expect primary data and research reports; they want recommendations based on these, as well as suggestions on how to operationalize them into workable guidelines and procedures (Cernea, 1991).

Agency Factors

Collaborative research is more likely to succeed if one understands the structure and organization of the agency, community or group that may be client or beneficiary, as well as the political context within which the research and knowledge use is to occur; in other words, by doing an ethnography of the research situation. Becoming informed about the ways in which communities and groups may be affected by the research process or outcomes, and about the client group and its decision making process, provides the researcher with some understanding of the relationships among relevant groups, who the key decision makers and community leaders are, as well as the potential areas of conflict and possible forums for resolving them.[5]

    In studying the nature of the client-agency, one can focus on questions such as:

- Who are relevant decision makers and potential users of the information?
- What are the relationships among relevant participants?
- How are decisions made within the organization?
- What are the usual channels of communication?
- What are the constraints and/or incentives to use of the information within the agency? These may be ideological or related to organizational structures or political processes.
- Is the research supply- or demand-driven? An agency or program will be more likely to use data that they requested.[6]

Guides for developing additional questions can be found in Glaser *et al.* (1983), Patton (1986), and Rothman (1980).

Community and Political Factors

It is important to be aware of the potential impact of research findings, and to understand the relationship that exists between the client agency and those individuals, groups or communities that may be affected. In many instances, the client may be in a position of relative power *vis-a-vis* the community, and the agency's values and bureaucratic needs may conflict with those of community members (van Willigen, 1986). Recommendations perceived as threatening by those outside the agency may enable a community to mobilize public support to defeat such action. Conversely, the agency may decide not to act on recommendations perceived as going against its best interest, even if they are beneficial to the community that it serves.

Awareness of political relationships is also crucial in situations where the anthropologist is working on behalf of a community. Differences may be only indirectly evident through varying viewpoints expressed concerning an issue or problem, or they may be highly visible in the form of factions or competing organizations. In addition, research that is based in a publicly recognized and established community institution with political clout has greater likelihood of having an impact and bringing about desired social change (Schensul, 1987).

Political factors at the regional or national level may also affect the extent to which knowledge gets used, how, by whom, and to what purposes. Awareness of political realities can inform research design and dissemination plans so as to maximize the likelihood of successful impact (Murray, 1987). Perhaps less obvious is the fact that values can play an important role in determining the extent to which knowledge influences the political process. Measurable knowledge use may require the accumulation of social research in conjunction with a favorable set of ideological, social and political conditions (Barber, 1987).

Research Process Factors

Research needs to be designed, from the onset, with utilization in mind (Patton, 1986). We focus on four features of the research process that increase the potential for use.

Diversity of research methods, in particular the creative combination of quantitative and qualitative methods and analysis, can provide an insightful, valid, and convincing representation of social reality, while meeting time constraints, as well as criteria of reliability and generalizability that policy makers often expect (Beyer and Trice, 1982; Fetterman, 1989; Schenusl, 1987; Trotter, 1987).

Use is directly related to the *credibility* of the research process and findings (Caplan, 1977; O'Reilly and Dalmat, 1987; Weiss and Bucuvalas, 1980; Whiteford, 1987). This includes perceived accuracy, fairness, understandability and face validity of research design and methods (Patton, 1986).

High *quality* research (that meets established scientific criteria) also enhances credibility, but does not necessarily ensure that data will be used, since other factors, including values, political expediency, and the extent to which findings are understandable to users may be more salient in certain situations (Beyer and Trice, 1982). However, there is evidence that quality takes on more importance in situations of political debate, where the policy maker cannot afford to have the research discounted due to uncertain methodology (Weiss and Bucuvalas, 1980).

The potential for use also increases if the research focuses on variables that can be acted upon, that are accessible to control (Gouldner, 1957; Rossi, Wright, and Wright, 1978). We call this *applicability*. Several studies suggest that decision makers are more likely to use findings if recommendations are feasible, and the results conform to users' expectations or existing knowledge (Caplan, 1977; Leviton and Hughes, 1981; Patton *et al.*, 1977; Weiss and Bucuvalas, 1980).

However, one has to be sensitive to the potential dangers that exist in focusing primarily on problems and variables that are perceived as manipulable. Such research may have little explanatory value and may avoid raising issues or offering recommendations that are controversial but provide a more accurate picture of the situation or problem. Co-optation of the researcher can also occur, since decision makers may perceive as changeable those factors that do not challenge their own political power or role within the organization (Beyer and Trice, 1982).

Time Factors

Policy research often has a short time frame, and recognition of this has led to a number of developments by anthropologists doing policy research (van Willigen and DeWalt, 1985). These include use of large research teams, smaller samples, and secondary data, or refocus of research done for other purposes.

Perhaps most notable is the development of problem-focused, short-term research techniques such as focus groups and rapid appraisal (van Willigen and Finan, 1991). One example is the *sondeos* or rapid rural reconnaissance done in farming systems research, where there is a heavy reliance on key informant interviewing, judgmental sampling, reading of documents, and on-site observation. Another example is 'rapid assessment procedures', such as those developed for evaluating and improving primary health services (Scrimshaw and Hurtado, 1987).

Advocacy for Research Findings

Promoting one's research findings and recommendations can also improve the prospects for use (Barber, 1987; Jones, 1976; Rothman, 1980; Siegel and Tuckel, 1985). Such advocacy is enhanced if one has identified relevant decision makers and information users, and if one understands the decision making process of the client agency and the constraints that may limit utilization. One way of personally ensuring that research is used is to take on an advisory role to decision makers. However, it is much harder to influence the policy process from the outside, and some have suggested that social scientists need to actually become involved in policy making roles (Cernea, 1991), a step that anthropologists have largely been reluctant to take in the past (Chambers, 1987).

Application of the Framework to Cases

Content analysis of fourteen case studies in applied anthropology provides insights into the applicability of this knowledge utilization framework to anthropological work. These case studies are collected in one volume, *Making Our Research Useful* (van Willigen *et al.*, 1989), and were written independently by authors who were asked to reflect on how they designed, conducted and disseminated research findings so as to increase use and have an impact on the policy process. They deal with a variety of cultural groups in the United States, Central America, and Africa, and cover a broad cross-section of topics including delivery of health and social services, land relocation, agricultural development and family law. These cases are a judgmental sample; however, their analysis provides an example of the kind of approach that can be used to develop an empirically-based understanding of how knowledge is converted into action.

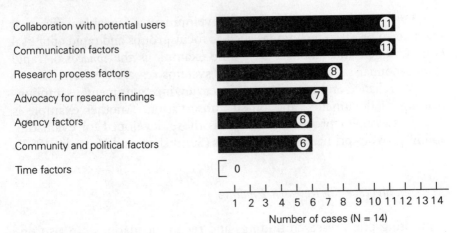

Figure 11.2   Frequency with which various knowledge utilization factors were present in 14 case studies

The content analysis focused on identifying various factors that authors used to enhance the potential for knowledge utilization and policy impact. The content analysis also revealed that each factor may be dealt with using a variety of strategies. The number of factors presented by the authors in the discussion of their research ranged from two to five, with four being the modal number. While no single pattern emerged, the large variability in the number and types of strategies used in each case underscores the value of integrating several key strategies into various phases of the research process.

Figure 11.2 summarizes the frequency with which the various factors appeared. It is clear that two of these factors, *collaboration with potential users* and *communication* were relevant in the majority (eleven) of these cases. In many instances, the collaboration evolved as the project proceeded and often focused on a particular phase, such as involvement in training workshops or development of data collection instruments. More significant are the examples where collaboration was planned from the start of the project, and was incorporated into many phases (Barger and Reza, 1989; DeWalt and DeWalt, 1989; Drake, 1989; Kendall, 1989; Scheinfeld *et al.*, 1989; Warren, 1989).

This was facilitated by the identification of all parties who might have an interest or stake in the research. Involvement of such stakeholders was accomplished in a number of ways, including the establishment of alliances with key people, development of a committee of representatives from various interested groups, and having stakeholders serve as consultants or as members of an advisory board (Drake, 1989; Scheinfeld *et al.*, 1989; Warren, 1989). In one instance, collaboration

146

was taken in its fullest meaning, through the use of a 'community action model', where the anthropologist's expertise was used to support the goals and efforts of a community-based group (Barger and Reza, 1989).

Another strategy for collaboration was the development of various channels and forms of communication for providing on-going feedback of results and opportunities for interaction between researchers and users. In one hospital-based project, researchers initially presented on-going data at the weekly meeting of an already existing committee of directors and ward leaders. As the project evolved, they broadened their collaboration network by negotiating the creation of a sub-committee that dealt specifically with the planning of data feedback to staff and other groups throughout the hospital (Scheinfeld *et al.*, 1989). In such cases, collaboration and communication become mutually reinforcing, since preliminary progress reports and ongoing feedback give clients and users immediate information, provide opportunities for input and participation, and thus help to inform the research process (Coreil, 1989; Drake, 1989; Iris, 1989; Poland and Giblin, 1989).

The cases also provide examples of other communication strategies mentioned earlier in the paper. In particular, they stress the importance of presenting findings in the language and style of users, and the need to go beyond the traditional written report, by using a variety of media and formats for communicating information (Boone, 1989; Gilbert, 1989; Girdner, 1989; Warren, 1989).

In one case, the researcher organized a day-long conference for key decision makers and political leaders as a way of disseminating the findings from a needs assessment study for state-wide medical rehabilitation (Greenwood, 1989). In another case where biological and agricultural scientists were the potential users of data, the anthropologists adopted the communication style commonly used in those disciplines, which included short, focused talks and substantial use of slides with data presented in the form of tables (DeWalt and DeWalt, 1989).

Timing of data dissemination can also be critical, and requires that one be informed about key decision making events and deadlines (Coreil, 1989; Poland and Giblin, 1989). Finally, returning to the research site to share findings with interested individuals and organizations can also improve utilization. Community-based workers, in particular, have a great need for information, but may not have access to technical reports and scholarly journals (Gilbert, 1989).

The latter is also an example of how one can personally ensure that research findings get used. In fact, *advocacy for research findings* was a relevant factor in seven of the cases. The most common strategy was active dissemination of data by providing press releases, public lectures, organizing conferences, and meeting with key decision makers. In some cases the researchers made knowledge available directly to those who could apply it in the course of their work, through in-service training sessions and workshops for professionals and others (Gilbert, 1989; Girdner, 1989). Several anthropologists appeared as expert witnesses at legislative hearings during which they were able to present their data and recommendations (Boone, 1989; Wood, 1989).

Perhaps the most direct form of advocacy was involvement in the policy process itself, by taking on advisory and policy making roles (Girdner, 1989; Greenwood, 1989; Poland and Giblin, 1989). In one example that spanned a period of over fifteen years, the researcher served in a variety of capacities, as a member of the board of directors of a local non-profit service agency, on county-level commissions and advisory boards, and eventually on statewide committees and program review panels (Gilbert, 1989). These activities allowed her many opportunities to bring anthropological data and perspectives into the policy process.

Factors relating to the *research process* were evident in eight out of the fourteen cases, and dealt primarily with the value of a mixed methodology, which increases the potential for producing valid and useable results (Barger and Reza, 1989). Several authors observed that while quantitative data were important for statistical analysis and credibility with decision makers, qualitative data were valuable in fleshing out abstract numbers and demonstrating that the results were about real people with real problems (Boone, 1989; Coreil, 1989; DeWalt and DeWalt, 1989; Gilbert, 1989; Scheinfeld *et al.*, 1989).

Strategies that dealt with the nature of the *client-agency* were mentioned in a slightly smaller number of cases (six), and they generally dealt with the importance of understanding the structure, organization, and decision making process of the agency or institution. For example, the hierarchy that exists in many organizations can create barriers to knowledge dissemination and use. In one case, efforts to directly communicate data on a regular basis with not only program participants but also agency directors, meant that key decision makers were informed about program progress as well as policy and service issues, thereby increasing the chance that such information would be considered in policy decisions (Iris, 1989).

Awareness of agency factors may be especially important in international development research, where programs may be funded and managed by a number of government and international agencies that have competing goals and priorities (Coreil, 1989; DeWalt and DeWalt,

1989). Finally, several cases also demonstrate the value of understanding the broader service delivery system within which specific agencies are located (Gilbert, 1989), particularly in situations where there may be a number of diverse stakeholders with an interest in the project and the potential to affect its outcome (Drake, 1989).

This latter case also demonstrates that understanding the power relations between stakeholders was important in successfully collaborating with them, in promoting negotiation, and resolving issues as they came up during the research process (Drake, 1989). This was one of six cases where strategies dealing with *community and political factors* were relevant. Others pointed to the need to study the political process that the research is hoping to impact (Wood, 1989), and the potential credibility and support gained by involving those in positions of power and responsibility in some aspect of the project or issue (Girdner, 1989; Greenwood, 1989; Warren, 1989).

Finally, *time effectiveness* (in the sense of how long it takes to complete a project) was not stressed in any of the cases, despite the fact that it is mentioned by others as a relevant factor in successful policy research (Weaver, 1985a). It may be that the recent development of rapid ethnographic assessment techniques has addressed this problem in anthropology to some extent.

Instead, a number of the cases demonstrated the value of a long-term commitment to studying a particular problem or cultural group. They described cumulative research efforts, which led to a broad knowledge base, extensive network of contacts and an in-depth understanding of agencies, policy-making bodies, and community groups. The authors were able to use this experience creatively so as to have an impact on decision making and policy implementation (Boone, 1989; Gilbert, 1989; Girdner, 1989; Poland and Giblin, 1989; Warren, 1989).

Conclusion

The content analysis of these fourteen cases demonstrates the relevance for anthropology of the knowledge utilization framework presented earlier in this chapter. It also points to the value of integrating several strategies into the research plan. The most significant factors in getting research findings used were collaboration with potential users and communication. A smaller but significant number of cases also relied on advocacy for research findings, combining qualitative and quantitative methods, as well as agency, community and political factors to enhance knowledge use.

There are, of course, many different ways of conceptualizing such a framework and categorizing salient factors. The critical points are (1) that we need to plan for utilization, and (2) that efforts toward improving the use of anthropological knowledge need to be systematic and have empirical basis.

There are a number of examples (most from other disciplines) of how this can be accomplished. Policy-makers have been interviewed to find out what factors affect their use of social science (Caplan, 1976, 1977; Mitchell, 1980; Weiss and Bucuvalas, 1980). Other studies have looked at specific applied projects to identify factors related to the project's impact on decision making, by analyzing written reports, and interviewing project researchers as well as decision makers who were likely to use this information (Patton, 1986; Patton *et al.*, 1977; van de Vall and Bolas, 1980). Also of value are in-depth studies of policy planning and implementation in social sectors or institutions. One recent example is the analysis of foreign aid and health development in Nepal done by Judith Justice (1986), which demonstrated the many ways in which the culture, structure, organization, and needs of agencies and bureaucracies can impede the use of social science knowledge.

Future studies could focus on policy-making sectors where anthropologists have been particularly active (e.g., farming systems, primary health care, educational evaluation, social impact assessment, etc.). Additional collections of cases, as well as exploratory and structured interviews with anthropologists who have had experience in policy research can also increase our understanding of which strategies or factors are especially useful under what circumstances. It may even be revealing to examine the careers of anthropologists who have a long-term record of effectiveness in influencing policy as well as shaping theory. This was the strategy used by Barber (1987), who interviewed eight prominent social scientists.

It is important to remember that ethical dilemmas may arise when we try to make our research more applicable to clients' needs or when we involve stakeholders collaboratively in the research process. By focusing primarily on making our research more useful, we may overlook the manner and purpose for which it is being used. The issue of unintended use concerns both applied and basic research. However, the potential for misuse is greater for policy research since it focuses on questions of specific relevance to the client, and it is value-laden because of its association with policy decision making (Chambers and Trend, 1981; Weaver, 1985a). As Patton (1986) has pointed out, knowledge reduces uncertainty and facilitates action, thereby allowing the accumulation of power.

The existence of such ethical dilemmas should not discourage us.

Rather, it should increase sensitivity and challenge us to find new and better ways of making our research useful while 'being ethically and politically effective' (Partridge, 1987, p. 231).

There are many different ways of approaching this task. The important point is that as a discipline we need to identify factors which relate to high use of our findings and develop a practical, comprehensive utilization method for doing applied research. In addition, we need to recognize that the single most important factor associated with successful knowledge utilization is personal commitment, on our part as well as that of policy makers, to having it occur.

Notes

1 This framework is a refinement of an earlier version presented in the first chapter of the book, *Making Our Research Useful* (van Willigen, Rylko-Bauer, and McElroy, 1989). The framework was derived from a cross-disciplinary review of studies on this topic and our understanding of work in applied anthropology. The fourteen case studies also appear in this book.
2 For a brief summary of such studies, see Rylko-Bauer *et al.* (1989, pp. 8–10).
3 These points were raised during a session 'The Impact of Anthropological Research on the Development of Policy', that took place at the 1991 annual meeting of the Society for Applied Anthropology. The participants included Arthur Rubel, Norman Schwartz, Ann McElroy, Barbara Pillsbury, Carl Kendall, Barbara Rylko-Bauer, John van Willigen, as well as Joan Atherton and Nancy Pielmeyer.
4 Patton (1986, p. 43) defines stakeholders as 'people who have a stake — a vested interest — in [research] findings'. He also points out that there are often multiple stakeholders, including program funders, staff, administrators, clients, and others with a direct or indirect interest in the research process or outcomes.
5 Being aware of the broader research context may also alert the researcher to the potential occurrence of random processes and unanticipated events (such as political upheaval, changes in agency personnel, etc.) that can either facilitate or obstruct knowledge use (Coreil, 1989; see also note 3 above).
6 This point was first brought to our notice during the SfAA session mentioned above, in note 3.

References

ALKIN, M. (1985) *A Guide for Evaluation Decision Makers.* Beverly Hills, CA, Sage.

BALLARD, S.C. and JAMES, T.E. (1983) 'Participatory Research and Utilization in the Technology Assessment Process', *Knowledge*, **4**, 3, pp. 409–27.

BARBER, B. (1987) *Effective Social Science*, New York, Russell Sage Foundation.

BARGER, W.K. and REZA, E. (1989) 'Policy and Community-Action Research: The Farm Labor Movement in California', in VAN WILLIGEN, J. *et al.* (Eds) *Making Our Research Useful*, pp. 257–82, Boulder, CO, Westview.

BEYER, J.M. and TRICE, H.M. (1982) 'The Utilization Process: A Conceptual Framework and Synthesis of Empirical Findings, *Administrative Science Quarterly*, 27, pp. 591–622.

BOONE, M.S. (1989) 'A Utilization Study Using Network Analysis: Maternal and Infant Health Policy Change in Washington, DC', in VAN WILLIGEN, J. *et al.* (Eds) *Making Our Research Useful*, pp. 89–121. Boulder, CO, Westview.

BURRY, J. (1984) *Synthesis of the Evaluation Use Literature. NIE Grant Report*, Los Angeles, CA, UCLA Center for the Study of Evaluation.

CAPLAN, N. (1976) 'Social Research and National Policy: What Gets Used, By Whom, For What Purposes, and With What Effects?' *International Social Science Journal*, **28**, 1, pp. 187–94.

CAPLAN, N. (1977) 'A Minimal Set of Conditions Necessary for the Utilization of Social Science Knowledge in Policy Formulation at the National Level', in WEISS, C.H. (Ed.) *Using Social Research in Public Policy Making*, pp. 183–98, Lexington, MA; D.C. Heath.

CAPLAN, N., MORRISON, A. and STAMBAUGH, R.J. (1975) *The Use of Social Science Knowledge in Policy Decisions at the National Level*, Ann Arbor, MI, Institute for Social Research, University of Michigan.

CERNEA, M.M. (1991) 'What Policy-Makers Require of Anthropologists', unpublished paper presented at annual meetings of Society for Applied Anthropology, 1991.

CHAMBERS, E. (1987) 'Applied Anthropology in the Post-Vietnam Era: Anticipations and Ironies', *Annual Review of Anthropology*, 16, pp. 309–37.

CHAMBERS, E. and TREND, M.G. (1981) 'Fieldwork Ethics in Policy-Oriented Research, *American Anthropologist*, **83**, 3, pp. 626–28.

COREIL, J. (1989) 'Lessons from a Community Study of Oral Rehydration Therapy in Haiti', in VAN WILLIGEN, J. *et al.* (Eds) *Making Our Research Useful*, pp. 143–57. Boulder, CO, Westview.

DAVIDSON, J.R. (1987) 'The Delivery of Rural Reproductive Medicine', in WULFF, R.M. and FISKE, S.J. (Eds) *Anthropological Praxis*, pp. 262–72. Boulder, CO, Westview.

DAVIS, H.R. and SALASIN, S.E. (1975) 'The Utilization of Evaluation', in STRUENING, E. and GUTTENTAG, M. (Eds) *Handbook of Evaluation Research*, Vol. 1, pp. 621–66, Beverly Hills, CA, Sage.

DAWSON, J.A. and D'AMICO, J.J. (1985) 'Involving Program Staff in Evaluation Studies: A Strategy for Increasing Information Use and Enriching the Data Base', *Evaluation Review*, **9**, 2, pp. 173–188.

DELORIA, D. and BROOKINS, G.K. (1982) 'The Evaluation Report: A Weak

Link to Policy, in TRAVERS, J.R. and LIGHT, R.J. (Eds) *Learning From Experience: Evaluating Early Childhood Demonstration Programs*, pp. 254–71. National Academy Press.

DEWALT, K.M. and DEWALT, B.R. (1989) 'Incorporating Nutrition into Agricultural Research: A Case Study from Southern Honduras', in VAN WILLIGEN, J. *et al.* (Eds) *Making Our Research Useful*, pp. 179–99. Boulder, CO, Westview.

DRAKE, H.M. (1989) 'Using Stakeholders in the Research Process: A Case Study in Human Services', VAN WILLIGEN, J. *et al.* (Eds) *Making Our Research Useful*, pp. 237–55. Boulder, CO, Westview.

FETTERMAN, D.M. (1989) *Ethnography: Step by Step*, Newbury Park, CA, Sage.

GILBERT, M.J. (1989) 'Policymaking Roles for Applied Anthropologists: Personally Ensuring that Your Research Is Used', in VAN WILLIGEN, J. *et al.* (Eds) *Making Our Research Useful*, pp. 71–88. Boulder, CO, Westview.

GIRDNER, L. (1989) 'Custody Mediation: Taking the Knowledge Act on the Policy Road', in VAN WILLIGEN, J. *et al.* (Eds) *Making Our Research Useful*, pp. 55–70, Boulder, CO, Westview.

GLASER, E.M., ABELSON, H.H. and GARRISON, K.N. (1983) *Putting Knowledge to Use. Facilitating the Diffusion of Knowledge and the Implementation of Planned Change*, San Francisco, Jossey-Bass.

GOULDNER, A.W. (1957) 'Theoretical requirements of the applied social sciences', *American Sociological Review*, 22, pp. 92–102.

GREENWOOD, J. (1989) 'The Politics of Planning and Implementing a Statewide Health Service: Medical Rehabilitation in West Virginia', in VAN WILLIGEN, J. *et al.* (Eds) *Making Our Research Useful*, pp. 123–41. Boulder, CO, Westview.

IRIS, M.A. (1989) 'The Use of Feedback in a Model Project: Guardianship for the Impaired Elderly', in VAN WILLIGEN, J. *et al.* (Eds) *Making Our Research Useful*, pp. 219–36, Boulder, CO, Westview.

JONES, D.J. (1976) 'Applied Anthropology and the Application of Anthropological Knowledge', *Human Organization*, 35, pp. 221–9.

JUSTICE, J. (1986) *Policies, Plans, and People*, Berkeley, University of California Press.

KENDALL, C. (1989) 'The Use and Non-Use of Anthropology: The Diarrheal Disease Control Program in Honduras', in VAN WILLIGEN, J. *et al.* (Eds) *Making Our Research Useful*, pp. 283–303. Boulder, CO, Westview.

LEVITON, L.C. and HUGHES, E.F.X. (1981) 'Research on the Utilization of Evaluations: A Review and Synthesis', *Evaluation Review*, 5, pp. 525–48.

MARK, M.M. and SHOTLAND, R.L. (1985) 'Stakeholder Based Evaluation and Value Judgements', *Evaluation Review*, 9, 5, pp. 605–625.

MITCHELL, D.E. (1980) 'Social Science Impact on Legislative Decision Making: Process and Substance', *Educational Researcher*, 9, 10, pp. 9–12, 17–19.

MURRAY, G.F. (1987) 'The Domestication of Wood in Haiti: A Case Study in Applied Evolution', in WULFF, R.M. and FISKE, S.J. (Eds) *Anthropological Praxis*, pp. 223–40. Boulder, CO, Westview.

O'REILLY, K.R. and DALMAT, M.E. (1987) 'Marketing Program Evaluation: Birth Attendant Training in Kenya', *Practicing Anthropology*, **9**, 1, pp. 12–13.

PARTRIDGE, W.L. (1987) 'Toward a Theory of Practice', in EDDY, E.M. and PARTRIDGE, W.L. (Eds) *Applied Anthropology in America*, pp. 211–33. New York, Columbia University Press.

PATTON, M.Q. (1986) *Utilization-Focused Evaluation*, 2nd ed. Beverly Hills, Sage.

PATTON, M.Q., GRIMES, P.S. GUTHRIE, K.M. *et al.* (1977) 'In Search of Impact: An Analysis of the Utilization of Federal Health Evaluation Research', in WEISS, C.H. (Ed.) *Using Social Research in Public Policy*, pp. 141–64. Lexington, MA, D.C. Heath.

PELZ, D.C. (1978) 'Some Expanded Perspectives on the Use of Social Science in Public Policy', in YINGER, J.M. and CULTER, S.J. (Eds) *Major Social Issues: A Multidisciplinary View*, New York, Free Press.

POLAND, M.L. and GIBLIN, P.T. (1989) 'Prenatal Care and Pregnancy Outcome: Applications of Research Findings to the Reduction of Infant Mortality in Detroit', in VAN WILLIGEN, J. *et al.* (Eds) *Making Our Research Useful*, pp. 39–54. Boulder, CO, Westview.

RICH, R.F. (1975) 'Selective Utilization of Social Science Related Information by Federal Policy Makers', *Inquiry*, 12, pp. 239–45.

RICH, R.F. (1977) 'Uses of Social Science Information by Federal Bureaucrats: Knowledge for Action Versus Knowledge for Understanding', in WEISS, C.H. (Ed.) *Using Social Research in Public Policy Making*, Lexington, MA, Lexington Books.

ROSSI, P.H., WRIGHT, J.D. and WRIGHT, S.R. (1978) 'The theory and practice of applied social research', *Evaluation Journal*, 2, pp. 171–91.

ROTHMAN, J. (1980) *Using Research in Organizations*, Beverly Hills, CA, Sage.

RYLKO-BAUER, B., VAN WILLIGEN, J. and McELROY, A. (1989) 'Strategies for Increasing the Use of Anthropological Research in the Policy Process: A Cross-Disciplinary Analysis', in VAN WILLIGEN, J. *et al.* (Eds) *Making Our Research Useful*, pp. 1–25. Boulder, Co, Westview.

SCHEINFELD, D.R. (1987) 'A Collaborative Approach to Research Utilization', *Practicing Anthropology*, **9**, 1, pp. 4–5.

SCHEINFELD, D.R., MARSHALL, P.A. and BEER, D.W. (1989) 'Knowledge Utilization Structures, Processes and Alliances in a Psychiatric Hospital Study', in VAN WILLIGEN, J. *et al.* (Eds) *Making Our Research Useful*, pp. 201–218. Boulder, CO, Westview.

SCHENSUL, J.J. (1987) 'Knowledge Utilization: An Anthropological Perspective', *Practicing Anthropology*, **9**, 1, pp. 6–8.

SCRIMSHAW, S.C.M. and HURTADO, E. (1987) *Rapid Assessment Procedures for Nutrition and Primary Health Care: Anthropological Approaches to Improving Program Effectiveness* (RAP). Los Angeles, CA, UCLA Latin American Center Publications.

SIEGEL, K. and TUCKEL, P. (1985) 'The Utilization of Evaluation Research. A Case Analysis', *Evaluation Review*, **9**, 3, pp. 307–28.

STERN, G. (1985) 'Research, Action, and Social Betterment', *American Behavioral Scientist*, **29**, 2, pp. 229–48.

STULL, D.D. and SCHENSUL, J.J. (Eds) (1987) *Collaborative Research and Social Change. Applied Anthropology in Action*. Boulder, CO, Westview.

TROTTER, R.T., II. (1987) 'A Case of Lead Poisoning from Folk Remedies in Mexican American Communities', in WULFF, R.M. and FISKE, S.J. (Eds) *Anthropological Praxis*, pp. 146–59. Boulder, CO, Westview.

VAN DE VALL, M. and BOLAS, C. (1980) 'Applied Social Discipline Research or Social Policy Research: The Emergence of a Professional Paradigm in Sociological Research'. *The American Sociologist*, **15**, pp. 128–137.

VAN WILLIGEN, J. (1986) *Applied Anthropology: An Introduction*. South Hadley, MA, Bergin and Garvey.

VAN WILLIGEN, J. and DEWALT, B.R. (1985) *Training Manual in Policy Ethnography*. A Special Publication of the American Anthropological Association, No. 19. Washington, DC: The Association.

VAN WILLIGEN, J. and FINAN, T.L. (Eds) (1991) *Soundings: Rapid and Reliable Research Methods for Practicing Anthropologists*, NAPA Bulletin No. 10. Washington, DC: American Anthropological Association.

VAN WILLIGEN, J., RYLKO-BAUER, B. and MCELROY, A. (1989) *Making Our Research Useful. Case Studies in the Utilization of Anthropological Knowledge*, Boulder, CO, Westview.

WARREN, D.M. (1989) 'Utilizing Indigenous Healers in National Health Delivery Systems: The Ghanaian Experiment', in VAN WILLIGEN, J. *et al.* (Eds) *Making Our Research Useful*, pp. 159–78. Boulder, CO, Westview.

WEAVER, T. (1985a) 'Anthropology as a Policy Science: Part I, A Critique', *Human Organization*, **44**, 2, pp. 97–105.

WEAVER, T. (1985b) 'Anthropology as a Policy Science: Part II, Development and Training', *Human Organization*, **44**, 3, pp. 197–205.

WEISS, C.H. (1977) 'Introduction', in WEISS, C.H. (Ed.) *Using Social Research in Public Policy Making*, pp. 1–22. Lexington, MA, D.C. Heath.

WEISS, C. (1981) 'Measuring the Use of Evaluations', in CIARLO, J.A. (Ed.) *Utilizing Evaluation*, pp. 17–33. Beverly Hills, CA, Sage.

WEISS, C. and BUCUVALAS, M. (1980) 'Truth Test and Utility Test: Decision Makers' Frame of Reference for Social Science Research', *American Sociological Review*, **45**, pp. 302–313.

WEISS, J.A. and WEISS, C.H. (1981) 'Social Scientists and Decision Makers Look at the Usefulness of Mental Health Research', *American Psychologist*, 36, pp. 837–47.

WHITEFORD, L.M. (1987) 'Staying Out of the Bottom Drawer', *Practicing Anthropology*, **9**, 1, pp. 9–11.

WOOD, J.J. (1989) 'Political Action and the Use of Anthropological Research: Land and Religion at Big Mountain', in VAN WILLIGEN, J. *et al.* (Eds) *Making Our Research Useful*, pp. 27–37. Boulder, CO, Westview.

12 Ethnography and Policy: Translating Knowledge into Action

David M. Fetterman

Ethnographers and policy makers all too often believe that they work at cross purposes and come from separate worlds. In fact, ethnography and policy share a long history and a rich tradition. The relationship between these two disciplines traces back to both academic and applied anthropological work, although applied anthropological endeavors have a stronger track record. The work of Spicer, Holmberg, Tax, Spradley, and many others has demonstrated ethnography's relevance for policy. More recently, as discussed in the first chapter of this collection, ethnographic educational evaluators have established a tight link between educational policy and ethnography. This concluding chapter expands the discussion of a national ethnographic evaluation of dropouts begun in chapter one. This evaluation and other ethnographic studies of gifted and talented education provide specific first-hand examples of how ethnography has informed policy decision making on many levels. The lessons learned from these policy-relevant studies serve to further inform our current discussion.

The Applied Tradition

The question of whether ethnography and policy decision making can be combined is moot; the two have been combined for years. A brief list of examples of how ethnography and policy have walked hand in hand provides insights into the rich tradition that practicing anthropologists have established. The examples include a study of a semifeudal Indian hacienda in Peru, an investigation of tramps on skid row in Seattle, Washington, and the long list of studies in this collection. The list underscores ethnography's historical relevance for policy.

Historical Examples

Edward Spicer was involved in both policy formulation and execution. He served as a program facilitator in the implementation of the War Relocation Authority during World War II. He was a cross-cultural interpreter, attempting to find out what Japanese Americans thought about the relocation camps. His task required sensitivity, political dexterity, and an appreciation of different cultural orientations in order to avoid misinterpretations that might have resulted in charges of disloyalty during wartime. Spicer also served as an ethnographer/policymaker as an Office of Economic Opportunity project director. He used ethnographic knowledge of the Yaqui community to help mediate agency programs to meet the needs of the Yaqui Indians.[1] (See Spicer, 1976.)

As a joint enterprise between Cornell University and the Peruvian government, the Vicos project, Allan Holmberg's work, stands out as a notable achievement in planned organizational change. The project successfully transformed a semifeudal Indian hacienda in Peru into a democratic community within five years. (See Holmberg, 1958. See also Doughty, 1987.) His work had considerable impact in the policy arena, shaping the transformation of many other similar hacienda communities in Peru. In addition, this ethnographic effort produced contexts in which Mestizos and Indians were able to interact under conditions of social equality, thus influencing traditional notions about segregation and prejudice.

As an ethnographic researcher, Sol Tax (1958) directly influenced the community policy of the Fox Indians. He clarified issues and listed options for change in the community. The decision to select and implement an alternative remained in the hands of the Fox. However, Tax, functioning as an ethnographer, served as a significant catalyst in policy development and implementation.

Ethnographic fieldwork has also significantly influenced policies concerning such issues as the social function of ghettos, minority unemployment, the causes of poverty, ethnic affairs, and the structure and function of family services.[2] (See Gans, 1962; Liebow, 1967; Bott, 1957; Hicks and Handler, 1987; Valentine, 1966; and Lewis 1966). Ethnographic concepts and techniques have yielded much in the area of dealing with public drunkenness and mediating sentencing (Spradley, 1970; 1973). Spradley's success in eliciting the viewpoint of tramps on skid row in Seattle helped develop a blueprint for change to stop the phenomenon of the jailhouse 'revolving door'.

Pelto and Schensul (1987) provided recommendations to the federal Bureau of Education for the Handicapped about parental involvement in special education decision making, focusing on the placement of children in special education classes. They also illustrated how ethnographic work generated recommendations that influenced legislation. Wulff and Fiske (1987) produced a collection of award-winning cases studies in which anthropological knowledge was successfully applied to real-world problem solving, including policy formulation, implementation, and evaluation.

Ethnographic Educational Evaluation

Ethnographic evaluation has made a significant contribution to policy decision making, as discussed in chapter one.[3] Ethnographic educational evaluation highlights ethnography's contemporary role in policy decision making, drawing on examples ranging from a study of disadvantaged youth in an Israeli town to analyses of bilingual bicultural preschool curriculum models in California, New York, Texas, and Wisconsin. Two national case studies provide depth to the discussion and explore specific policy implications.

Smith and Robbins's (1984) US Department of Education-funded study of four federal elementary and secondary education programs provided a contextualized picture of parental involvement. Their efforts also illustrated clearly the compromises and tradeoffs requisite in policy research, while informing policy decision making.[4] In a study of disadvantaged youth in an Israeli town, Goldberg (1984) highlighted the importance of matching a research site to appropriate policy research questions (and the hazards of a mismatch). In a study of a school for the deaf, sponsored by the Department of Health, Education, and Welfare (now the Department of Health and Human Services), Hemwall (1984) demonstrated the value of ethnography in exploring the policy question of mainstreaming the hearing-impaired. In a nonprofit research and demonstration organization-sponsored study, Simon (1986) used anthropological theory and ethnographic research methods and analysis to examine how youth employment and training programs and public incentives affected hiring decisions. An ethnographic understanding of the hiring process enabled the ethnographers to develop 'marketing tools' to demonstrate how hiring youth would benefit employers. Studstill (1986) used ethnographic techniques to evaluate ten secondary schools in Zaire. The study was specifically designed to inform policy makers and to recommend ways to decrease extremely high student attrition. Chesterfield (1986) studies bilingual bicultural preschool curriculum models in California, New York, Texas, and Wisconsin for the

Head Start Bureau of the Administration for Children, Youth and Families. This study's qualitative analysis furnished information about issues of concern to teachers, program staff, and policy planners. For example, the qualitative data documented how some children used a majority of English in the classroom by the end of the year — even though the test data continued to judge them as dominant Spanish speaking in the classroom. Ferrell and Compton (1986) used ethnographic techniques to evaluate a school district's gifted and talented education program. Their work had an impact on students, parents, teaching staff, and the district's administration and Board of Education. They recommended the development of job descriptions for teachers, specification of how the gifted and talented program curriculum differed from the basic curriculum, and development of improved approaches to the identification of gifted minority students. Similarly, Marotto's (1987) ethnographic study of in-school truancy had an impact on students, teachers, school administrators, and the Board of Education, as well as an effect on the school's disproportionate number of minority suspensions.

Quantitative researchers, including Cronbach (1982) and Hoaglin *et al.* (1982), have reinforced ethnography's position in policy decision making by acknowledging a role for qualitative research in policy and evaluation studies. Numerous quantitative and qualitative researchers — including Cook and Reichardt (1979), Fetterman (1982a, 1988a, 1988b, 1989a, 1989b), Goetz and LeCompte (1984), LeCompte and Goetz (1982), Patton (1980), Smith and Louis (1982), and Weiss and Rein (1972) — have also made a case for the value of ethnographic and case study methods in the pursuit of knowledge about policy issues of implementation and change in school systems. (See Firestone and Herriott 1984 for a discussion about multisite qualitative research and federal policy decision making.)

The following discussion about two ethnographic evaluations further illustrates the link between ethnography and policy decision making. The first case focused on a national ethnographic evaluation of dropouts. The second study focused on gifted and talented students in the United States and internationally.

A National Ethnographic Evaluation of Dropouts

As part of a research firm, I conducted the ethnographic evaluation of the Career Intern Program (CIP) — the national program for dropouts and potential dropouts discussed briefly in chapter one. The formative and summative reports stemming from the ethnographic evaluation had a significant impact on the survival and potential prosperity of the CIP schools.

The CIP schools offered students a high school diploma and a career-oriented education. The schools were designed to handle both academic and personal problems. The CIP schools had as many counselors as they had teachers, recognizing that management of personal problems was essential to the program's academic mission. CIP schools successfully placed former dropouts in college and career-oriented positions. CIP represented one of the few exemplary programs for disenfranchised and economically disadvantaged minority youth in the late 1970s and early 1980s.

The CIP study represented an important shift in emphasis from the urban educational anthropology research of the previous decade because it focused on school success for minority youth rather than on school failure. It differed from the traditional ethnography of schooling in incorporating findings from a multidisciplinary evaluation effort. The research concerned not a single school, but an entire demonstration project in several sites across the United States. The analyses examined classrooms, program components, community environments, local and national affiliates, government agencies, and evaluators. The study differed also in its multidimensional emphasis, discussing federal involvement, evaluation design, and the role of reinforcing world views (Fetterman, 1981a). It expanded an understanding of the process by which values and ideas are passed on from one generation to the next. In providing educational evaluators with a model of detailed description on several levels, the ethnographic component of the study demonstrated the means of contextualizing data. By locating data more precisely in a multilevel context, educational evaluators and ethnographers can arrive at a more comprehensive interpretation of its meaning. The CIP study also demonstrated how ethnography can be adapted to the language, timelines, and political concerns of policy makers, including advocacy. (See Fetterman, 1987, 1989a, as well as chapter one.)

Policy Implications

The CIP study had a policy impact on many levels. During the study, the federal sponsors considered closing one of the schools. They were concerned that the program was not serving the target population because of low attendance: approximately 60 per cent to 70 per cent. This concern was legitimate, from their perspective, because they did not want to waste taxpayer money. The attendance in the CIP school was somewhat lower than that in neighboring urban high schools. However, I reminded the sponsoring agency that the baseline with which to compare 60 per cent to 70 per cent attendance was zero attendance. These students were systematically different from the students attending the neighboring urban high school. The CIP students had routinely skipped school when enrolled in the neighboring urban high schools. The contextualized data helped policymakers make a more informed decision about the program. In this case, ethnographic data ensured that the program would continue serving former dropouts.

The most significant policy implications of the study, however, involved the concepts of replicating schools and of using the experimental design in studying dropouts. The federal government's goal was to replicate an existing exemplary program throughout the United States. It expected an almost clone-like duplication of the original program. The ethnographic report stated that this expectation was conceptually off-target. Replication is a biological not an anthropological or sociological concept. Programs take on new shapes and forms in the process of adapting to the demands of their environments. Studying how these programs respond to their differing environments would have been more fruitful than noting whether they were in or out of compliance with a given model. The ethnographic report specifically recommended that: 'The process of adaptation should be the focus of inquiry' (Fetterman, 1981b).

A second, and more controversial, policy impact involved the use of the experimental design in federal evaluations. One part of this study included a treatment-control design. Students were required to pass specified tests for admission into the program. Half the candidates were randomly assigned to the treatment group — admitted to the alternative high school — while the other half were denied admission. The ethnographic portion of the study concluded that this behavior was maladaptive and inappropriate. Ethically, the use of the treatment-control design was problematic because it prevented dropouts from taking the first step back into the educational system. Parents referred to this rejection as a 'slap in the face'. Methodologically, the design had serious flaws: It was not double-blind. The teachers, counselors, and administrators providing the program knew that they were delivering the treatment. The students admitted to the program knew that they were receiving the 'treatment' and thus received a positive treatment. No true control group existed. Students who passed the entrance tests but were selected as part of the control group knew they were not participating in the program or treatment. Thus the 'control' group was actually a negative treatment group. In addition, because the control group had little incentive to return for post testing, the students who did return represented a biased sample, producing misleading comparisons with the treatment group. All these forms of reactivity and contamination severely undermined the credibility of any outcome. (See Fetterman, 1982a, for a detailed discussion of this problem.)

The study (Fetterman 1981b) delivered a strong set of recommendations to policy-makers:

1 Abandon the use of randomized treatment-control designs to evaluate social programs, particularly when ethical standards have been violated. All available program positions should be filled; individuals should not be excluded from participation for the sake of constructing a control group.

2 Re-evaluate the selection of an experimental design when methodological requirements can not be met. The most significant methodological concerns in this case involve constructing a negative treatment group instead of a control group, and comparing groups without considering the effects of differential attrition at post test time. (See Fetterman, 1982a; Tallmadge, 1979).

These recommendations were made during a period in which evaluators and policy makers were attempting to legislate the use of specific evaluation designs, 'especially randomized experiments'. During the same period, academia was demonstrating much resistance to criticism of this sacred cow in educational research. (See Fetterman, 1982b, for a detailed discussion about academic resistance to substantive criticism.)

As a result of this ethnographic study, CIP program sponsors made and implemented a variety of additional policy and programmatic recommendations. The findings and recommendations provide another demonstration of ethnography's relevance for educational policy. The relevance of ethnography for policy, however, extends beyond the written word. One of the ethnographer's most important roles may be as a consultant for policy questions. In the case under discussion, both government policy makers and program officials asked the ethnographer for information and advice regarding short- and long-term intervention strategies.

Researchers have a moral responsibility to serve as advocates — after the research has been conducted — if the findings merit it. In this case, the evaluators disseminated the generally positive findings to appropriate individuals in governmental and quasi-governmental institutions. Future funding for the program depended on the dissemination of the evaluation findings and the recommendations of various agencies. The evaluation team also prepared a Joint Dissemination Review Panel Submission substantially based on the ethnographic findings to improve the program's credibility and its chances of securing future funding. This task was accomplished in the face of significant resistance: It was politically hazardous to favor social programs during this period. These actions were in accord with Mill's (1959) position that: 'There is no necessity for working social scientists to allow the potential meaning of their work to be shaped by the "accidents of its setting", or its use to be determined by the purposes of other men. It is quite within their powers to discuss its meaning and decide upon its uses as matters of their own policy'. (p. 177)

Gifted and Talented Education and Policy Implications

During a study of dropouts and potential dropouts, I identified a handful of gifted and talented students from limited-English-speaking and lower socioeconomic class groups. This study evolved into a decade of work on the gifted and talented in the United States and abroad. These efforts culminated in the publication of a book for both the lay person and the professional in the field: *Excellence and Equality: A Qualitatively Different Perspective on Gifted and Talented Education* (1988a). The book depicted the plight of gifted and talented children in a system geared toward the mean — an attempt to inform an educated and concerned citizenry about these children's special needs and individual differences. It discussed mythologies supporting neglect and explored simplistic conceptions of democracy that equated equality of rights with equality of ability and results. Comparisons of gifted selection procedures with athletic selection procedures helped to dispel the myth that Americans are equally egalitarian in all arenas. This work was primarily ethnographic in nature and successfully informed policy makers on the state and national level.

A review of all 433 gifted and talented programs in California, reported in *Excellence and Equality*, resulted in continued funding and overall program improvements, including legislation maintaining a broad conception of giftedness. As a result of a cross-cultural review of gifted education worldwide — and of my recommendation that the US government establish a national gifted and talented center — I received an appointment to a US Department of Education panel to select a consortium to create a national gifted and talented education research center. Highlighting the disenfranchised, I specifically recommended that the center focus on identifying gifted and talented children who may not be identified through traditional assessment methods. This group includes limited English speakers, the economically disadvantaged, the physically handicapped or disabled, and women. As an instance of a recommendation becoming a reality, in this case, ethnography had an impact on various policy levels and provided both the groundwork for change in terms of concrete policy recommendations and the actual construction and implementation of policy recommendations in terms of participation in the selection process of a national center for the gifted.

Policy decision making is both an art and a craft (Wildavsky, 1979). It is fundamentally a political process in which research — ethnographic or otherwise — plays one part. The exchange of information, however, does not presuppose a substantial voice in policy decisions; it only ensures participation in the game. The insights and findings of the most capably conducted research are useless if researchers abdicate their responsibility and choose not to play in this game.

Playing the Game

Playing the game does not mean behaving unethically. On the contrary, it requires honesty, candor, and commitment. Educators, anthropologists, and well-informed public citizens have an obligation to take a position and to become involved in addressing the social and educational problems that lie at their doorstep.

Participation in the process of decision making is what playing the game is all about. Sensitivity to the decision maker's world view can enhance one's effectiveness. The CIP and gifted studies were successful because they overcame traditional obstacles by translating academic language into bureaucratese, internalizing the dynamics of policy decision making, producing results in a timely fashion, assuming the role of advocate when appropriate, and providing the type of process information useful to policy decision makers.

A Common Thread

A common thread running through this collection is the attempt to speak to power — in the language of the power broker. Researchers' roles vary and include the rhetorician and expert witness. Strategies involve participating in the political process by testifying on the hill and serving on governmental panels. Guidelines are often learned along the way, ranging from the simple and straightforward, such as explaining who you are and what you are doing to collaborating with clients and desensitizing them throughout an evaluation — to enhance acceptance of the findings and recommendations.

There are a multitude of obstacles along the path, as ethnographers attempt to communicate qualitative findings to power brokers. Specific strategies are required to address adversarial audiences, including colleagues and sponsors. Exposure — in the field or in the class — can help to demystify ethnography and convince detractors of the utility of qualitative research. Other useful strategies are borrowed from cross-cultural communication (listening to others and trying to address their issues from their framework), adopted from innovations literature (meeting a perceived need and providing concrete examples of how qualitative methods are useful), and drawn from negotiation literature (avoid viewing the critic as the enemy and creating options for mutual gain). If none of these approaches work, a good old-fashioned Orwellian fable might be in order. Ideally these strategies are designed to alter a critic's world view about qualitative research.

There are many ways to give voice to the people we work with and bring them forth to policy brokers. This collection provides a framework, in both general and specific terms, for thinking about how knowledge is transformed into action. The last chapter is a useful lens through which to see themes that emerge from a review of ethnographic studies. Some of the most striking and successful strategies cross-cutting studies demonstrated in this collection include collaboration and advocacy. An additional strategy worthy of consideration is timeliness. However, in applying all of these strategies, the researcher depends heavily on the foundation of language. Specific examples drawn from the studies in this collection illustrate and highlight the power of these strategies.

Collaboration

Weeks and Schensul, for example, emphasize the value of collaborating with project staff on various levels, ranging from administrative staff to social workers in data collection. A collaborative orientation helped staff gain a sense of the needs and interests of injection drug users and prostitutes, providing invaluable information for recruitment purposes and in designing appropriate interventions. In a complementary fashion, outreach workers and social workers enriched the data because of the strategic data collection positions they occupied in the street. Weeks and Schensul also highlight the role of collaboration with related agencies, such as research, health care, and support services. These collaborative efforts have helped to serve the needs of people with HIV and AIDS more effectively.

Parker and Langley also focus on the instrumental role of collaboration — in this case with the Coushatta Tribe of Louisiana. Parker explains how (after swallowing her anthropological pride) she listened to Langley's advice about how to work with the Coushatta Tribe, using traditional ethnographic tools to work with them. Parker talked to tribal members, spent time with them on the reservation, and asked them what they wanted to achieve. Her experience culminated in a list of protocol guidelines that will help others work with people they want to help.

Christman and Simon demonstrate how collaboration with their clients was essential to the successful completion of their evaluation. Their clients refined the accuracy of the findings and the relevance of their recommendations. In addition, working in close proximity with their clients throughout most of the evaluation sensitized the clients to their interim findings and recommendations and helped them to embrace many of the evaluation conclusions. As in most collaborative efforts, this collaboration continues well after the formal study has been concluded. Christman and Simon work together with the program planners responsible for implementing new program directions — which the planners adopted directly from the evaluators' contributions.

My own work with the CIP and gifted studies relied on a close collaborative relationship with teachers, students, parents, and administrators. Descriptions of events as well as strategies to improve curricula, rules and regulations, program design and operations, and school climates were shared with participants. Their feedback and participation in the process improved the accuracy and effectiveness of the ethnographic effort. Moreover, participants in the dropout and gifted programs helped adapt policies and programmatic recommendations to each school program across the country — as they evolved from the study.

Advocacy

A few examples of the advocacy role (adopted after the research was conducted) have been discussed in this chapter. The CIP study included the dissemination of generally positive findings to appropriate policy makers and the preparation of a Joint Dissemination Review Panel Submission. The gifted studies culminated in a book recommending that the US government establish a gifted and talented center. In addition, I took an active role in selecting a consortium to create such a center.

There are many appropriate roles to adopt. Educators can seek the assistance of unions, public relations offices, and lobbyists to represent them in the policy arena. Politically savvy researchers can work with senators and representatives. For example, Hess, in chapter three, testified before a congressional committee in support of an act to establish a National Demonstration Project of Educational Performance Agreements for School Restructuring that would provide locals schools with more flexibility in the use of federal funds, in exchange for commitments to improve student performance. (See Hess, 1989, 1991.)

Hopper's work represents another avenue of advocacy. His work as an expert witness in 'right-to-shelter' lawsuits and in drafting enabling legislation have spoken eloquently to the role ethnographers can play. Hopper and Fetterman have also used the media to build a case for the people they work with, attempting to inform a concerned and educated citizenry. In this discussion, Hopper also reminds us about ethnography's ability to focus on the larger structural influences and the competing cultural beliefs that blind us to the facts. He demonstrates how to make links between specific social agendas and the underlying social and structural conditions that contribute to real social and economic problems. However, Hopper also turns a critical eye on ethnography's potential in public policy decision making. He highlights problems that may emerge when the ethnographer leaps from the native's point of view to useful solutions to immediate needs. The gains may be short-lived if the recommendations focus on surface remedies. Hopper also reminds us of the ethnographic advocate's role in correcting distortions and misused research findings.

Weeks and Schensul demonstrate how ethnographic research can be used to empower people as a tool of advocacy. Program staff were able to use descriptions of the cultural aspects of various interventions and information about injection drug users and prostitutes' attitudes toward needle exchange to better inform policy discussion and decision making. Project researchers were able to turn city-wide collaborative efforts toward prevention. Weeks and Schensul also discuss how qualitative research was used to advocate better access and minimize barriers to services for HIV-positive people. Specifically, qualitative data was used to advocate sustained funding for AIDS prevention programs on local, state, and national levels.

Parker's role as an economic development consultant for the Coushatta Tribe is also a form of advocacy. She used her knowledge of the government grant systems and Langley's knowledge of the Tribe to help them accomplish their objectives. Writing grant proposals and getting some of them funded to serve tribal needs represents a concrete accomplishment in furthering the goals of self-determination.

Brown, Maxwell, Mertz, and Abascal-Hildebrand are methodological advocates attempting to alter world views about the value of qualitative research. Brown's strategies focus on the role of formal and informal education — required naturalistic methods courses as well as opportunities for anti-naturalistic colleagues and policy makers to observe us in the field. Maxwell provides tools designed to enhance mutual communication and understanding. He emphasizes the importance of speaking the language of the people you want to communicate with; solving recognized problems; and looking for win-win situations. Mertz provides a clever and entertaining alternative narrative — a fable — to change world views. Mertz uses the folk tale in a traditional manner — to illustrate a parable and to distance the reader enough to see the maladaptive web of meaning they have spun for themselves. Abascal-Hildebrand uses critical hermeneutics and traditional ethnographic tools to promote participants' voices. She retained the participants' voices from the field, but she also acknowledged the school board's world view by adding attendance and survey data. By making these modifications, she convinced the School Board to accept the report and thus 'hear' the participants' words.

Timeliness

One of the most important features of the federal and state policymaker's perspective is timeliness. Knowledge is power, but the information must be available at prespecified periods to play a part in the decision-making process. Hess's testimony is an excellent example. It had to be carefully orchestrated and presented at the appropriate time. A day early or a day late would be meaningless — as no one would be there to hear it.

The CIP and gifted studies also attempted to recognize and adapt to these needs. These studies were completed within the specified periods of time to allow for maximum policy impact. In addition, I produced interim reports and delivered them without jeopardizing complex research relationships or the quality of work. In fact I found that memoranda and other interim communications improved the accuracy of the effort by providing a reality check on the accuracy and appropriateness of the interim findings and recommendations. In addition, I made an effort to be responsive to premature policy-maker inquiries in the middle of the research effort. Shifting political pressures had compelled well-intentioned policy makers to seek information before agreed-on timelines. Knowing that the decisions would have been made with or without the desired input, I provided what information I could. Fortunately, policy decision makers preferred limited and imprecise information to no information at all.

Language

A brief salute to language brings this collection full circle. Language, as discussed in chapter one, is a powerful force that can shape thoughts and influence minds. Policy-makers funding Simon and Christman, Brown, Abascal-Hildebrand, and my work with the CIP and gifted research needed executive summaries about the studies' findings and recommendations written in their own language. As Cronbach stated, 'when an avalanche of words and tables descends, everyone in its path dodges' (Cronbach *et al.*, 1980, p. 184). The full, thorough, and scholarly investigations (the basis for the executive summaries) were also reported in a lengthy technical report for program personnel and policy-maker staff members. In addition, academic, newspaper, and magazine articles and books about dropouts, gifted children, the homeless and the environment came out of the studies reported in this collection and served to educate and inform a concerned citizenry, with the aim of influencing other policy-makers from the grass roots.

Anthropological knowledge can shed light on classroom practices as well as on the dark and often mysterious political corridors. The same tool required to navigate inside the school district can be used to navigate around the Capitol. Sensitivity to the perspective of insiders — whether student or politician can go a long way in increasing one's effectiveness.

Conclusion

Anthropological tools represent only one approach to removing edifices of social injustice.[5] However, they are a powerful force when combined with policy decision making. The leap from policy to practice is often difficult, but not impossible. Ethnography already has an established tradition in the policy field. Lessons learned from that relationship can be applied to a host of socially relevant concerns. (See also Griffin, [1986, 1991] on his work in the area of racial discrimination and young women entering the job market for additional excellent examples.) Sensitivity to people, context, language, timelines, and political concerns are imperative if a policy impact is desired. (See Shipman, 1985, for an edifying discussion of the topic.) A few of these concerns have been highlighted in this discussion. As members of a global community, we can enable our children to achieve their full potential only if we continue to toil in the educational and social vineyards of our time.

Notes

1 Spicer's efforts were not always successful, but they represent a significant step in the development of the interrelationship of ethnography and policy.
2 Angrosino and Whiteford (1987) discuss how anthropologists assist in the process of policy formation by conducting ethnographic work. Their studies of community-based treatment for mentally retarded and emotionally disturbed clients — together with a fact-finding advocacy group designed to trace how the loss of federal monies affected health care to children — served to question the existing conception of policy formation. They demonstrate how policy developed at the initiation of the community-based program, rather than of the federal bureaucracy. They also demonstrate how practicing anthropologists can have an impact on policy at the local level, often the foundation of state and national policies.
3 These contributions can be found in a multitude of areas and on various levels. For example, Maxwell *et al.* (1986) combined ethnographic and experimental methods to study physicians' participation in medical care evaluation committees at Michael Reese Hospital and Medical Center in Chicago. The work contributed to an understanding of the educational processes that occur in these committees, benefiting physicians, administrators, and patients. Pitman and Dobbert (1986) illustrated the value of using ethnography to evaluate a teacher training program in a day-care center at a private urban college.
4 Similarly, focusing on the limitations of the federal government to make comprehensive change, the US Office of Education-funded Rural Experimental Schools Study provided an insight into policy decision making processes that was as valuable as the final assessment of the program (Messerschmidt, 1984).
5 During my presidency of the American Evaluation Association, I created the concept empowerment evaluation. Empowerment evaluation is the use of evaluation concepts and techniques to foster self-determination. In

essence, empowerment evaluation is the 'give someone a fish and you feed her for one day, teach her to fish and she will feed herself for the rest of her life' concept applied to evaluation. This evaluation approach is problem focused and collaborative. It requires both qualitative and quantitative methodologies, is highly flexible, and can be applied to evaluation in any area.

It can take many forms, including training, facilitation, advocacy, illumination, and liberation. Evaluators can teach people to conduct their own evaluations and thus become more self-sufficient. This process desensitizes and demystifies evaluation and ideally helps organizations internalize evaluation principles and practices, making evaluation an integral part of program planning. Evaluators can also serve as coaches or facilitators to help others conduct their evaluation. They may also conduct the evaluation, after the goals and evaluation design have been collaboratively established. Evaluators may even serve as direct advocates — helping to empower groups through evaluation (as long as the findings merit such advocacy).

Empowerment evaluation will create a new niche in the intellectual landscape of evaluation. My preliminary conception of empowerment evaluation has many sources, including community psychology and action anthropology. Community psychology focuses on people, organizations, and communities working to establish control over their affairs. The literature about citizen participation and community development is extensive. Rappaport's 'Terms of empowerment/exemplars of prevention: Toward a theory for community psychology' is a classic in this area. Sol Tax's work in action anthropology focuses on how anthropologists can facilitate the goals and objectives of self-determining groups, such as Native American tribes.

This collection of socially concerned scholars has also strongly influenced my conception of empowerment evaluation. The aim of this collection is to explore successful strategies, share lessons learned, and enhance our ability to communicate with an educated citizenry and powerful policy-making bodies. In the process of communicating this message, the concept of empowerment evaluation became crystallized in my thinking. It laid the foundation for this new evaluation approach to helping others help themselves. (See Fetterman, D.M. (1993) Empowerment Evaluation for a more detailed discussion about this approach.)

References

ANGROSINO, M. and WHITEFORD, L. (1987) 'Service, Delivery, Advocacy, and the Policy Cycle', in EDDY, E. and PARTRIDGE, W. (Eds) *Applied Anthropology in America*, Second Edition, New York, Cambridge University Press, pp. 482–504.

BOTT, E. (1957) *Family and Social Network*, New York, Free Press.

CHESTERFIELD, R. (1986) 'Qualitative Methodology in the Evaluation of Early Childhood Bilingual Curriculum Models', in FETTERMAN, D.M. and PITMAN, M. (Eds) *Educational Evaluation: Ethnography in Theory, Practice, and Politics*. Beverly Hills, CA, Sage.

COOK, T. and REICHARDT, C. (Eds) (1979) *Qualitative and Quantitative Methods in Evaluation Research*, Beverly Hills, CA, Sage.

CRONBACH, L., AMBRON, S., DORNBUSCH, S., HESS, R., HORNIK, R., PHILLIPS, D., WALKER, D. and WEINER, S. (1980) *Toward Reform of Program Evaluation*, San Francisco, CA, Jossey-Bass.

CRONBACH, L. (1982) *Designing Evaluations of Educational and Social Programs*, San Francisco, CA, Jossey-Bass.

DOUGHTY, P. (1987) 'Vicos: Success, Rejection, and Rediscovery of a Classic Problem', in EDDY, E. and PARTRIDGE, W. (Eds) *Applied Anthropology in America*, Second Edition. New York, Cambridge University Press, pp. 433–459.

FERRELL, B.G. and COMPTON, D. (1986) 'Use of Ethnographic Techniques for Evaluation in a Large School District: The Vanguard Case', in FETTERMAN, D.M. and PITMAN, M. (Eds) *Educational Evaluation: Ethnography in Theory, Practice, and Politics*, Beverly Hills, CA, Sage.

FETTERMAN, D.M. (1981a) 'Blaming the Victim: The Problem of Evaluation Design and Federal Involvement, and Reinforcing World Views in Education', *Human Organization*, **40**, pp. 67–77.

FETTERMAN, D.M. (1981b) *Study of the Career Intern Program. Final Report — Task C: Program Dynamics: Structure, Function, and Interrelationships*. Mountain View, CA, RMC Research Corporation.

FETTERMAN, D.M. (1982a) 'Ethnography in Educational Research: The Dynamics of Diffusion', *Educational Researcher*, **11**, 3, pp. 17–29.

FETTERMAN, D.M. (1982b) 'Ibsen's Baths: Reactivity and Insensitivity (A Misapplication of the Treatment-Control Design in a National Evaluation)', *Educational Evaluation and Policy Analysis*, **4**, 3, pp. 261–279.

FETTERMAN, D.M. (1987) 'Ethnographic Educational Evaluation', in SPINDLER, G.D. (Ed.) *Interpretive Ethnography of Education: At Home and Abroad*, Hillsdale, NJ, Lawrence Erlbaum Associates, pp. 79–106.

FETTERMAN, D.M. (1988a) *Excellence and Equality: A Qualitatively Different Perspective on Gifted and Talented Education*, Albany, NY, State University of New York Press.

FETTERMAN, D.M. (1988b) *Qualitative Approaches to Evaluation in Education: The Silent Scientific Revolution*, New York, NY, Praeger Publications.

FETTERMAN, D.M. (1989a) 'Ethnographer as Rhetorician: Multiple Audiences Reflect Multiple Realities', *Practicing Anthropology*, **11**, 2, p. 2, pp. 17–18.

FETTERMAN, D.M. (1989b) *Ethnography: Step by Step*, Newbury Park, CA, Sage.

FETTERMAN, D.M. (1993) 'Empowerment Evaluation', *Evaluation Practice*, **14**, 1.

FIRESTONE, W. and HERRIOTT, R. (1984) 'Multisite Qualitative Policy Research: Some Design and Implementation Issues,' in FETTERMAN, D.M. (Ed.) *Ethnography in Educational Evaluation*, Beverly Hills, CA, Sage.

GANS, H. (1962) *The Urban Villagers*, New York, Free Press.

GOETZ, J. and LeCOMPTE, M. (1984) *Ethnography and Qualitative Design in Educational Research*, New York, NY, Academic Press.

GOLDBERG, H. (1984) 'Evaluation, Ethnography, and the Concept of Culture: Disadvantaged Youth in an Israeli Town', in FETTERMAN, D.M. (Ed.) *Ethnography in Educational Evaluation*, Beverly Hills, CA, Sage.

GRIFFIN, C. (1991) 'The Researcher Talks Back: Dealing with Power Relations in Studies of Young People's Entry into the Job Market', in SHAFFIR, W.B. and STEBBINS, R.A. (Eds) *Experiencing Fieldwork: An Inside View of Qualitative Research*, Newbury Park, CA, Sage.

GRIFFIN, C. (1986) *Black and White Youth in a Declining Job Market: Unemployment Among Asian, Afro-Caribbean and White Young People in Leicester*, Leicester, UK, Centre for Mass Communication Research, University of Leicester.

HEMWALL, M. (1984) 'Ethnography as Evaluation: Hearing-Impaired Students in the Mainstream', in FETTERMAN, D.M. *Ethnography in Educational Evaluation* (Ed.). Beverly Hills, CA, Sage.

HESS, G.A. (1989) 'Testimony in Favor of: Educational Performance Agreements for School Restructuring', Testimony Presented to the United States House of Representatives Committee on Education and Labor Subcommittee on Elementary, Secondary, and Vocational Education. Chicago, Illinois, Chicago Panel on Public School Policy and Finance.

HESS, G.A. (1991) *School Restructuring, Chicago Style*, Newbury Park, CA, Corwin Press.

HICKS, G.L. and HANDLER, M. (1987) 'Ethnicity, Public Policy, and Anthropologists', in EDDY, E. and PARTRIDGE, W. (Eds) *Applied Anthropology in America*, Second Edition, New York, Cambridge University Press, pp. 398–432.

HOAGLIN, D., LIGHT, R., McPEEK, B., MOSTELLER, F. and STOTO, M. (1982) *Data for Decisions: Information strategies for Policymakers*, Cambridge, MA, Abt Books.

HOLMBERG, A. (1958) 'The Research and Development Approach to the Study of Change', *Human Organization*, **17**, 1, pp. 12–16.

LeCOMPTE, M. and GOETZ, J. (1982) 'Problems of reliability and validity in ethnographic research', *Review of Educational Research*, **52**, pp. 31–61.

LEWIS, O. (1966) The Culture of Poverty, *Scientific American*, **215**, pp. 19–25.

LIEBOW, E. (1967) *Tally's Corner*, Boston, MA, Little, Brown.

MAROTTO, R. (1986) 'Posin' to Be Chosen': An Ethnographic Study of In-School Truancy', in FETTERMAN, D.M. and PITMAN, M. (Eds) *Educational Evaluation: Ethnography in Theory, Practice, and Politics*, Beverly Hills, CA, Sage.

MAXWELL, J., BASHOOK, P. and SANDLOW, L. (1986) 'Combining Ethnographic and Experimental methods in Educational Evaluation: A Case Study', in *Educational Evaluation: Ethnography in Theory, Practice, and Politics*. FETTERMAN, D.M. and PITMAN, M. (Eds) Beverly Hills, CA, Sage.

MESSERSCHMIDT, D. (1984) 'Federal Bucks for Local Change: On the ethnography of experimental schools', in FETTERMAN, D.M. (Ed.) *Ethnography in Educational Evaluation*. Beverly Hills, CA, Sage.

MILLS, C. (1959) *The Sociological Imagination*, New York, NY, Oxford University Press.

PATTON, M. (1980) *Qualitative Evaluation Methods*, Beverly Hills, CA, Sage.

PELTO, P. and SCHENSUL, J. (1987) 'Toward a Framework for Policy Research in Anthropology', in EDDY, E. and PARTRIDGE, W. (Eds) *Applied Anthropology in America*. Second Edition, New York, Cambridge University Press, pp. 505–527.

PITMAN, M. and DOBBERT, M. (1986) 'The Use of Explicit Anthropological Theory in Educational Evaluation: A Case Study', in *Educational Evaluation: Ethnography in Theory, Practice and Politics*, FETTERMAN, D.M. and PITMAN, M. (Eds) Beverly Hills, CA, Sage.

SHIPMAN, M. (1985) 'Ethnography and Educational Policy-Making', in BURGESS, R.G. (Ed.) *Field Methods in the Study of Education*, London, Falmer Press.

SIMON, E. (1986) 'Theory in Education Evaluation: Or, What's Wrong with Generic-Brand Anthropology', in FETTERMAN, D.M. and PITMAN, M. (Eds) *Educational Evaluation: Ethnography in Theory, Practice, and Politics*. Beverly Hills, CA, Sage.

SMITH, A. and LOUIS, K. (Eds) (1982) 'Multimethod policy research: Issues and applications', *American Behavioral Scientist*, **26**, 1, pp. 1–144.

SMITH, A. and ROBBINS, A. (1984) 'Multimethod Policy Research: A Case Study of Structure and Flexibility', in FETTERMAN, D.M. (Ed.) *Ethnography in Educational Evaluation*. Beverly Hills, CA, Sage.

SPICER, E. (1976) 'Anthropology and the Policy Process', ANGROSINO, M. (Ed.) in *Do Applied Anthropologists Apply Anthropology?*' Southern Anthropological Society, Athens, GA, University of Georgia Press.

SPRADLEY, J. (1970) *You Owe Yourself a Drunk: An Ethnography of Urban Nomads*, Boston, Little Brown.

SPRADLEY, J. (1973) 'The Ethnography of Crime in American Society', in NADER, L. and MARETZKI, T. (Eds) *Cultural Illness and Health*. Washington, DC, American Anthropological Society, pp. 23–34.

STUDSTILL, J. (1986) 'Attrition in Zairian Secondary Schools: Ethnographic Evaluation and Sociocultural Systems', in FETTERMAN, D.M. and PITMAN, M. (Eds) *Educational Evaluation: Ethnography in Theory, Practice, and Politics*, Beverly Hills, CA, Sage.

TALLMADGE, G. (1979) 'Avoiding problems in evaluation', *Journal of Career Education*, **5**, 4, pp. 300–08.

TAX, S. (1958) 'The Fox Project', *Human Organization*, **17**, 1, pp. 17–19.

VALENTINE, C. (1966) *Culture and Poverty: Critique and Counter Proposals*, Chicago, University of Chicago Press.

WEISS, R. and REIN, M. (1972) 'The evaluation of broad-aim programs: Difficulties in experimental design and an alternative, in WEISS, C.H. (Ed.) *Evaluation Action Programs*: (1972) *Readings in Social Action and Education*, Boston, MA, Allyn and Bacon.

WILDAVSKY, A. (1979) *Speaking Truth to Power: The Art and Craft of Policy Analysis*, Boston, MA, Little, Brown (1979).

WULFF, R. and FISKE, S. (1987) *Anthropological Praxis: Translating Knowledge into Action*, Boulder, CO, Westview Press.

Note about Editor

David M. Fetterman: Editor

David M. Fetterman is a Professor of Education at Stanford University,
the California Institute of Integral Studies, and Sierra Nevada College.
Formerly, he was Principal Research Scientist at the American Institute
for Research. He received his Ph.D. from Stanford University in educational and medical anthropology. He has conducted fieldwork in both
Israel (including living on a kibbutz) and the United States (primarily

in inner-cities across the country). David works in the fields of educational evaluation, dropout programs, gifted and talented education, and Judaic education.

David is President of the American Evaluation Association. In addition, he is past president of the American Anthropological Association's Council on Anthropology and Education. He has also served as the program chair for each of these organizations — organizing the annual conference meetings.

He has conducted extensive multisite evaluation research on local, state, and national levels. David's multisite work has been primarily in urban settings. He conducted a three year national evaluation of dropout programs for the Department of Education. In addition, he served as the Director of an Anti-poverty Program. He has also conducted research on migrant and bilingual education programs. David has taught in an inner-city high school, two Hebrew schools, and in various university settings. He is currently involved in the national educational reform movement and has a contract from the Department of Education on self-determination and individuals with disabilities. He is also creating a new form of evaluation called empowerment evaluation which is designed to help people help themselves.

David was awarded the George and Louise Spindler Award for outstanding contributions to educational anthropology as a scholar and practitioner and the Ethnographic Evaluation Award from the Council. He received the President's Award from the Evaluation Research Society for contributions to ethnographic educational evaluation. He was also awarded the Washington Association of Practising Anthropologists' Praxis Publication Award for translating knowledge into action. David has been elected a fellow of the American Anthropological Association and Society for Applied Anthropology.

David has also worked on the state, national, and international level in the field of gifted and talented education. He received one of the 1990 Mensa Education and Research Foundation Awards for Excellence. Mensa Education and Research Foundation encourages research into the nature, characteristics, and uses of intelligence. The award was made for Fetterman's book *Excellence and Equality: A Qualitatively Different Perspective on Gifted and Talented Education* and articles on gifted and talented education in *Educational Evaluation and Policy Analysis* and *Gifted Education International*.

Fetterman was appointed by the US Department of Education to serve on a panel to select a national center for the gifted and talented. He was selected in part because of his recommendation to create a national center in his book *Excellence and Equality*. The center is in operation and Fetterman is a member of the Center's Consultant Bank.

He has consulted for a variety of federal agencies, foundations, corporations, and academic institutions, including the US Department of Education, Centers for Disease Control, National Institute of Mental Health, Kellogg Foundation, Walter S. Johnson Foundation, Syntex, and universities throughout the United States and Europe.

Fetterman is the author of *Ethnography: Step by Step, Qualitative Approaches to Evaluation in Education: The Silent Scientific Revolution, Excellence and Equality: A Qualitatively Different Perspective on Gifted and Talented Education, Educational Evaluation: Ethnography in Theory, Practice, and Politics,* and *Ethnography in Educational Evaluation.*

Notes on Contributors

Mary Lopez de Abascal-Hildebrand is an independent scholar pursuing interdisciplinary applications of anthropology, philosophy, and narrative theory to educational research, evaluation, and community development. She served as a member of the faculties of the California State University, Hayward, and The University of Toledo where she was also an associate member of the graduate faculty; she is a fellow of the Society for Applied Anthropology. Her publications include her chapter, 'Tutor and Student Relations: Applying Gadamer's Notion of Translation' in *Essays on Theory in the Writing Center*, edited by Joan A. Mullin and Ray C. Wallace, National Council for the Teachers of English, and her chapter, 'Understanding Education, Democracy, and Community Development in Thailand: Applying Gadamer's Theory of "Play" in Participatory Research,' in *Language and Community: Applications of Critical Hermeneutics*, edited by Ellen A. Herda, Bergin Garvey. She conducts research and evaluation in a variety of contexts; her most recent projects are a unique application of Writing Across the Curriculum at The University of Toledo, and a large, cultural anthropology study funded by the Corporation for Public Broadcasting through KQED-TV9 in San Francisco to examine how public television might promote parent education and family services. She currently serves on several public policy boards, including the California State Supreme Court Office of Family Court Services Advisory Board. She is just completing a second doctorate in literary criticism.

Mary Jo McGee Brown is Assistant Professor in the Educational Psychology Department at The University of Georgia. She serves as the Council on Anthropology and Education's Contributing Editor and Chair of the Committee on Ethnographic Approaches to Evaluation in Education. Her areas of specialization include community ethnography, African-American culture, educational ethnography, ethnographic evaluation, qualitative research design and data collection methods, and qualitative data analysis. In the area of education, she has conducted an ethnography of the Georgia team of Project 2061: Science for All Americans and conducted ethnographic evaluation on a variety of innovation and reform projects such as parent-child preschool curriculum reform; teacher collaboration to enhance basic skills of vocational students; elementary school teaming, interdisciplinary instruction and literacy instruction; school system climate change; reduction of dropout rates in at risk populations; and non-graded primary school reform. Her work in educational ethnographic evaluation is reflected in her chapter, 'Rural Science and Mathematics Education: Empowerment through Self-Reflection and Expanding Curricular Alternatives' in G. Alfred Hess, Jr. (Ed.) *Empowering Teachers and Parents: School Restructuring Through the Eyes of Anthropologists.*

Jolley Bruce Christman Dr. Christman is Director of Research for Action, which provides a variety of planning, research and evaluation services to the educational community. She is also Associate Faculty at the University of Pennsylvania, Graduate School of Education. Christman received her Ph.D. in Educational Administration from the University of Pennsylvania. She has a particular interest in working with organizations to develop their capacity for organizational learning through evaluation processes which are closely linked to reflection and planning activities. She also has extensive experience in conducting qualitative research in urban settings and received the 1992 Ethnographic Evaluation Award for excellence in the scholarly application of ethnographic procedures to policy decision making from the Council on Anthropology and Education of the American Anthropological Association. Dr. Christman is currently involved in a variety of research projects including: the creation of Charter Schools — schools within schools which is a central piece of high school reform in Philadelphia; parenting education for teen mothers; science and math enrichment programs for minority youth; and, a dropout prevention project involving a comprehensive high school and its 16 elementary and middle feeder schools. With Frederick Erickson of the Center for Urban Ethnography, she is co-director of a project funded by the Knight Foundation to implement a three year school self-study process, which is designed to support Philadelphia elementary schools' restructuring efforts.

G. Alfred Hess, Jr. is the executive director of the Chicago Panel on Public School Policy and Finance, a multi-racial research and advocacy non-profit agency. The Panel is the primary independent monitor of the implementation and effectiveness of the Chicago School Reform Act, an Illinois law which establishes site-based management in all city schools as a vehicle for educational improvement. Over the past decade, the Panel has produced more than 30 research reports on the policies and practices of the Chicago Public Schools. Hess received his Ph.D. in educational anthropology from Northwestern University. Hess is the author of a participant-observer account of the development and early implementation of Chicago's reform legislation, *School Restructuring, Chicago Style* (Corwin Press, 1991). He is the editor of a volume of anthropological studies in restructuring school systems across the United States entitled *Empowering Teachers and Parents* (Bergin & Garvey, 1992). Hess is also a consultant on urban education and served as an expert witness for the St. Louis Public Schools on the costs of educating 'at risk' students in the successful 1992 Missouri school finance suit. He has served as Chair of the Council on Anthropology and Education's Committee on Ethnographic Approaches to Evaluation in Education.

Kim Hopper received his Ph.D. in Sociomedical Sciences from Columbia University, and is now Research Scientist at the Nathan S. Kline Institute for Psychiatric Research. He has taught at Columbia University, Rutgers University, the City University Medical School, and most recently was Visiting Assistant Professor of Anthropology at the New School for Social Research. Since 1979, he has done ethnographic and historical research on homelessness, chiefly in New York City. He was a co-founder of both the New York and the National Coalitions for the Homeless and is past president of the latter organization. The author (or co-author) of numerous articles, reports and reviews on homelessness, its historical and contemporary configurations, its relationship to mental illness and to contemporary poverty, Dr. Hopper is a frequent consultant to the National Institute of Mental Health, New York State governmental agencies, and private foundations. He has testified as an expert witness in four lawsuits involving the rights of the homeless poor in New York City. Since 1989, he has also been involved in a WHO collaborative research project on cross-cultural differences in the long-term course of severe psychiatric disorders.

Bertney Langley is President of Bayou Indian Enterprises and a member of the Koasati Indian Tribe in Elton, Louisiana. His work includes on-going efforts to 'change the image of American Indians' and provide alternative activities and positive role models for Indian youth. He has recently been appointed to the Small Business Advisory Board for Louisiana.

Joseph A. Maxwell is Assistant Professor of Education at Harvard Graduate School of Education, where he teaches courses on qualitative research design and methods and on integrating qualitative and quantitative methods. He has a Ph.D. in anthropology from the University of Chicago. His dissertation was a study of kinship in an Inuit community in northern Canada. He was Chair of the Council on Anthropology and Education's Committee on Ethnographic Approaches to Evaluation in Education. He has published 'Combining Ethnographic and Experimental Methods in Educational Evaluation: A Case Study' in Fetterman, D.M. (Ed.) *Educational Evaluation: Ethnography in Theory, Practice, and Politics*. He has also published other papers on qualitative methodology and on medical education. His current research interests include the philosophy of the social sciences, intracultural diversity, qualitative evaluation, the adoption of innovations, and how people learn to do qualitative research.

Ronald Mertz is an Assistant Director of the Division of Research, Evaluation, and Assessment in the St. Louis Public School system. He received his Ph.D. in anthropology at the University of Arizona. He has served as a Council on Anthropology and Education Board Member-at-Large, Contributing Editor, and Chair of the Committee on Ethnographic Approaches to Evaluation in Education. He has taught elementary school in Liberia and Michigan, operated a Head Start Center for the Seminole Tribe of Florida, taught anthropology at Jacksonville State University and educational research in Taiwan. He has conducted research on two American Indian reservations, and in Belize and Taiwan.

Linda Parker is an Assistant Professor of Anthropology and Sociology at Louisiana State University at Eunice. Her current research includes on-going substance abuse prevention efforts in the Koasati Indian community of southwestern Louisiana, as well as ethnographic evaluation of a prevention program run by the Rhode Island Indian Council and participation in an alcohol treatment outcome study conducted by Brown University.

Barbara Rylko-Bauer is an adjunct Assistant Professor in the Department of Anthropology at Michigan State University. She received her PhD in Anthropology from the University of Kentucky in 1985. She has served as contributing editor for the Society for Medical Anthropology since 1991. Current research interests include exploration of the ways in which medical education shapes physicians, crosscultural studies of abortion, other issues relating to women's health, and a continuation of her interest in the use of anthropological knowledge in programs and policy. Recent publications include *Making Our Research Useful: Case Studies in the Utilization of Anthropological Knowledge*, co-edited with John van Willigen and Ann McElroy (1989); 'Patients' Use of Freestanding Emergency Centers: A Multimethod Approach to Health Services Research,' In *Anthropological Research; Process and Application*, J. Poggie, B. DeWalt, and W. Dressler, eds. (1992); and 'The Development and Use of Freestanding Emergency Centers: A Review of the Literature,' *in Medical Care Review*.

Jean Schensul is Executive Director and Founder of the Institute for Community Research, an applied and policy research institute based in Hartford, Connecticut, with projects in the northeastern United States. She received her Ph.D. in anthropology from the University of Minnesota. She is also a faculty member in the Department of Anthropology and Community Medicine at the University of Connecticut. She is a past president of the Council on Anthropology and Education. She is the recipient of the American Anthropological Association's Solon T. Kimball Award for Public and Applied Anthropology, 1990, and has been involved for almost 20 years in federally funded applied research in urban areas in the United States, Latin America, and South East Asia. Her recent publications include, 'Theory and practice in policy research,' in E. Eddy and W. Partridge (Eds), *Applied Anthropology in America*, New York: Columbia University Press; 'Urban Comadronas,' in *Collaborative Research and Social Policy: Anthropology in Action*, D. Stull and J. Schensul (Eds); 'Ethnographic evaluation of AIDS programs: Better data for better programs,' special issue on Evaluation of AIDS Programs, *New Directions for Program Evaluation*; and 'Methods in Collaborative Research,' in J. Goetz and M. LeCompte (Eds) *Handbook on Qualitative Methods in Educational Research*.

Elaine Simon is currently the Co-director of the Urban Studies Program at the University of Pennsylvania and an Associate at Research for Action. She has a M.S. in Education from the University of Pennsylvania and a Ph.D. in Anthropology from Temple University. She has served as the Council on Anthropology and Education's Contributing Editor, Board Member-at-Large, and Chair of the Committee on Ethnographic Approaches to Evaluation in Education. She was also the President of the Philadelphia Association of Practising Anthropologists from 1986–88. Over the past twenty years, she has conducted ethnographic research and evaluation studies in the fields of education, employment and training, work, and community development. Most recently, she has been involved in studying school reform efforts in Chicago and Philadelphia. In 1992, she won the Council on Anthropology and Education's Ethnographic Evaluation Award for the evaluation of PATHS/PRISM, The Philadelphia Partnership for Education, with Jolley Christman and Carla Asher. Simon has also been recognized for her teaching talent. In 1991, she was awarded the Provost's Award for Excellence in Teaching at the University of Pennsylvania. In addition to the many reports she has written and shared with clients as part of her evaluation work, she has published a book, *Job-Saving Strategies: Worker Buyouts and QWL* (with Arthur Hochner, Cherlyn Granrose, Judith Goode, and Eileen Appelbaum), and several articles including 'Women's Work Culture and the Transition to Leadership Among Supermarket Workers,' 1991 (*in Frontiers: A Journal of Women's Studies*), 'Constraints on the Contribution of Anthropology to Interdisciplinary Policy Studies,' 1989 (in *Urban Anthropology*), and 'Theory in Ethnographic Evaluation or What is Wrong with Generic Brand Anthropology?,' 1986 (in *Educational Evaluation: Ethnography in Theory, Practice, and Politics* edited by David M. Fetterman.) She has also presented numerous papers at scientific meetings and invited sessions and participated in symposia on topics related to her research and practice.

John van Willigen is Professor of Anthropology at the University of Kentucky. He is also the Director of Applied Studies in the Anthropology Department. His research program includes policy research in Kentucky agriculture and assessment of current management practice among industrial firms in the US owned by Japanese companies. In addition, he directs the Applied Anthropology Documentation Project. He is an active member of the Society for Applied Anthropology and the National Association for the Practice of Anthropology. A few of his publications include: *Applied Anthropology: An Introduction; Training Manual in Policy Ethnography Making Our Research Useful: Case Studies in the Utilization of Anthropological Knowledge; Becoming a Practising Anthropologist: A Guide to Careers and Training Programs in Applied Anthropology; and Anthropology in Use: A Sourcebook on Anthropological Practice.*

Margaret Weeks is Associate Director of the Institute for Community Research. She received her Ph.D. from the University of Connecticut. She is an applied social anthropologist with expertise in women's issues, health, community program development, and contemporary Chinese political economy. She is currently Co-Principal Investigator and Project Director of COPE (Community Outreach Prevention Effort), a National Institute on Drug Abuse (NIDA) cooperative agreement for community-based AIDS prevention with injection drug users, and Assistant Director of Project CONNECT (Community Outreach Neighborhood Network for Education, Counseling, and Treatment), a Center for Substance Abuse Treatment (CSAT) project to prevent HIV among drug users. She is Co-Facilitator of the Community Alliance for AIDS Programs, a community consortium that develops, implements, and evaluates AIDS programs in Hartford, Connecticut. She has published articles on a variety of topics including 'AIDS Prevention and the African American Injection Drug User,' *Transforming Anthropology*, and 'Virtuous, Wives, and Kind Mothers: Concepts of Women in Urban China,' *Women's Studies International Forum*.

Author Index

Subject Index